Re-Circuiting Trauma Pathways in Adults, Parents, and Children

Re-Circuiting Trauma Pathways in Adults, Parents, and Children presents the evidence-informed and substantiated Intergenerational Trauma Treatment Model (ITTM), with an emphasis on up-to-date trauma theory, the development of specialized clinical skills, and the replicability of methods. Grounded in original research, experiential practice, and mathematical principles of logic, the ITTM targets and treats both the child's and the caregiver's complex trauma, providing the content and the process for supplying an effective and brief caregiver-first treatment option. It delivers an innovative, multigenerational approach to complex trauma treatment that strengthens the caregiver-child relationship by motivating and teaching caregivers to help their children cope with the effects of trauma.

Valerie Copping, PsyD, is the developer, lead trainer, and clinical consultant for the Intergenerational Trauma Treatment Model (ITTM). She currently provides training, courses, and consultation to students, professionals, and mental health organizations.

Re-Circuiting Trauma Pathways in Adults, Parents, and Children

A Brain-Based, Intergenerational Trauma Treatment Method

Valerie Copping

Routledge
Taylor & Francis Group
NEW YORK AND LONDON

First published 2018
by Routledge
711 Third Avenue, New York, NY 10017

and by Routledge
2 Park Square, Milton Park, Abingdon, Oxon, OX14 4RN

Routledge is an imprint of the Taylor & Francis Group, an informa business

Library of Congress Cataloging-in-Publication Data
Names: Copping, Valerie, author.
Title: Re-circuiting trauma pathways in adults, parents, and children : a brain-based, intergenerational trauma treatment method / Valerie Copping.
Description: New York, NY : Routledge, 2018. | Includes bibliographical references and index.
Identifiers: LCCN 2017041978 | ISBN 9781138223134 (hardcover : alk. paper) | ISBN 9781138223127 (pbk. : alk. paper) | ISBN 9781315392066 (e-book)
Subjects: MESH: Stress Disorders, Traumatic—therapy | Parent-Child Relations | Professional-Family Relations | Psychotherapy—methods
Classification: LCC RC552.T7 | NLM WM 172.5 | DDC 616.85/210651—dc23
LC record available at https://lccn.loc.gov/2017041978

ISBN: 978-1-138-22313-4 (hbk)
ISBN: 978-1-138-22312-7 (pbk)
ISBN: 978-1-315-39206-6 (ebk)

Typeset in ACaslon
by Apex CoVantage, LLC

Contents

Acknowledgments vii

Introduction: The Intergenerational Trauma Treatment Model **1**

PART 1
Theory **11**

Chapter 1 Hope and Motivation: Working With Adult and Child Victims of Childhood Complex Trauma **13**

Chapter 2 Starting With the Brain: Childhood Complex Trauma, Neuroscience, and the ITTM **25**

Chapter 3 Reconstructing Negative Self-Beliefs: The ITTM's Early Childhood Deductive Reasoning Theory **43**

PART 2
Practice **59**

Chapter 4 Phase A: How the Model Works—Caregivers and Children **61**

Appendix 4.1: Phase A: Trauma Information Sessions Checklist 73
Appendix 4.2: Phase A, B, and C Diagram Examples 76
Appendix 4.3: The Caregiver's Unresolved Childhood Trauma Impact: Group Discussion 80
Appendix 4.4: Testimonial From a Parent 96
Appendix 4.5: Our Trauma Treatment 106
Appendix 4.6: ITTM Implementation 109

Appendix 4.7: Reflections on the Intergenerational Trauma Treatment Model (ITTM) 111
Appendix 4.8: Endorsement for the Intergenerational Trauma Treatment Model (ITTM) 117

Chapter 5 Phase B: The Caregiver Sessions **118**

Chapter 6 Phase C: Bringing the Child Back In **149**

Appendix 6.1: Adult Therapeutic Letter 190

Conclusion: Re-Circuiting Trauma Pathways **193**

Index 199

Acknowledgments

I dedicate this book with love to my mother, Mary-Lorraine Buchan; to my father, Philip D. Rosengarten; and to my sisters, Darlene B. Donovan and Sunny Savage; each of whom nurtured and expanded my understanding, sensitivity, and compassion to the negative impact of complex trauma and implanted my hope in every person's potential for healing.

I am especially indebted to my editor, Dr. Cynthia Comacchio, whose generosity, expertise, and uncanny ability to read my mind now enables the model, in its description and organization, to finally be shared with a wider audience. Words cannot express my gratitude for your guidance, genius, encouragement, and tireless determination.

Children, caregivers, clinicians, and mentors have meaningfully assisted in the ongoing development of the ITTM in research, practice, and implementation across Canada, the United States, New Zealand, Poland, and the United Kingdom. The mentors are: Gordon Greenway, Dr. Donald Woodside, Dr. Katreena Scott, Dr. Bill Bergquist, Dr. Linda Paige, Dr. Ian Manion, Heather Cook, and Kirk Donald.

Best friends—Chantal Hollander, Arden Ryshpan, Kae Dee, Christine Von Maydell, Brigid Porter, Dr. Kimberly Blyden-Taylor, Ana Maria Mendez Dardon, Julie Brown, Dr. Stephanie Von Dehn, Wendy Maynard, Valerie Van Wassenaer, Alison Miles, and Beverley Barnes—offered their expertise and encouragement each step of the way.

Every one of you has played a vital role in helping me to advance and actualize my life's work, and for this I am extremely grateful and infinitely gratified.

Introduction: The Intergenerational Trauma Treatment Model

> Experience has taught us that we have only one enduring weapon in our struggle against mental illness: the emotional discovery and emotional acceptance of the truth in the individual and unique history of our childhood.
>
> (Miller, 1997)

Renowned psychologist Alice Miller succinctly describes what is axiomatic for child practitioners of all types and ranks: that certain "truths" of childhood—truths that can just as readily be called "traumas"—are the core of both mental illness and recovery, in children and in adults. The corollary is that an effective method to uncover those truths and treat the resultant trauma is equally essential. What follows is an overview of the model that I have pioneered, practiced, taught to others, observed in its implementation, studied for outcomes, and continued to refine over the course of several decades since the completion of the doctoral research that was its foundation.

This book is intended to introduce, theorize, and contextualize the Intergenerational Trauma Treatment Model as an effective three-phase, brain-based, psychodynamic, metacognitive method that addresses the root causes and behavioral symptoms of childhood trauma in adults (usually parents/caregivers), children and adolescents.[1] In its theoretical basis, the ITTM is a refinement of research conducted in my therapeutic practice of the past 20 years or so. My findings were further tested, adapted, and revised in response to what I learned while teaching students and training psychologists and mental health clinicians (of varied professional designations) in child and family mental health clinics, in special workshops, and also in private practice. The model is dynamic: the operationalization of each phase provides opportunity for rigorous evaluation of the methods employed in each phase. These years of practical application and re-examination of the ITTM as a primary treatment for complex trauma have provided substantial evidence to validate it as an effective and sustainable adult/caregiver and caregiver/child therapy (Scott & Copping, 2008, Copping, 2001). Drawing carefully from other disciplines, the ITTM builds upon and advances extant therapeutic models, is applicable in diverse situations, requires a relatively brief learning period for students and clinicians, and can be quickly implemented with adults and children in need. Most important, the ITTM identifies initial childhood trauma impact at its roots to enable sustained resolution.

Complex trauma in childhood is defined as "the experience of multiple, chronic and prolonged, developmentally adverse traumatic events, most often of an interpersonal nature, often within the child's caregiving system" (Van der Kolk, 2005, p. 295). In most cases, such trauma involves repeated exposure to sexual, physical, and/or psychological abuse or neglect in childhood. (Briere et al., 2015; Cook et al., 2005; Van der Kolk, 2005). Multiple and severe forms of trauma, especially in childhood, generally have multiple and severe psychological results. The list is long: dissociation; relational, identity, and affect regulation disturbance; cognitive distortions; somatization; "externalizing" behaviors such as self-mutilation, dysfunctional sexual behavior, and violence; substance abuse; eating disorders; susceptibility to revictimization; and traumatic bereavement associated with loss of family members and other significant attachment figures (Maguire et al., 2015). Current research demonstrates how negative beliefs about the self, left unacknowledged and unresolved, increase the risk for persistent, and worsening, psychological symptoms and outcomes across the lifespan (Van der Kolk, 2016, p. 269; Wesley et al., 2015; Kaya Tezel, 2015; Thimm, 2010). Trauma researchers and clinicians have long stressed the need for effective short-term treatments that address both the negative self-deductions in adults/caregivers who have experienced childhood traumas, and their formulation in trauma-impacted children who risk repeating the cycle (Gardner et al., 2014; Cyr & Alink, 2017, p. 82.).

Mental health treatments for children typically focus on the child, and are delivered in individual clinician-directed sessions. The caregiver is usually peripheral to the clinician's treatment plan, even though parental participation may be listed as a component of the treatment modality. Adult participation often means simply that the clinician updates caregivers about the child's thoughts, feelings, and behaviors, as well as the particulars of treatment or the child's responses to it. Recent research supports a more definite, active caregiver involvement in treatment of children (Van der Kolk, 2016; Betancourt et al., 2015; Gardner et al., 2014). The recommendations for this vital involvement do not, however, specify its timing, nature, and extent, an ambiguity that has led to generalized and ill-defined interpretations of what form caregiver participation and involvement needs to take in order to achieve the most efficacious treatment outcomes.

According to the World Health Organization (WHO), every year 40 million young people experience maltreatment before reaching 14 years of age (Svevo-Cianci, 2010; Ijzendoorn, 2015). Even more disturbing is the fact that caregivers are the source of most of this maltreatment. In the United States, parents are identified as the perpetrators in 83.9% of cases; mothers were the sole perpetrators in 40.8% of the cases, and were reported to be nearly twice as likely to be involved in child maltreatment than fathers (Rosenberg et al., 2006). It is estimated that between one-quarter and one-third of the young victims are, in turn, likely to sexually, physically, or emotionally abuse others (Noll & Shenk 2010). As adults, they are more likely to abuse their own children than are caregivers who were not maltreated in childhood (Kaufman et al., 1987; Widom et al., 2006). Regardless of external variables, every maltreated child is at greater risk for becoming an abusive caregiver who perpetuates the intergenerational cycle of abuse and neglect with their own children (Noll & Shenk, 2010; Finzi-Dottan & Harel, 2014; Cyr & Alink, 2017).

In Canada, statistical studies on the national level, as well as on the provincial level,[2] also affirm that child maltreatment occurs primarily at the hands of caregivers. These caregivers (most often mothers) were, in the majority, also subjected to this abuse as children, in an adult domestic partnership, or in both situations. In Ontario, the most populous province, of the 125,281 investigations conducted in 2013 (a rate of 53.3 per 1,000 children), 78% investigated concerns about abuse or neglect (41.7 investigations per 1,000 children), while a considerable 22% concerned the risk of future maltreatment (11.6 investigations per 1,000 children) (Fallon et al., 2013, pp. 11–12; Jones et al., 2015).

On record for the first time in the 2008 national study, and a key point of follow-up investigation for the 2013 provincial study, is one crucial fact: child welfare authorities have been amassing "many more reports about situations where the primary concern is that a child may be at risk of future maltreatment," even in situations where "there are no specific concerns about a possible incident of maltreatment that may have already occurred" (Fallon et al., 2013, pp.11–12). A significant number of children, as their caseworkers acknowledge, are living in fear of future maltreatment. Sixty-seven percent of the Ontario subjects studied had been referred to child welfare authorities at least once before (Fallon et al., 2013, p. 11–12).

The ITTM is fundamentally concerned with complex trauma and its acknowledged potential for intergenerational transmission. It was specifically designed to remedy the threat, as well as the incidence, of repeated abuse by making the caregivers' own childhood trauma the initial focus of treatment. As such, the ITTM is one of the first programs to receive endorsement as an appropriate model of treatment for Indigenous populations, whose particular history of colonial oppression has sustained this inter- and cross-generational breakdown in healthy self-belief systems, with demonstrably negative individual, family, and community repercussions.

The forced removal of Indigenous children from their families has been widespread across the world for generations. Exactly as was the case with Canada's Indigenous children, at the start of colonization in the mid-18th century, Aborigine children in Australia were forcibly taken from their parents and placed in residential schools in a deliberate program to eradicate the practice of their language and culture. In Canada and Australia, the schools were sites of everyday neglect, malnutrition, emotional, physical, and sexual abuse. To this day, in both situations as well, Indigenous peoples struggle with problems of domestic violence, family breakdown, alcoholism, addiction, and any number of medical health issues in far higher proportion than do the white populations of either country. In Australia, their mental health hospital admittance rates 2–4 times the average of American rates (Gone & Trimble, 2012; Hunter, 2007). The final reports of the Truth and Reconciliation Commission in Canada, especially the volumes *Calls to Action and Survivors Speak* (www.trc.ca 2015), establish beyond question the special need for healing in Indigenous communities that have been traumatized for more than a century because of the imposed residential school system.

Over 80,000 survivors, whether from direct experience or from the impacts of their caregivers' trauma, are alive today. Many of the survivors have raised first- and second-generation families of their own. Canada has the highest concentration of residential school survivors, their adult children, and third-generation children in North America. As such, it likely also has the highest population of individuals enduring the consequences of unresolved intergenerational trauma. Gone and Trimble (2012) reported higher than average rates of alcohol abuse and post-traumatic stress disorder (PTSD) with three times the national average of youth suicides. During the infamous "Sixties Scoop," a 1960s federal program that authorized social workers in five provinces to remove children deemed to need "protection" from their families, some 20,000 children were forcibly removed, often without their caregivers' knowledge, separated from their siblings, and placed in the care of mostly non-Indigenous families across Canada and the United States. This "project" continued through the 1980s. A recent study for the province of Alberta confirmed that, for the vast majority who were adopted by non-Indigenous families, the severed connection from their birth families, communities of origin, and ancestral customs amounted to a loss of identity detrimental to their physical and mental health (Carriere, 2008, p. 61).

The well-documented rates of psychiatric and physiological distress facing Indigenous populations are exacerbated by the lack of research on the design and practice of effective and culturally informed mental health treatments. Indigenous people in Canada, the United States, Australia, and New Zealand face additional difficulties accessing mental health services and the negative realities of marginalization of status as invisible communities (Gone & Trimble, 2012; Hunter, 2007). Individual psychotherapy for adolescents is completely lacking, research on adults is negligible, and there is no research on Indigenous children under the age of 11. There is no over-statement in remarking on the *urgent* need for attention to this lack of research and services in a population demonstrating such a serious extent of mental health problems. A large part of what exacerbates this situation is our absolute commitment to the empirically supported treatments of so-called "Western" science. Especially in view of the historical, intergenerational nature of the trauma, we must pay attention to the cultural knowledge that has been deliberately suppressed, but was nonetheless (and continues to be) transmitted generationally in Indigenous communities. As Indigenous professionals and advocates point out, "we already know what works in our communities" (Gone & Alcantara, 2007, p. 360). Indigenous therapeutic approaches should be accorded their rightful status in mental (and physical) health contexts.

Although unfamiliar to mental health professionals trained in evidence-based practice, traditional therapies need to be considered in terms of "practice-based evidence" (Isaacs et al., 2005). Despite recent initiatives and state funding commitments, there are to date few extant therapies that integrate Indigenous knowledge with current scientific approaches (Gone, 2016; Rowan et al., 2015). The challenge of fashioning assessment and treatment in culturally appropriate ways that nonetheless build on contemporary psychological findings is enormous, but it is one that must be accepted by mainstream science. It is clear that "science" has done little of consequence in addressing the myriad problems of colonially oppressed Indigenous communities around the world. One position is that mental health services for Indigenous clients are generally of such low quality that promoting empirically supported treatments in these settings without the distraction of cultural adaptation is already challenging enough. Inarguably, clinicians must prioritize their own cultural understanding in any attempt to design specific therapies, and this knowledge and experience of cultural differences is clearly essential in professional training (Sue et al., 2009). Also feasible is adapting established protocols to reflect (at least symbolically) the cultural tenets of local groups before their actual implementation (Venner et al., 2006). Close consultation with Indigenous groups is obviously the best way to proceed in any case. The principal objective is to develop effective therapies with solid community consultation and support in order to center—at long last—cultural relevance and self-determination (Williamson, 2014).

The Intergenerational Trauma Treatment Model has been recognized by Indigenous mental health directors, coordinators, and clinicians as appropriate and effective for Indigenous communities. As employed to date, the ITTM has been adapted to incorporate and combine traditional Indigenous practices with evidence-based approaches contingent on the needs and wishes of each reserve. The ITTM's diagrammatic approach naturally accommodates the changes required to ensure and increase affiliation with cultural and spiritual differences across diverse populations. One example of how the model combines traditional healing practices with evidence-based practice is the "telling of the trauma story." Traditional healing often involves the telling and retelling of personal stories in traditional sweat lodge practices. Most important, the model's intergenerational basis is demonstrably efficacious in dealing with the particular mental health matters that are endemic in 21st century Indigenous societies. Because treatment begins with, and consistently involves, the primary caregiver, whether an elder, foster, adoptive biological parent, grandparent, or other kin, it effectively starts at the heart of the problem. Translators are welcome to participate as needed, although the diagrammatic structures utilized often lessen this need because spoken language and understanding are not as important as in conventional therapy.

It is inarguably important to address the maltreatment that has already been suffered by children. But the noted "primary concern . . . that a child may be at risk" (Fallon et al., 2013, pp. 11–12, 17) emphatically directs child welfare workers, clinicians, social workers, and other practitioners to the childhood trauma imprinted in and reproduced by abusive adult caregivers. The body of evidence underscores the need for effective, rapid interventions that will definitively interrupt the generational transmission of trauma by confronting its physical and emotional repercussions at their childhood/caregiver sources. While complex trauma (CT) evidence-based treatments are now emerging, current treatment methods are largely informed by interventions for Type I, acute, one-time events—such as the sudden death of a parent or other primary caregiver—rather than the more challenging Type II complex trauma that involves prolonged traumatic conditions over an extended period, most often effected by a trusted person or persons in the child's life.

To provide direction, the American Academy of Child and Adolescent Psychiatry (cited in Dauber, 2015) developed a set of best-practice guidelines for the treatment of complex trauma in which the need for and value of a phase-based treatment method was first identified. The initial treatment phase should focus on safety and the development of competencies in emotional and behavioral regulation (**ITTM: Phase A**). The second phase should then focus on trauma processing, in order to integrate memories and meaning into a unified sense of self (**ITTM: Phase B**). The strengthened emotional foundation and resilience that is the objective of these two phases ideally sees effective gains, to the extent of full self-engagement with family and community, in the final phase (**ITTM: Phase C**).

The ITTM is the only treatment model to date that deals specifically with the unresolved complex trauma history of the caregiver (**Phase A & Phase B**) *before* the child is treated (**Phase C**). Various approaches address event-specific abuses such as physical, emotional, and sexual abuse, but none of the extant models directly assess and treat intergenerational patterns of complex trauma transmission. By beginning with advanced cognitive behavioral diagrams, the ITTM provides cutting-edge instruction to caregivers and clinicians about the impact of trauma. The diagrams, as later chapters will detail, are created by the client (both caregiver and child) with the clinician's help, and are employed as interactive process and progress tracking tools. As visual representations "drawn" according to specific guidelines established by the clinician, they allow clients to circumvent most educational, cultural, and language barriers to obtaining complex trauma treatment for themselves and their child. We know that therapies designed to increase caregiver sensitivity by strengthening their emotional attunement, attachment, and increased mentalizing capacity produce the most successful results. The ITTM fortifies this relational sensitivity by having caregivers participate in the model's Phase A. Phase A is designed and implemented to acquire valid information about the child's behaviors and symptoms, for both caregiver and clinician. All the information is presented within the context of child/adolescent development and perceptions.

Caregivers may initially believe that they are attending sessions in order to work toward improving outcomes for their children, a correct perception, but they are also being supplied with the knowledge and tools to repair their personal, individual, unresolved trauma impacts. In the ITTM framework, understanding their own negative childhood experiences is fundamental to successful treatment of their children. Phase B of ITTM treatment has the clinician carrying out specific tasks with the adult(s) individually to gradually uncover the earliest and most impactful details of trauma impact in their own childhood. They are taught that when the developing human brain innately formulates a negative self-deduction, the outcome is a disarrangement in the belief systems of the self and others, across and between generations. The ITTM is based on the principle that the most successful approach to complex trauma is to accurately assess, address, and resolve the caregiver/adult's **Primary Negative Belief System** (PNBS) which is formulated during childhood. This must be accomplished for the caregiver prior to assessing and resolving the child's PNBS.

The ITTM also demonstrates the importance of developing interdisciplinary as well as intergenerational approaches to increase the likelihood of resolving the complex mental health problems of contemporary societies. A chief distinguishing feature is its integration of theoretical and practical elements from other disciplines. The model is informed by up-to-date research in developmental traumatology, complex traumatology, attachment theory, Cognitive Behavioral Theory, and neuroplasticity. It is theorized within a framework of philosophical and mathematical principles of practice. The ITTM's theoretical basis and its practical applications, consequently, are in line with the restructuring, re-building, and resolution of key trauma factors defined in recent findings on brain development, attachment, developmental trauma and self-system development. Its core treatment is founded on a foolproof, logic-based method that uses the requisites of reason and mathematical logic to deconstruct and reconstruct Primary Negative Belief Systems in caregivers and children.

In a comprehensive but economical and efficient process, the ITTM sets out 15 sessions for adults and 21 sessions for caregivers and their children. Because of its comprehensive and relatively short-term structure, its adoption helps to mitigate the lengthy—sometimes dangerously so—wait times for diagnosis and treatment that characterize contemporary mental health treatments. Dr. Paul Kurdyak, director of health systems research at Toronto's Centre for Addiction and Mental Health (CAMH), found that, among Ontario children and youth aged 10–24 with mental health issues, there was a 33% rise in emergency department visits between 2006–2011. For many, the wait time is simply too long and damaging. The rate of hospital admissions also rose by 53% over the five-year study period (Ubelacker, 2015).

In my experience, child and family welfare agencies and clinicians turn to ITTM training precisely because their experience with current models are both long in delivery and short in demonstrating long-term resolution and "successes." There is often a frustrating number of "drop-outs" along the way. First and foremost, the ITTM provides complex trauma treatment to caregivers to deal with their own childhood experiences. In effect, it treats two generations at once, increasing the functioning of both child and adult caregiver(s). The method provides additional, and frequently shorter, treatment options for clinical practitioners, psychologists and social workers, and their clients; there are no wait lists for Phase A, the Trauma Information Sessions (TIS), which can be started at any time.

In sum, the ITTM differs from current child trauma treatments in that:

- It accurately assesses and addresses adult caregivers' Primary Negative Belief System (PNBS) from childhood, because the unresolved impact of the PNBS is reinforced and intensified through adulthood when it remains unrecognized.
- It deconstructs and reconstructs the caregiver's PNBS by means of its foolproof mathematical logic method before treating the child. This approach allows the child to experience the caregiver differently, as their primary, autonomous agent of positive change, and not because they are directed to refer the child for treatment by a therapist, or under the requirements of a child and family welfare agency, for example.
- The caregiver's role as the child's primary guide is preserved and reinforced by teaching caregivers to act as "co-therapist" to the child rather than assigning this expertise to the therapist alone. This process is important to reducing caregiver depression, increasing the caregiver's motivation and hope, and strengthening the essential parent-child attachment that is the child's core emotional health determinant.

The ITTM's Early Childhood Deductive Reasoning Theory (EC-DRT) captures the reasoning processes of the brain in that life stage and delivers a step-by-step, clinical method for accurately determining, deconstructing, and reconstructing primary negative self-beliefs, the very heart of much intergenerational trauma. It is, in effect, a theory of thinking that seeks to explain the calculation, induction, creation, and the association of ideas (Johnson-Laird & Byrne, 1993, p. 323). The ITTM's brain-based method is a mathematical structure that represents how a child's brain formulates general and self-beliefs. With the application of the same mathematical method and propositional calculus principles to achieve this end, it works to disprove and correct the faulty negative self-beliefs formulated by adults, caregivers, and children in early childhood. In the ITTM schema, effective treatment succeeds at finally and lastingly separating the client's protracted, overly personalized assignment of themselves—the "I" from within the brain's automatic structuring of their primary negative self-deduction equation. In so doing, the authentic self is freed from "other-generated" evidence and free to emerge and be informed, often for the first time, by their own, first-hand, self-based generated evidence.

Part 1 of this book concentrates on the ITTM's conceptual and contextual frameworks. Three chapters outline its historical and theoretical frameworks, and situate the model within the expanding multidisciplinary trauma literature—and particularly that of neurotraumatology. I also explain the innovative methodology that it brings to bear on adults (caregivers) and their children. The ITTM operates from the top down: it effectively uncovers the specific root issue(s) underlying the individual's negative self-belief system. The ITTM's brain-based approach aims to recircuit the brain's traumatic pathways. In so doing, caregivers and children experience sustainable improvements in trauma-related behaviors, symptoms, and interactions. Dealing with both generations at once also interrupts the circuits that facilitate trauma's potential for intergenerational transmission.

Part 2 is an abbreviated version of the model's therapeutic application. It provides specific examples and instruction on the elements of Phase A, Phase B, and Phase C as they are carried out by ITTM-certified clinicians. Methods within each phase of the 21-session model are described and elaborated upon by means of research and practical findings and illustrated with experience-based examples and case studies.[3]

I will close this brief introduction as I began, with a quote that has inspired me and countless others who work with traumatized children and family. It captures the essence of how, relying on the requisite mix of compassion and science, we can best approach those we hope to help. As eminent child psychiatrist Dr. Kyle Pruett so eloquently expresses this imperative,

> Ultimately . . . it is how children are loved and protected by the ones they hold most dear that makes their days, and often their lives, matter. It is here, in the primacy of intimacy and trust, that trauma works its toxic and corrosive mischief . . . the child's first self image is mirrored in the eyes of his or her parents . . . Frightening self images may emerge that can take even the young child beyond the limits of trust and endurance, or the emotional reach of his or her loved ones. This is precisely what makes trauma a family affair—whether in perpetration or resolution. Those who ignore this maxim are generally less than helpful in the attempts they make to intervene on behalf of the traumatized child and family.
>
> (Pruett, 2004)

What follows is a systematic exploration of the potential for truly helpful interventions in these "family affairs" through an instrument for assessment and treatment of my own design: the Intergenerational Trauma Treatment Model.

Notes

1. For consistency and brevity, and to acknowledge that biological caregivers are not the only adults responsible for children's nurture, and that children might well be cared for by grandparents, other adult family members, foster or adoptive caregivers, in agency group homes, and so on, I use the term "caregiver" throughout this book. Likewise, I use the plural pronoun "they" or "them" in reference to caregivers, clinicians, and children to maintain gender-neutral language.
2. *Canadian Incidence Study of Reported Child Abuse and Neglect* (2008); *Ontario Incidence Study of Reported Child Abuse and Neglect* (2013).

3. The practical applications that constitute the 21-session ITTM program are fully laid out in the *ITTM Training Manual* (Copping, 2001) for use in training seminars with professionals involved in childhood trauma treatment. Clinicians are required to complete ITTM training, either through their clinic or on-line. Training and certification requirements can be viewed on the ITTM website: www.theittm.com.

References

Betancourt, T. M., et al. (2015). The intergenerational impact of war: Longitudinal relationships between caregiver and child mental health in postconflict Sierra Leone. *Journal of Child Psychology and Psychiatry* 56:10, pp. 1101–1107.

Briere, J. S. et al. (2015). Complex trauma in adolescents and adults: Effects and treatment. *The Psychiatric Clinics of North America* 38:3, p. 515.

Carriere, J. (2008). The soul work of adoption and Aboriginal children. *Pimatisiwin: A Journal of Aboriginal and Indigenous Community Health* 6:1, pp. 61–78.

Cook, A. S., Spinazzola, J., & Ford, J. (2005). Complex trauma. *Pediatrics, Psychiatric Annals* 35:5, pp. 1–9.

Copping, V. W. (2001). A child trauma treatment pilot study. *Journal of Child and Family Studies* 10:4, pp. 467–475.

Cyr, C. & Alink, L. (2017). Child maltreatment: The central roles of parenting capacities and attachment. *Current Opinion in Psychology* 15, pp. 81–86.

Dauber, S. L. (2015). Treatment of complex trauma on the front lines: A preliminary look at child outcomes in an agency sample. *Child and Adolescent Social Work Journal* 32:6, pp. 529–543.

Fallon, B., Van Wert, M., Trocmé, N., MacLaurin, B., Sinha, V., Lefebvre, R., Allan, K., Black, T., Lee, B., Rha, W., Smith, C., & Goel, S. (2015). Ontario Incidence Study of Reported Child Abuse and Neglect-2013 (OIS-2013). Toronto, ON: Child Welfare Research Portal. p. 11–12.

Finzi-Dottan, R. & Harel, G. (2014). Parents' potential for child abuse: An intergenerational perspective. *Journal of Family Violence* 29:4, pp. 397–408.

Gardner, S. L., et al. (2014). Family live: Parental skill building for caregivers with interpersonal trauma exposures. *Clinical Social Work Journal* 42:1, pp. 81–89.

Gone, J. P. (2016). Alternative knowledge and the future of community psychology: Provocations from an American Healing tradition. *American Journal of Community Psychology* 58:3–4, pp. 314–321.

Gone, J. P. & Alcantara, C. (2007). Identifying effective mental health interventions for American Indians and Alaska Natives: A review of the literature. *Cultural Diversity and Ethnic Minority Psychology* 13:4, pp. 356–363.

Gone, J. P. & Trimble, J. E. (2012). American Indian and Alaska Native mental health and diverse perspectives on enduring disparities. *Annual Review of Clinical Psychology* 8, pp. 130–160.

Hunter, E. (2007). Disadvantage and discontent: A review of issues relevant to the mental health of rural and remote Indigenous Australians. *The Australian Journal of Rural Health* 15:2, pp. 88–93.

Ijzendoorn, M. H. (2015). The prevalence of child maltreatment across the globe: Review of a series of meta-analyses. *Child Abuse Review* 24, pp. 37–50.

Isaacs, M. H., Huang, L. N., & Hernandez, H. (2005). *The Road to Evidence: The Interaction of Evidence-Based Practices and Cultural Competence in Children's Mental Health*. Chicago: National Alliance of Multi-Ethnic Behavioral Health Associations.

Jiang, Q., Wang, Q., Li, P., & Li, H. (2016, October). The neural correlates underlying belief reasoning for self and for others. *Frontiers in Psychology* 7, p. 1501. www.frontiersin.org.

Johnson-Laird, P. & Byrne, R. M. J. (1993). Precis of Deduction. *Behavioral and Brain Sciences*, Vol. 16, 232–380.

Jones, A., Sinha, V., & Trocmé, N. (2015). Children and youth in out-of-home care in the Canadian provinces. CWRP Information Sheet #167E. Montreal, QC: McGill University Centre for Research on Children and Families.

Kaufman, J., et al. (1987). Do abused children become abusive parents? *American Journal of Orthopsychiatry* 57, pp. 186–192.

Kaya Tezel, F. T. (2015). Relationships between childhood traumatic experiences, maladaptive schemas and interpersonal styles. *Arch Neuropsychiatry* 52, pp. 226–232.

Lawson, A. (2004). The nature and development of scientific reasoning: A synthetic view. *International Journal of Science and Mathematics Education*, Vol. 2, pp. 307–338.

Maguire, S. A., Williams, B., Naughton, A. M., Cowley, L. E., Tempest, V., Mann, M. K., Teague, M., & Kemp, A. M. (2015). A systematic review of the emotional, behavioral and cognitive features exhibited by school-aged children experiencing neglect or emotional abuse. *Child: Care Health Development* 41, pp. 641–653.

Miller, A. (1997). *The Drama of the Gifted Child: The Search for the True Self.* New York: Harper Collins Publishers.

Noll, J. S. & Shenk, C.E. (2010). Introduction to the special issue: The physical health consequences of childhood maltreatment-implications for public health. *Journal of Pediatric Psychology* 35:5, pp. 447–449.

Pruett, K. (2004). Foreword. In J. D. Osofsky (Ed.), *Young Children and Trauma: Intervention and Treatment*. New York: Guilford Press.

Rosenberg, J. W., et al. (2006). The importance of fathers. In *Fatherhood and Child Welfare: Fatherhood Curriculum* (pp. 1–10). Maine: Office on Child Abuse and Neglect.

Rowan, M., Poole, N., Shea, B., & Mykota, D. (2015). A scoping study of cultural interventions to treat addictions in Indigenous populations: Methods, strategies and insights from a two-eyed seeing approach. *Substance Abuse Treatment, Prevention, and Policy* 10:26, pp. 1–9.

Scott, K. & Copping, V. (2008). Promising directions for the treatment of complex childhood trauma: The intergenerational trauma treatment model. *The Journal of Behavior Analysis* 1:13, pp. 273–283.

Sue, S., Zane, N., Nagayama Hall, G. C., & Berger, L. K. (2009). The case for cultural competency in psychotherapeutic interventions. *Annual Review of Psychology* 60, pp. 525–548.

Svevo-Cianci, K. H. (2010). Protecting children from violence and maltreatment: A qualitative comparative analysis assessing the implementation of U.N. CRC Article 19. *Child Abuse and Neglect* 34, pp. 45–56.

Thimm, J. C. (2010). Relationships between early maladaptive schemas and psychological developmental task resolution. *Clinical Psychology and Psychotherapy* 17, pp. 219–230.

Trocme, N. F. (2008). *Canadian Incidence Study of Reported Child Abuse and Neglect*. Ottawa: Public Health Agency of Canada.

Ubelacker, S. (2015). More kids, youth visiting hospital ERs for mental health issues: Report. *The Canadian Press* 7 May.

Van der Kolk, B. (2005). Developmental trauma disorder: Toward a rational diagnosis for children with complex trauma histories. *Psychiatric Annals* 35, pp. 401–408.

Van der Kolk, B. (2016). Commentary: The devastating effects of ignoring child maltreatment in psychiatry. *Journal of Child Psychology and Psychiatry* 57:3, pp. 267–270.

Venner, K. L., Wall, T. L., Lau, P., & Ehlers, C. L. (2006). Testing of an orthogonal measure of cultural identification with adult Mission Indians. *Cultural Diversity and Ethnic Minority Psychology* 12:4, pp. 632–643.

Wesley, M. A., et al.(2015). Early maladaptive schemas and early trauma experiences in depressed and non-depressed individuals: An Indian study. *Journal of Psychosocial Research* 10:1, p. 125.

Widom, C. M., et al. (2006). Childhood victimization and illicit drug use in middle adulthood. *Psychology of Addictive Behaviors* 20, pp. 394–403.

Williamson, L. (2014). Patient and citizen participation in health: The need for improved ethical support. *The American Journal of Bioethics* 14:6, pp. 4–16.

Part 1

Theory

Chapter 1

Hope and Motivation: Working With Adult and Child Victims of Childhood Complex Trauma

> We didn't really escape (the trauma of residential schools) . . . it visited us every day of our childhood through the replaying over and over of our parents' childhood trauma and grief which they never had the opportunity to resolve in their lifetimes . . . [Our mother] blames herself for not being able to protect us and not being able to help us when we were suffering.
>
> Vera Manuel[1]

Indigenous author Vera Manuel and her brother were spared the residential school experience, but their parents' childhood suffering became their own. Manuel's memories capture the schools' traumatic impact on the children compelled to attend: for about 150,000 Indigenous children in Canada, across all generations, for more than a century, neglect and abuse were the central motifs of their childhood experiences. Very few escaped the painful realities that shaped their own caregivers' experiences as these manifested in their own childhoods, even if, like Manuel and her brother, they did not personally attend these schools. The continuous repetitive result of unresolved childhood trauma is a destructive pattern of intergenerational trauma transmission.

Although the specific case of unresolved intergenerational trauma in Indigenous communities—not only in Canada, but around the world wherever racist colonial practices were employed to suppress Indigenous populations—provides a textbook example of enormous magnitude, it is nonetheless evident that childhood trauma is not isolated to subjugated peoples. Popularly depicted as a lightning-bolt experience, trauma is a universal phenomenon, regardless of the singular aspects of each person's traumatic experiences, and whether they are objectively classified as major or minor, "big T" or "little t," by victims or by others on their behalf. In its infinite variants, trauma is likely to occur at least once, if not many times, in any individual's lifespan. More than a distinct event, or even a series of distinct events, *trauma is a process* that has shifting, yet ongoing, effects on self-formation. The negative consequences of even one traumatic event obviously challenge the individual's well-being. Just as often, however, these repercussions touch their "inner circle" of family, caregivers, and close friends.

This is especially the case when the traumatized individual is a child or adolescent. Because the trauma occurs during the most important years of self-formation, its imprint is deep and lasting. The simple fact that traumatologist Bessel Van der Kolk points out is unassailable: children are "programmed" to regard their caregivers as their principal nurturers and protectors. Thus, "if the parents themselves are the source of distress, the child has no one to turn to for comfort and restoration of biological homeostasis" (Van der Kolk, 2016, p. 267). And when the impact of trauma is carried, unresolved, from childhood into adulthood, autonomy, inter-relatedness, personal competence, and their related behaviors invariably suffer. This chapter discusses how unresolved complex trauma—or recurrent trauma—in childhood affects the critical caregiver-child-clinician relationship in terms of building and reinforcing the three bases of intrinsic motivation, or behavior motivated by the inherent value of action-taking (Dreikus-Ferguson, 2000). It focuses on the ways in which correlated treatment of caregiver and child, as the keystone of the Intergenerational Trauma Treatment Model (ITTM), can effectively address the diminished hope and motivation of both, allowing for improved and lasting outcomes.

Motivation in Trauma Treatment Theories

"Motivation" is here defined as the influence of needs and desires on the intensity and direction of individual behavior. It is an internal process that shapes the individual's response to an external event or events (Dreikus-Ferguson, 2000, p. 7). Psychological studies on motivation generally include the evaluation of antecedents: traumatic past events experienced by an individual in conjunction with the attainment of such goals as improved personal and social functioning. More than a century past, Wundt (1902) identified three distinct dimensions of emotion: pleasurable *versus* non-pleasurable; exciting *versus* depressing; and stressing *versus* relaxing. Towards the close of the 20th century, psychologists such as Diener suggested that emotional intensity is a personality variable reflecting individual differences (Diener et al., 1985, p. 71–75). Others linked task variables to emotions, and emotions to effort, connecting emotion and motivation. Not surprisingly, depressed people were found to have less energy (Bandura et al., 1981), less memory, and less capacity for applying themselves to daily tasks (Ellis, 1988). More recently, Ferguson (2002) classified arousal as the energizing and intensifying aspect of motivation that is manifested both physiologically and behaviorally. An increase in energizing arousal after each treatment session, for example, is clearly more beneficial than the experience of tense arousal (Dreikus-Ferguson, 2000). Intrinsic motivation is the most significant "wellspring" of further motivation, inciting individuals to continue working toward their goals, even when there is no outside incentive to keep doing so (Ferguson, 2008).

Building motivation is at once the most important and the most challenging objective of the therapeutic professions. We know that motivated behavior is more likely to occur when specific sub-goals are defined first, securing the foundation for the attainment of larger goals. Definite short-term sub-goals are clear guidelines and immediate incentives for achievement; focusing on distant, generalized gains, such as improved functioning or a reduction in negative behaviors, can be overwhelming, with the effect of making the goal or goals seem beyond reach. Focusing on long-range goals tends to set the stage for free-floating "preparations" for a nebulous future, rather than immediate and achievable "first steps." Treatment that works towards specific, tangible, quickly attained goals can direct the individual to quickly attainable—and consequently motivational—successes (Bandura et al., 1981).

The starting point for understanding the causal relationship between caregiver motivation and successful treatment for children is identification of the underlying factors that discourage the caregivers. Uncovering these influences will assist clinicians to implement effective tools and strategies for enhancing caregiver motivation levels, thereby increasing their hopefulness for the child. Caregivers tend to postpone seeking treatment until they are overwhelmed by the child's problems, by which time personal and caregiving strategies have likely failed repeatedly. Their own untreated—even unacknowledged—traumatic childhood events, and their present emotional stress levels, especially in response to their child's needs, further deplete the necessary energy to encourage healthy relationships with their children as with others. Reduced effectiveness in personal interactions, in turn, increases the risks associated with isolation. When caregivers are unable to improve their own child's functioning, and put off referring the child for treatment, the outcome is often further impairments to already-damaged personal competence.

Caregiver hope and motivation improve the prospects that caregivers will see their children's treatment to its close.

In current practices, the initial indicator of a caregiver's motivation is also the most easily measured: how regularly they bring their child to scheduled treatment sessions. Using consistency of attendance as a measure, however, poses problems. Mental health clinicians generally accept that if a caregiver walks through the doors of a clinic, they are sufficiently motivated to participate in treatment. Yet this is often a critical error of assumption. The pressure to quickly assess the type and direction of treatment for children at intake can't help but take the clinician's attention from hidden problematic motivation factors in caregivers. Yet the most common explanation for negative treatment outcomes is premature dropout, which is usually the caregivers' decision. In short, the highest instances of negative outcomes are directly related to unmotivated, or inconsistently motivated, caregivers in bringing their child to treatment, which too often leads to stopping altogether (Willis-Shattuck, 2008).

When caregivers drop out of treatment, clinicians can conclude that the caregivers' motivation is insufficient. The explanation for failures in caregiver motivation and follow-through is a weak or absent sense of caregiver commitment; these shortcomings that so affect their children are therefore the caregivers' problem and responsibility, and not those of the clinician (Maclean et al., 2000). It's often a small step to viewing those who don't follow the clinician's advice as "failures" themselves, negligent caregivers who nonchalantly dismiss important treatment for their child because *they* lose interest. Since children usually can't pursue treatment on their own initiative, it's the caregivers' fault when treatment is not carried out to its necessary end. Ironically, these common assumptions about caregiver motivation often compound the problem itself.

The apparent absence of motivation is usually, and primarily, the product of the caregivers' own long-diminished and currently weakened personal competence levels. For all human beings, of all ages, competencies are developed and integrated in direct correlation to the number and frequency of tangible successes. Aware as they are of the larger problem, a significant number of service providers request practical applications to minimize lapses and set-backs caused by sporadic attendance. Research has demonstrated that interventions producing solid evidence of success are most likely to lead to the improvement and reinforcement of competence levels. The experience of relatively quick successes raises hope in caregivers, as their personal/caregiver capacity to commit for the long term is strengthened.

Clinicians do not intentionally minimize the importance of motivation-building in treatment programs. Yet child and family trauma treatment research invariably focuses on recommendations for "what" treatment issues need to be addressed and "why" doing so is important. Often the crucial "how" aspects are scarcely touched on, or even left out. The growing need for service, as reflected in historically high caseloads and the reduced funds that commonly lead to short staffing, have also distracted clinicians from working to develop interventions that specifically encourage motivated behaviors in adults. The result is a notable paucity of motivational behavior building tools and strategies to help caregivers participating in child trauma treatment. What follows is a discussion of some of the main strategies and how the ITTM utilizes and expands upon these in order to effectively treat complex childhood trauma in both children and caregivers.

Among the most efficacious of potential motivation-building strategies is **motivational interviewing** (MI), a direct, person-centered style of counseling. Motivational interviewing was originally designed to be used with alcoholics, who often experience ambivalence about changing their drinking behavior (Britton et al., 2008). Its goal is to buoy the client's healthy need for autonomy by working with them to examine their ambivalence, and then directing them in making carefully mapped, measured, behavioral changes (Rollnick, 1992). Motivational interviewers rely primarily on non-verbal listening, reflective listening, and selective reflection. Ultimately, MI is intended to help individuals define and express their own reasons for either changing or maintaining the status quo, and to understand how their current behavior affects their ability to achieve their life goals. As such, they chart their own path to recovery. As a clinical approach, however, motivational interviewing lacks the theoretical framework to describe its mechanisms and functions. Studies by Britton and associates indicate that, after providing suicidal adults with combined CBT and MI interventions within a **Self-Determination Theory** framework, the method's effectiveness in improving client engagement or treatment outcomes still could not be established. This may help to explain why MI is reported to work best in increasing the client's engagement in treatment and in improving outcomes when it is used to complement other treatments (Britton et al., 2008).

Self-Determination Theory, first described by Ryan et al. (1997), emphasizes the crucial relationship between an individual's inner resources and their personality development and behavioral self-regulation. The three essential inner resources—autonomy, inter-relatedness, and competence—must be established before high levels of self-determination and motivation can occur (Deci & Ryan, 1985). Degrees of self-determination are relative to age, strength, and the functioning of the three specific intrinsic elements. The higher the level of each element, the higher the concentration of self-determination levels in every individual. Heightened levels of self-determination in turn spark heightened levels of hope in the personal capacity to set and achieve goals. Higher concentrations of self-determination then help to increase the frequency of intrinsically motivated behaviors.

Expanding on theories concerning intrinsic and extrinsic motivation, Deci and Ryan (1985) developed **Organismic Integration Theory** (OIT). This theory posits that the value of each type of motivation is dependent upon the degree to which each form of behavior is internalized and integrated into the individual's "sense of self." The more evidence of competence, autonomy, and inter-relatedness, the stronger the likelihood of increased value in each area. The stronger the strength of each component, the more the individual will value intrinsically motivated behavior. By these measures, a caregiver who does not refer a child for treatment despite escalating post-traumatic symptoms is situated at the lowest end of the motivated behavior continuum. Deci and Ryan (1985) characterize such a caregiver as extrinsically unmotivated and therefore unable to perceive the value of initiating treatment. The caregiver's lack of motivation might bring about a style of non-regulatory, non-intentional behavior, demonstrating a significant absence of control and a growing experience of incompetence (Bandura, 1981).

Extrinsic motivation is the participation in activities or tasks to avoid punishment or to gain external rewards. A caregiver can be identified as extrinsically motivated if they seek treatment because they believe good and responsible caregivers want their children to experience fewer negative behaviors and symptoms and better overall health. Denying that treatment is valuable might consequently challenge their self-perception as responsible and caring caregivers. People engage in extrinsically motivated behaviors largely to mirror and valorize the behaviors of those with whom they already feel a connection, or to bring about that connection (Deci & Ryan, 1985). Of the three other levels of extrinsically based motivation, **identified regulation** is perhaps most applicable to caregivers who make referrals to trauma treatment. It occurs when the amount of motivation required to achieve a goal is consistent with the individual's core values and beliefs. Identified regulation behavior, therefore, reflects the conscious value of the behavior that the individual holds to be personally important (Britton et al., 2008).

Self-Determination Theory also provides a useful explanation of intrinsic motivation in relation to "innate" or "inherent" individual characteristics. It puts forward three foundational ideas about "inherency" in human development:

- Humans are inherently able to master their inner drives and emotions;
- Humans inherently tend toward growth, development, and integrated functioning;
- Although optimal development and action are inherent, they do not occur automatically.

(Vansteenkiste, 2004)

Self-determination theorists are not nearly as concerned with *how* inherent tendencies and innate psychological needs form, as they are with distinguishing the internal processes that motivate people at intrinsic levels (Deci & Ryan, 1985). They identify autonomy, inter-relatedness, and competence as intrinsic and essential psychological needs that are internally established by everyone, to various points of functionality, such as personality development and the capacity to regulate the self (Deci & Ryan, 1985). Importantly, SDT also recognizes that individual strengths will vary even within each of the three innate need categories. Such variations account for individual differences of degree in satisfying each need (Deci & Ryan, 1985). The ITTM uses a variety of motivational interviewing techniques within an SDT framework, modified in accordance with the client's age and developmental stage, to encourage and reinforce engagement and positive outcomes in caregiver and child (McCormack & Thomson, 2017, p. 156).

Caregiver Involvement in Child Trauma Treatment

As are all health professionals, child trauma treatment specialists are in the business of caring for others. Clinicians work to reduce relational distances between children and caregivers, and take every possible step to intensify levels of compassion between them, especially considering any historical and current trauma and its related impacts on the family. A caregiver who has experienced childhood trauma, and whose child has been referred for trauma treatment, presents an important opportunity to work with them to strengthen their individual levels of autonomy, capacity for inter-relatedness, and personal competence. This is decidedly *not* about blaming caregivers. It is a simple recognition that even well-intentioned caregivers need help to overcome the very traumas that have damaged their own caregiving practices. As well as encouraging several clinically significant treatments, this timely adult intervention can build the caregiver's motivation to bring in the child for regular treatment.

Acknowledging the need for intervention to build caregiver capacity for completing the prescribed treatment involves further consideration of the three levels of intrinsic motivation function. To begin, a caregiver's need for **autonomy** derives from the requirement to experience themselves as causal agents of their own actions when their child is referred for trauma treatment. Bandura et al. (1981) defines autonomy according to Self-Determination Theory as the need to feel the power of choice in personal actions, not in terms of a need for dependency or independence in relation to others. Often, however, by the time a caregiver feels the need to request professional assistance for their child, their capacity to maintain personal autonomy has already been further weakened. But autonomy does not mean operating alone or independently of others. If autonomy is a universal urge in humans to be causal agents in their own lives, and if a child's exposure to life events and conditions is largely determined by caregiver realities, children and trauma therapists both need caregivers' participation in child trauma treatments (Ratelle, 2004).

Inter-relatedness, the "universal want to interact, be connected to and experience caring for others," is the second of the three basic psychological needs (Baumeister et al., 1995). The negative impact of a single traumatic event, or a series of traumatic events, will demand all the individual's available emotional and psychological energy for coping. Energy that would normally be available to interact, connect and provide care sufficient for both the self and others can become inaccessible. Like an injured animal, the individual may feel the need to retreat into isolation in an attempt to conserve personal energy for self-needs. If they do not improve within a reasonable time, their isolation and lack of inter-relatedness to self and others is likely to grow. Caregiver stress levels, therefore, strongly influence the degree to which a caregiver will maintain active participation in a child's life (Ratelle, 2004; Van der Kolk, 2012; Cyr & Alink, 2017, p. 81).

Where the psychological need to feel a satisfactory measure of personal competence is concerned, a caregiver who has experienced trauma in childhood, and who must face the impact of a separate trauma experienced by their child, will see their personal sense of competence undermined. They may report feeling depressed, anxious, or worthless. According to Friendly et al. (2008) the need for competence is closely related to "a person's sense of self-efficacy or mastery over his or her environment" (p. 68). They further posit that "the environmental dimension associated with the need for competence is structure versus lack of structure" (p. 68). Structure is essential to the stability that encourages individuals to shape "reasonable expectations about their environments" (p. 69) and thereby to gain mastery over them (Friendly et al., 2008). Any area of life that appears to lack structure will fuel a sense of incompetence in that area.

To actualize inherent potential, individuals require the nurturing that is obtained within social environments. Every caregiver-child-clinician relationship has, at once, both the potential to meet needs, and to prevent needs from being met (Friendly et al., 2008). A caregiver's need to break through self-isolation and to feel greater personal competence may be unintentionally circumvented by the mental health system if the primary participants in the child's treatment are the child and therapist alone. Caregivers of children who have experienced trauma can be helped by attendance in psycho-educational courses with other caregivers in similar situations. The child's clinician can provide individual attention to the caregiver for their own trauma history prior to treating the child, as discussed. These interventions will reinforce and recover the caregiver's abilities to inter-relate.

Despite their centrality in recovery, child-focused trauma treatments may unintentionally diminish hope in caregivers and undermine their sense of their child's competence, autonomy, and inter-relatedness functioning. If this occurs, such treatments cannot help but reduce the child's own attainment of strength in these essential psychological areas. As this lower available energy affects caregivers' ability to inter-relate with children, it also automatically reduces their felt sense of autonomy. The ITTM is designed to assess, address, and resolve a caregiver's trauma impact history, and strengthen their levels of competence, autonomy, and inter-relatedness through exercises that produce tangible results in each phase of treatment. Most clinician-led child trauma treatment programs allow little opportunity for children to understand their caregiver's own issues with competence, autonomy, and inter-relatedness. This lack of substantive day-to-day evidence of the caregiver's capacity to change, and commitment to doing so, is the outcome of making the child the single recipient of treatment, as most trauma treatment methods do. The results negatively affect the child's faith in the caregiver, the therapist, and the treatment itself. The hope and motivation of both child and caregiver are substantially curtailed at exactly the moment when everything should be done to encourage their growth.

Developing Intrinsic Motivation-Based Platforms

The creators of Self-Determination Theory (Deci & Ryan, 1985) do not prioritize the imperatives of reconstructing, strengthening, or enhancing autonomy, inter-relatedness, and competence. It is nonetheless evident that, without a history of demonstrated successes, a caregiver's competence level will likely remain diminished to the point that the caregiver has difficulty even meeting the regular challenges of day-to-day life for themselves and their child, and may suffer from depression and anxiety. Competence is therefore the first intrinsic motivation-based platform addressed in the first phase of ITTM treatment. A client with proven evidence of self-capacity is much more likely to experience greater interest and energy to interact and relate to others. The ITTM supports Self-Determination Theory by providing specific interventions to strengthen the three intrinsic need levels (in this order): competence, autonomy, and inter-relatedness.

Strengthening the caregivers' competence and autonomy *even before* seeing the child in treatment works to build their hopefulness and energy for inter-relating with both the child and the clinician. Finally, the caregiver will feel less controlled by their own and their child's unresolved trauma. Real, current evidence of their own growing competencies brings about recognition of a strengthened and autonomous self. The adult, as an individual and a caregiver, is prepared and eager to assume the vital role of primary active participant and agent of change during each trauma treatment session with the child; hence, in the child's life. In sum, the ITTM is a practical, evidence-based application of Self-Determination Theory.

The ITTM is informed by three original **intrinsic motivation-based platforms** (IMBP) that can assist clinicians in recognizing the strength or weakness levels of competence, autonomy, and inter-relatedness in caregivers who are referring their child for treatment following trauma (Figure 1.1). Specific treatment interventions are then applied to build, strengthen, or enhance each caregiver's IMBP level. A description of the three most commonly presented categories of intrinsic motivation-based platforms follows.

This **Shattered IMBP** (Figure 1.2) caregiver treatment program, guided by the clinician, focuses on the building of competence, inter-relatedness, and autonomy, informed by first-hand, tangible experiences of small successes evidenced in each treatment session, every step of the way. The caregiver's experience of witnessing their own incremental successes in each treatment session provides a starting point for demonstrating a self-incurred competence platform. Solid examples of proven success will allow the caregiver to experience competence in incremental steps.

Criteria for Shattered IMBP

- The caregiver has a history of minor or very few successes.
- The caregiver does not have a sense of personal competence.
- The amount of available energy the caregiver has to apply to inter-relatedness with others is virtually non-existent.
- Very few, if any, examples of autonomous behavior are reflected in day-to-day functioning.

FIGURE 1.1 The ITTM's Three Intrinsic-Motivation-Based Platforms (IMBPs)

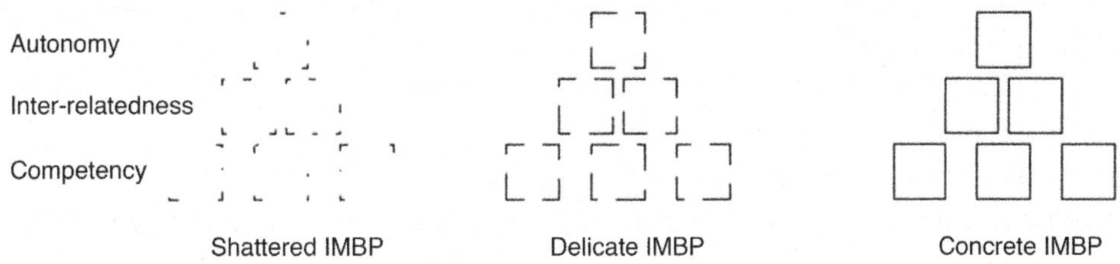

FIGURE 1.2 The Shattered IMBP

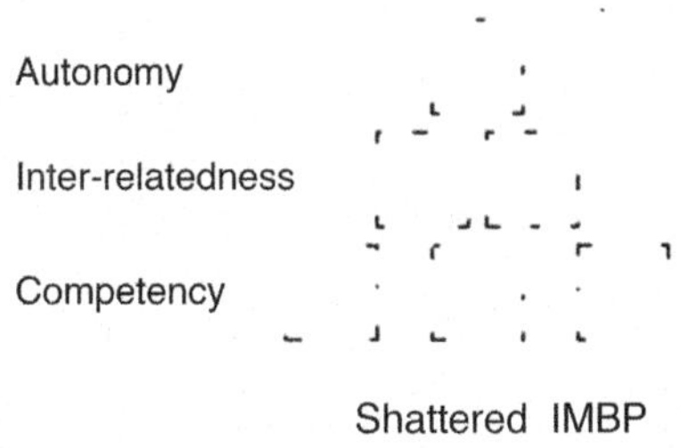

The Shattered IMBP lacks the essential building blocks of intrinsic-motivated behavior. It requires the construction of each level of the competence, inter-relatedness, and autonomous need platforms.

The available energy of the caregiver for continuing the practice of inter-relating with the clinician will also increase from the practical experience gained by improving relatedness to self and others as experienced first-hand through the treatment process with the clinician. Additionally, having the opportunity to metaphorically separate themselves from the trauma through the clinician provides the caregiver with a deliberate imposed distance from the trauma-created impact, so that they can begin, perhaps for the first time, to consider the trauma from a position of objectivity within themselves. The treatment goal of working to construct the **Shattered IMBP** of a caregiver is to build the groundwork that will eventually graduate the caregiver at least into the **Delicate IMBP** level.

The **Delicate IMBP** (Figure 1.3) caregiver's treatment works to strengthen their current felt sense of competence, inter-relatedness, and autonomy. **Delicate IMBPs** are capable of functioning at an average or near average level within themselves and with their children, providing stressful or traumatic events are not in the forefront of daily life. When a highly stressful or traumatic event does occur, the **Concrete IMBP** platform is likely to be shaken and can appear as though there are cracks or gaps of varying size within each platform level of competence, inter-connectedness, and autonomy. Negative symptoms and behaviors often escalate and the caregiver will need more structure within sessions to enable them to access and strengthen their own competencies, while building on examples of past autonomy efforts.

Treatment sessions will still need to design and provide medium-sized success opportunities. Witnessing their own successes in each treatment session will provide the caregiver with new tools to build additional strength for the **Delicate IMBP**. Reconstructed prior and present successes inform and support the **Delicate IMBP** caregiver. Demonstrated examples of success will naturally increase the caregiver's experience of autonomy and competence. The caregiver's available energy for continuing the practice of inter-relating with the clinician will also increase as they are reminded about the benefits of past and present self-supporting efforts. The clinician who works with a **Delicate IMBP** caregiver may find the caregiver already able to perceive the trauma and its damaging effects as clearly separate from themselves.

Criteria for Delicate IMBP

- The caregiver has a history of some successes.
- The caregiver has a frail sense of personal competence.
- The caregiver has a small amount of energy to apply to inter-relatedness to self and others.
- The caregiver has a few examples of experiences that have created intermittent experiences of autonomy-related behavior.

FIGURE 1.3 The Delicate IMBP

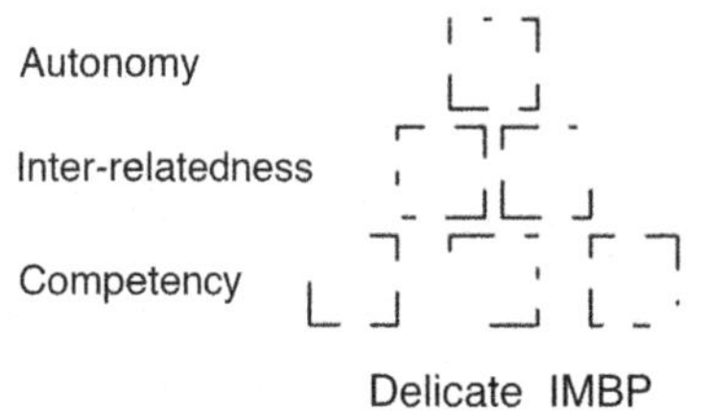

The Delicate IMBP depicts an intrinsic motivation-based platform that will require the clinician to strengthen each competence, inter-relatedness, and autonomy need platform level.

As a result, the clinician will be able to assist the caregiver's progression from the **Delicate IMBP** stage to that of the **Concrete IMBP**. This will improve the caregiver's ability to withstand and contain future stressors and the effects of their child's trauma on their own life.

The **Concrete IMBP** (Figure 1.4) caregiver's treatment is premised on the enrichment of their competence, inter-relatedness, and autonomy platforms. **Concrete IMBPs** typically function at a consistently healthy level with themselves and their children. When a highly stressful or traumatic event does occur, the **Concrete IMBP's** platform is likely to be questioned or challenged as a result of the caregiver attempting to return to pre-trauma thinking and behavior. The caregiver feels that they have not been able to do so over a reasonable period of time. As a result, their feelings of competence, inter-connectedness, and autonomy are diminished.

The **Concrete IMBP** caregiver's symptoms and behaviors likely will not be within clinically significant ranges. If they are, the behaviors and symptoms are likely related to situational effects and will be unlikely to fit the criteria of a *DSM-V* disorder. The clinician will need to assist and support the **Concrete IMBP** to demonstrate additional competencies, while drawing on current examples of autonomy. Treatment sessions will still need to design success-oriented opportunities for the **Concrete IMBP** caregiver, but the successes will be specifically related to the stressor or the traumatic event. The caregiver's experience of witnessing their own successes in each treatment session specific to the presenting issue will reinforce and return the **Concrete IMBP's** competence, inter-relatedness, and autonomy levels to a pre-trauma degree, reinforcing the **Concrete IMBP** caregiver's ability to cope and overcome future situational trauma effects. Above all, a complex phenomenon like client motivation requires a basis in theories that link motivation with beneficial outcomes. As discussed, it is consequently important to build caregiver motivation prior to the start of treatment with the child to maximize the chances of the child completing treatment, the foremost objective.

Criteria for Concrete IMBP

- The caregiver has a solid history of success.
- The caregiver has a strong sense of personal competence, even if slightly weakened at the point of referral.
- The caregiver has an adequate amount of energy to currently relate to self and others.
- The caregiver has a number of experiences that reflect autonomy-related behavior.

FIGURE 1.4 The Concrete IMBP

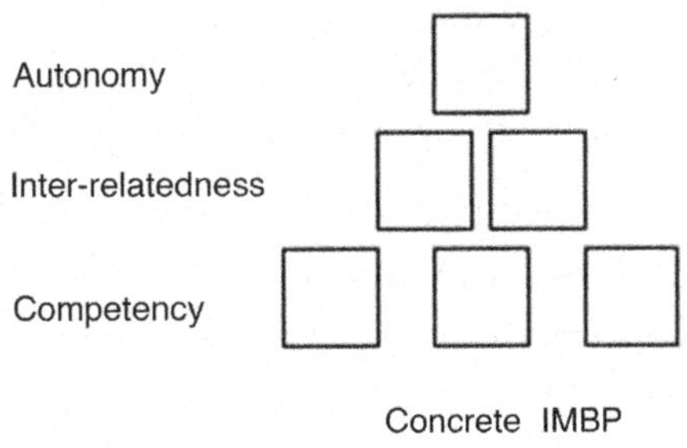

The Concrete IMBP depicts a high-functioning caregiver who has referred their child to trauma treatment. In this case, the clinician will be required to enhance a caregiver's competence, inter-relatedness, and autonomy need platforms.

Children with the most serious issues and the most complex social situations are less likely to attend the second treatment session and are also more likely to drop out from treatment prematurely (McKernan McKay et al., 1998; Kazdin et al., 1997). When Self-Determination Theory is applied in practice with caregivers who have referred their children to trauma treatment, increases in caregiver motivation can be expected. Therefore, providing caregivers with treatment specifically informed by Self-Determination Theory prior to commencing treatment with the child assists in ensuring that the child's treatment will be completed.

Caregivers typically access treatment services long after their personal coping methods and strategies for resolution have failed. Once an adult makes the choice to access treatment, the unexpected result may be a further reduction in the individual's already lowered sense of personal competence. Diminishment in the individual's sense of competence is likely to be coupled with a sense of being overwhelmed by the behaviors and symptoms generated in the child or triggered in the adult. As a result, much of a caregiver's energy is re-directed towards their own attempts at healing. The demand placed on the individual's energy to heal reduces the amount of available energy required to maintain a healthy level of inter-relatedness amongst and with others, including the child. Once a caregiver makes the courageous decision to access professional services with the goal of improving functioning, an inherent repercussion could lessen the adult's current level of autonomy. For this reason, the more supports a caregiver perceives their child or themselves to need to maintain a minimum or improved level of functioning, the greater the potential diminishment of the adult's current personal competence and autonomy functioning levels.

Because caregivers are a child's gateway to mental health treatment, those conducting child trauma treatment programs must seriously consider the short- and long-term benefits of strengthening adults' current functioning levels of intrinsic motivation platform elements. Making this the first course of action could significantly increase caregivers' commitment to getting themselves and their children to regularly scheduled treatment sessions. There are vital benefits for the child who witnesses tangible proof of their caregivers' individual choice, engagement, and capacity for change prior to commencing with trauma treatment interventions that target the behavioral symptoms of the child. The mental health outcomes for caregivers and children who *do not* receive treatment following trauma are significantly poorer, to the extent that some researchers recommend *mandating* mental health treatment for both caregivers *and* children known to have experienced significant trauma (Lundahl et al., 2006).

Conclusion

The most effective treatments for children impacted by complex trauma are those that provide a multimodal approach, follow a phase-based or sequential pattern, and involve the caregiver in treatment (Cloitre, 2009). Most opportunities for caregiver involvement are organized according to the child's primary presenting symptom(s). For example, such commonly offered group courses as "Managing Your Child's Anxiety," "Sexual Abuse Treatment," "Grief and Loss," and "Family Violence" typically focus on specific symptoms or events. Many "single focus" courses of this nature are also offered in post-secondary social work and psychology programs. Although a program such as "caring for your sexually abused child" is specifically designed for caregivers, this does not necessarily mean that the caregiver will be included in the treatment decisions or as an active participant in treatment sessions with their child. Not engaging the caregiver in the treatment of their child may unintentionally reinforce their feelings of lost autonomy. If caregivers have more than one professional involved in the child's treatment, their already-diminished sense of personal competence, autonomy, and self-determinism may be at risk for falling further.

At the same time, a caregiver's referral of a child to treatment denotes a small and unique opening for interventions that can strengthen motivation levels enough to sustain caregivers when children begin their own treatment. Caregivers who make referrals can be said to be perfectly positioned to receive their own treatment to strengthen current competencies, to increase opportunities for inter-relatedness, and to directly experience the benefits of individual autonomy. If higher levels of motivated behaviors in caregivers correlate with an increased probability of treatment completion, as they strongly appear to do, then bolstering the motivational platforms of caregivers prior to the commencement of the child's treatment should improve dropout rates and consequently treatment outcomes for both caregivers and children.

This chapter has considered how various theories of motivation inform the Intergenerational Trauma Treatment Model. Specific benefits, as detailed, are derived from **Cognitive Behavioral Theory** (CBT), **Self-Determination Theory** (SDT), and the application of **intrinsic motivation-based platforms** (IMBP). Chapter 2 will turn to ideas about brain development in childhood, as these have been formulated and tested by researchers in the past 20 years, with a view to situating the ITTM within the context of emerging neuroscientific inquiry.

Note

1. Vera Manuel, *The Abyss*, p. 107; cited in *First They Came for the Children*, v. 1, Truth and Reconciliation Commission, Ottawa: 2016, p. 79. Manuel is referring to the experience of compulsory residential school that faced all Indigenous children in Canada from the late 19th century until the last one was closed in 1986.

References

Bandura, A. S., et al. (1981). Cultivating competence, self-efficacy, and intrinsic interest through proximal self-motivation. *Journal of Personality and Social Psychology* 41:3, pp. 586–598.

Baumeister, R., et al. (1995). The need to belong: Desire for interpersonal connection as a fundamental human emotion. *Psychological Bulletin* 117, pp. 497–529.

Britton, P. W., et al. (2008). Self-determination theory, motivational interviewing, and the treatment of clients with acute suicidal ideation. *Journal of Clinical Psychology* 64:1, pp. 52–66.

Cloitre, M. S. (2009). A developmental approach to complex PTSD: Childhood and adult cumulative trauma as predictors of symptom complexity. *The Journal of Traumatic Stress* 22:5, pp. 399–408.

Cyr, C. & Alink, A. (2017). Child maltreatment: The central roles of parenting capacities and attachment. *Current Opinion in Psychology* 15, pp. 81–86.

Deci, E. & Ryan, R. (1985). *Intrinsic Motivation and Self-Determination in Human Behavior*. New York, NY: Springer.

Diener, E. E., et al. (1985). The satisfaction with life scale. *Journal of Personality Assessment* 49, pp. 71–75.

Dreikus-Ferguson, E. (2000). *A Biosocial and Cognitive Integration of Motivation and Emotion*. New York: Oxford University Press.

Ellis, H. C. (1988). Resource allocation model of the effects of depressed mood states on memory. In K. Fiedler (Ed.), *Affect, Cognition and Social Behavior* (pp. 25–43). Toronto: Hogrefe.

Ferguson, C. R. (2008). Violent video games and aggression: Causal relationship or byproduct of family violence and intrinsic violence motivation? *Criminal Justice and Behavior* 35:3, pp. 311–332.

Ferguson, M. H. (2002). Implicit motivation: Past, present, and future. In J. Y. Shah & W. L. Gardner (Eds.), *Handbook of Motivation Science* (pp. 1–43). New York, NY: Guilford Press.

Friendly, R. A., et al. (2008). Child adjustment to familial dissolution: An examination of parental factors using a self-determination theory framework. *Journal of Divorce & Remarriage* 50:1, pp. 66–80.

Kazdin, A. H., et al. (1997). Family experience of barriers to treatment and premature termination from child therapy. *Journal of Clinical Psychology* 65:3, pp. 453–463.

Lundahl, B. & Nimer, J. P. (2006). Preventing child abuse: a meta-analysis of parent training programs. *Research on Social Work Practice* 16:3, pp. 251–262.

Maclean, N. P., et al. (2000). A critical review of the concept of patient motivation in the literature on physical rehabilitation. *Social Sciences & Medicine* 50:4, pp. 495–506.

McCormack, L. & Thomson, S. (2017). Complex trauma in childhood, a psychiatric diagnosis in adulthood: Making meaning of a double-edged phenomenon. *Psychological Trauma: Theory, Research, Practice, and Policy* 9:2, pp. 156–165.

McKernan McKay, M. S., et al. (1998). Increasing access to child mental health services for urban children and their caregivers. *Journal of Health and Social Work* 23, p. 1.

Ratelle, C. V. (2004). Cognitive adaptation and mental health: A motivational analysis. *European Journal of Social Psychology* 34, pp. 459–476.

Rollnick, S. N. (1992). Negotiating behavior change in medical settings: The development of brief motivational interviewing. *Journal of Mental Health* 1, pp. 25–37.

Ryan, R. K., et al. (1997). Nature and autonomy: Organizational view of social and neurobiological aspects of self-regulation in behavior and development. *Development and Psychopathology* 9, pp. 701–728.

Truth and Reconciliation Commission (2016). *First They Came for the Children*. Ottawa, ON: TRC, p. 79.

Van der Kolk, B. (2012). Understanding interpersonal trauma in children: Why we need a developmentally appropriate trauma diagnosis. *American Journal of Orthopsychiatry* 82, pp. 187–200.

Van der Kolk, B. (2016). Commentary: The devastating effects of ignoring child maltreatment in psychiatry. *Journal of Child Psychology and Psychiatry* 57:3, pp. 267–270.

Vansteenkiste, M. S. (2004). Motivating learning, performance, and persistence: The synergistic role of intrinsic goals and autonomy-support. *Journal of Personality and Social Psychology* 87, pp. 246–260.

Willis-Shattuck, M. B. (2008). Motivation and retention of health workers in developing countries: A systemic review. *BMC Health Services Research* 8, pp. 247–254.

Wundt, W. (1902). *Grundzüge der physiologischen Psychologie* (5th ed.). (Principles of Physiological Psychology), 2. Leipzig: Engelmann.

Chapter 2

Starting With the Brain: Childhood Complex Trauma, Neuroscience, and the ITTM

> A child needs to feel from the very start that she or he is wanted and loved. They should grow up in the soil of affection and care. There is no replacement for that, it is the most important thing. If that isn't right from the very beginning then everything that follows is playing catch up—trying to make better that which isn't good.
>
> (Morpurgo, 2015)[1]

Who would dispute that childhood should be a life stage of creative exploration and self-formation, realized within the shelter of a loving family, where children are rooted "in the soil of affection and care" and seen by devoted caregivers safely along the path to growing up? Regrettably, this ideal childhood has little in common with the realities of many children's lives. Children obviously cannot select the families into which they are born or adopted. Whether as a singular event or an ongoing process, many are exposed to and experience trauma. Such children learn to distrust, and defend themselves against, the caregivers or other adults who don't protect them—or who are themselves the perpetrators. Their largely unformed self-image becomes distorted in its early and particularly vulnerable formative stages. They lose their capacity to believe that they are rightfully worthy of love, respect, and security. All too frequently, children who have suffered trauma are unable to grow up healthy, resilient, and emotionally equipped to deal with the stresses of everyday adult life. And as adults with histories of unresolved childhood trauma, they also frequently convey their own trauma to their children.

The 21st century has witnessed, more so than any other historic period of barely 20 years, an unrelenting process of rapid, intensive, accelerating, multifaceted change. Within this ever-shifting world context, what must be conceded is that complex trauma in childhood has been virtually normalized: such experiences are now more common than exceptional, contrary to long-held understandings of what "trauma" means. Quantitative data supports this lamentable conclusion (Scannapieco & Connell-Carrick, 2005). In 2016, an estimated 15 million children worldwide lived with domestic violence and 1 in 4 of those children died every day because of maltreatment (www.futureswithoutborders.com).

This chapter reviews how ongoing advances in neuroscience have influenced—and continue to influence—the development of the ITTM as a series of treatment interventions that can reverse, resolve, or at least improve the injurious neurophysiological effects of complex trauma in children, and in adults with unresolved childhood trauma. First to be discussed is the most relevant and up-to-date information available about neurobiological perspectives on brain development in children exposed to complex trauma. A critical review of the literature demonstrates how neuroscience supports the ITTM's brain-based method for deconstructing and reconstructing negative self-formulations in caregivers and children, individually and in joint treatment sessions (Copping et al., 2001). I am concerned with addressing two fundamental questions: Where select principles of mathematics and mentalization are applied to validate or negate faulty belief systems, does the brain's inherent drive to establish its reasoning capacity support the ITTM method? And how does neuroscience help us to understand some of the reasons why negative self-beliefs dominate the thoughts, feelings, and actions of adults, adolescents, and children who have experienced complex trauma in childhood?

Self-beliefs inform our sense-making of ourselves, and thus our self-making, in present and future, but the beliefs that guide our thoughts, feelings, and actions for the long term are those constructed in childhood. I contend that negative self-beliefs can be quickly and effectively reconstructed to reflect valid self-deductions when elements from neuroscience, the philosophy of reason, and mathematics are employed to formulate an intergenerational therapeutic method. I have developed an interdisciplinary, multidisciplinary approach that borrows philosophical perspectives on the brain's inherent and essential need to establish the capacity to reason. I have incorporated into this philosophical foundation the principles of mathematics that can be applied to disprove the validity of negative self-beliefs with adult and child victims of complex trauma. I have both used and trained other clinicians to use this method successfully with hundreds of adults, adolescents, and children.

Current studies, as will be discussed, report that changes in a child's neurophysiological development influence and alter beliefs, cognitions, identity development, and self-worth. The inter-relatedness of mathematics, neuroscience, the philosophy of reason, complex trauma theory, developmental psychology, and developmental traumatology is highlighted in this chapter. My goal is to demonstrate how neuroscience supports and influences specific treatment interventions for assessing and resolving the injurious neurophysiological effects of complex trauma in adult and child victims.

The Child's Brain and Complex Trauma

Multiple and severe forms of trauma, especially in childhood, generally have multiple and severe psychological results, a phenomenon referred to as "complex post-traumatic disturbance" or, more simply, complex trauma. The context is often one of emotional neglect and unsafe social environments (Briere & Scott, 2015; Cook et al., 2005). The development of psychological problems across the lifespan of people raised in dysfunctional and traumatic family settings is so well documented that it can be said to have passed into common knowledge (Goodman et al., 1999; Craighead & Nemeroff, 2005). The trauma literature repeatedly links unresolved behavioral and emotional difficulties in children to the later development of adult disorders such as depression, anxiety, and a wide range of health problems and antisocial behaviors (Felitti et al., 1998; Fletcher et al., 2003; Widom et al., 2006; Vachon et al., 2015). As Van der Kolk expresses its impact:

> trauma is not just an event that took place sometime in the past; it is also the imprint left by that experience on mind, brain and body. This imprint has consequences for how the human organism manages to survive in the present.
>
> (Van der Kolk, 2016, p. 21)

Caregivers with histories of unresolved trauma are often ill-equipped to help their children manage, regulate, and adapt to the impact of traumatic events. Thus, children are more likely to experience trauma symptoms if their caregivers also have traumatic childhood histories (Nader, 1998). The trauma literature generally agrees that family functioning is important in both the development of symptoms and the outcomes for the traumatized child. For example, after a natural disaster, separation from caregivers, maternal preoccupation, and altered family functioning are found to be more predictive of symptom development than trauma or loss (Pfefferbaum, 1997). Also evident is the fact that children whose caregivers were previously traumatized are more likely to experience symptoms following exposure to trauma than children of caregivers without histories of trauma (Nader, 1998; Van der Kolk, 2016, p. 86).

When children have experienced traumatic events, effective treatment hinges on the accurate assessment and resolution of trauma impact in their caregivers' histories. If trauma impact goes undetected, a wide range of negative effects can follow children through the lifespan, often becoming more frequent and severe as time goes on; for traumatized individuals, the trauma, then, "contaminates" all that happens in their lives (Scott & Copping, 2008; Van der Kolk, 2016, p. 53). Research confirms that the risk of behavior disorders increases when caregivers are burdened by maternal depression, caregiver discord, family stress, unresolved trauma impact, and social isolation (Copping et al., 2001; Davies & Cummings, 1994; Levine et al., 2005). One study found that 50% of mothers who referred children to treatment were clinically depressed. When indicators of additional mental health problems were present, disorder rates increased further (Hutchings et al., 2002). Children of sexually abused caregivers, for example, are more likely to be victims themselves, often due to caregivers' latent cooperation with the abuser or their "blindness" to the dangers of situations to which they expose their children (Lev-Wiesel, 2006).

The human brain, weighing three pounds at maturity and containing millions of cells, is the most complex organism ever investigated by science. Brain development is regulated by genes, and as De Bellis (2002) concludes, "genes interact with life experiences—specifically experienced in childhood (p. 540). Gene-environment interactions likely reflect genetic moderation of the brain's functional response to stress, including early life stress, which then transforms into anxiety and depression. That childhood maltreatment affects brain structure and function is an established fact (Maguire et al., 2015; Van der Kolk, 2016; Heim et al., 2008, p. 703; De Bellis, 2002).

A closer look at brain structure and function reveals that the first stages of visual processing involve the back portion of the cerebral cortex (the occipital lobe). The central sulcus is the frontal portion (frontal lobe) of the cerebral cortex responsible for motor behavior. Behind the central sulcus sits the portion of the cerebral cortex involved in processing tactile information (the parietal lobe). The prefrontal cortex is responsible for several of the most highly integrated functions of the individual's operating system. These includes the ability to plan and organize and to interweave cognitive and emotional streams of information. The anterior circular region of the medial prefrontal cortex is also a part of the executive attention system and involved in the extinction of conditioned fear responses (Hammer, 2002, p. 11). The prefrontal cortex continues to develop well into a person's third decade of life. Millions of axons, protected by a white substance called myelin, lie beneath the cortex. The myelin fills in the massive amounts of neurons or "gray matter" that is composed of neuronal cell bodies. The greatest increases in myelination are between the ages of 6 months and 3 years, and then again in the third decade (De Bellis, 2002). Most important for our purposes, the gray matter zones serve to process information; white matter can be described as the circuit system that sends information from one area of the brain to another. Gray matter also incorporates the basal ganglia that activates emotion and motivation levels. The basal ganglia's connection to motivational aspects is linked to the development and practice of addictive disorders (Hammer, 2002).

Also located within the gray matter zones are the amygdala and the hippocampus. The amygdala ascribes emotional meaning to events and objects, and significantly informs negative emotions such as fear. The hippocampus takes charge of converting and combining explicit and sporadic memories of people, places, and things. For example, periods of very brief separation of maternal rats from their offspring during infancy have been proven to affect the functioning of the limbic-hypothalamic-pituitary-adrenal axis, and hence the expression of the glucorticoid receptor gene in the hippocampus and frontal cortex

(Francis et al., 1999). Furthermore, sub-cortical gray matter and the limbic system structures composed of the septal area, hippocampus, and amygdala increase in volume through early adolescence, usually peaking at 16.6 years (De Bellis, 2002, p. 556).

Andersen et al. (2008) identified unique brain development sensitivities in young female adults (aged 18–22) who had experienced sexual abuse in childhood. Results from Multiple Resonance Imaging examinations (MRIs) revealed reduced hippocampal volume in association with childhood sexual abuse at 3–5 years and at 11–13 years of age. Corpus callosum was reduced with the experience of sexual abuse at 9–10 years of age, whereas frontal cortex volumes remained the same in young adult females who experienced childhood sexual abuse at ages 14–16 (Andersen et al., 2008, p. 292). This study supports earlier findings that physical or sexual abuse (and resulting psychopathology) are linked to hemisphere maturation, but also to changes in gray matter volume, symmetry, and neuronal integrity of the frontal cortex (p. 298).

Although hippocampal volume changes may not be evident in current MRI studies, the functioning of the hippocampal region has consistently been found to be adversely affected by maltreatment (De Bellis, 2002). In brief, stress in early childhood changes the brain's ability to make the best use of nutritive and growth component requirements. This can also create developmental differences in synaptic overproduction, which in turn can lead to changes in hippocampal volume properties that are evident in late adolescence or early adulthood (Andersen & Teicher, 2004; Teicher et al., 2012; Van der Kolk, 2016).

These associations between childhood abuse and stress reactivity have also been traced between fibromyalgia and childhood abuse, and between stress reactivity and fibromyalgia. Childhood abuse, consequently, is a possible etiological factor of abnormal brain development, but also appears to affect stress reactivity that can then lead to the development of fibromyalgia (Lee, 2010, p. 294). Other studies make similar connections between stress and emotional reactivity connected to childhood trauma and other chronic pain syndromes (Imbierowicz & Egle, 2003; Lee, 2010), gastrointestinal disorders (Leserman et al., 2007), and cardiovascular diseases (Dong et al., 2004; Heim, 2008, p. 703). The effects of maltreatment on a child's developmental process and the chance to create new syntactic connections in adults and children underscores the importance of mandating treatment to child victims of childhood maltreatment and to adults before they become caregivers.

Since the closing decade of the 20th century, and especially as functional magnetic resonance imaging is increasingly deployed to map brain activity, neuroscientific advances have been revolutionary, demanding an entirely revised approach to the brain and its capabilities. Research has disproved most earlier assumptions. Put simply, it is now generally accepted that the brain continues to manufacture neurons well into old age and that alternate segments of the brain can be activated when a particular area is injured or worn out: the brain recruits healthy neurons as necessary to carry out the tasks previously managed by the damaged or old ones (Ione, 2015; Simons et al., 2015).

The application of neuroscience to understanding complex trauma helps to identify the unique risks and mechanisms from which complex trauma conditions and other stressful events during childhood affect the brain development in children through the lifespan. Concerning the effects of maltreatment on the child's developing brain, Cicchetti & Lynch (1993) published a groundbreaking study in which they used a systems framework to situate current neuroscience findings and those of developmental scholars in order to foreground what both approaches recognized as the atypical brain development that appeared to result from maltreatment, and to propose hypotheses about how the trauma-affected brain might promote unusual behavior in children. When caregivers maltreat children, they exhibit a behavior outside the bounds of accepted, and expected, child nurture. The irregular environment created as a result will lead to unexpected, frequently deviant, effects on the child's self-formation, including learning ability (Allen & Oliver, 1982; Kirke-Smith et al., 2016). Childhood maltreatment can "switch on" certain genes that increase the potential for antisocial behavior later in life (Caspi & Moffitt, 2004).

There is also substantial evidence about the participant role of genetics in the development of mental health problems like depression, psychosis, anxiety, and drug and alcohol addiction, as well as learning challenges, including neurodevelopmental disorders such as autism (Rutter, 2006). Environmental influences, however, complicate the relationship of genes and human behavior, so that results are highly varied. Neuroscientists and geneticists alike warn against simplistic explanations such as "genes are destiny" and "nature versus nurture" (Woolgar, 2013, p. 243; Rutter, 2006). Environmental influences are established at the molecular level via "epigenetic" processes. The resulting developments constitute what is called an "epigenome" (Woolgar, 2013, p. 243). An organism's genetic code and the epigenetic effects of experience can be described in terms of having a "layering effect" on the genes. But the effect of the environment on genes modifies how they manifest themselves, which leads to the development of individual differences. However, just as environments can alter the impact of a child's genes, genes can similarly affect the impact of environments (Woolgar, 2013). Child welfare clinicians, and especially child and adult victims of complex trauma, can find purposeful directions for recovery in the now-significant evidence verifying how improvements in environmental conditions can alter neuropathways, a research focus that has been greatly facilitated using brain imaging technologies (Twadosz & Lutzker, 2010; Giedd, 2010). This potential for neural modification is also substantiated by a large body of research describing how the brain changes during different life stages in response to individual experiences (Greenough, 1987).

Life Experiences and Neuroplasticity

Based on more than 50 years of animal and human research concerning child development and maltreatment, Greenough and various co-researchers worked out a conceptual framework that distinguishes between childhood and adolescent brain plasticity, as well as confirming the brain's ability to adapt to experience throughout life (Greenough, 1987; Alcantara, 1993; Wilson, 2011). What resulted was a breakthrough neuroplasticity paradigm built on the critical notion that repeated experiences, activities, and thoughts alter gene expression and, in turn, the brain's structure (Simons et al., 2015, p. 576; Kennedy & Adolphs, 2012; Hughes et al., 2012). This process involves growth in cortical space devoted to functions used more frequently, and a corresponding decrease in cortical space devoted to those more rarely performed. Competitive operations are constantly at work in the brain, strengthening frequently used networks, and permitting those rarely utilized to disappear gradually (Merzenich, 2001). The thickness and breadth of the brain's diverse pathways, and the space that these occupy in individual brains—the brain's structure, including the size of different areas and the strength of connections between them—is literally shaped by individual experiences in everyday lives (Fishbane, 2007).

Both experience-expectant and experience-dependent brain plasticity occur during infancy and childhood, but the former type predominates. By early adulthood, it is thought that the essential "pruning" in the cerebral cortex is complete. Experience-dependent development—the modification and generation of new connections in response to experience—positions the brain to be continually affected by experience until death (Twadosz & Lutzker, 2010). The concept of experience-dependent plasticity draws attention to the informal and formal learning that occurs during childhood that is individually and culturally specific rather than universal. Such learning requires the consistent routines, responsive interaction, and specific teaching conditions that are less likely to be found in situations where maltreatment occurs. Instead, learning opportunities may revolve around surviving the abuse or neglect. Lifelong brain plasticity is also relevant for considering the impact of interventions for caregivers who must change their behavior to retain custody of their children; the stress experienced by these adults in their own lives may interfere with such learning (Sapolsky, 2003).

Neuroplasticity also relates to the nature of caregiver-child attachment. The quality of caregiver (usually maternal) care affects the infant's brain development. Recent studies in attachment psychology that utilize brain science clearly underscore the crucial role played by a child's primary caregiver in the biological, physiological, neurological, and intergenerational effects of individual development in and beyond childhood (Siegel, 2015). Children who are strongly attached to their mothers demonstrate higher capacity to manage real or perceived stress in adulthood. They are also more likely to provide a higher quality of caregiving to their infants (Siegel, 2015; Twadosz & Lutzker, 2010).

Considering what is known about brain functions, and how those functions affect individual belief systems and consequently behavior, it stands to reason that individuals have their entire store of available energy available to expend each day, no matter what age or size they are. Healthy happy children in healthy happy families can draw from the wellspring of all available psychological, neurological, and physiological energy to grow and learn about themselves in varying ways during various developmental stages. In contrast, most of the energy and capacity of children living in stressful, unsafe conditions will necessarily be depleted as they focus on their own anxiety, anticipatory worry, and the need to be hypervigilant (Ford et al., 2015, p. 62).

The child's age and gender, among other life circumstances, shape a response to trauma in the form of hyperarousal or dissociation. As either of these becomes a habitual, conditioned response, they will each demonstrate their own neurobiology, initial adaptive function for the child, and related psychiatric symptoms. In this manner, a response that was originally adaptive often becomes a "trait" defined by specific externalizing or internalizing patterns of behavior. Because these coping patterns are now part of the brain's organization, observers can classify these children as malleable rather than resilient. That is, children's agency is limited to adaptation for survival. They may appear to recover but often the neural changes will affect their mental health in adulthood in ways that are not directly traceable to earlier unresolved trauma. Early intervention is essential to minimize the severity of the child's response to trauma, and to curtail the possibility of neural changes leading to problems in adulthood, despite the appearance of recovery (Twadosz & Lutzker, 2010).

If there is little question about the ways in which environmental influences can alter neuropathways, what remains is to explore these influences with respect to neuroplasticity in children. MRI and fMRI (functional MRI) studies indicate that harsh and unpredictable childhood conditions (e.g. caregiver neglect) are associated with greater volume and reactivity in the amygdala, the portion of the brain responsible for vigilance and emotional responsiveness to threat (Pechtel, 2014), and with alterations of the prefrontal cortex, the area responsible for executive control (Herringa, 2013; Szczepanski et al., 2014). This can be seen in the brain structures of adopted children: those adopted at younger ages have smaller amygdala volume than those adopted later in childhood (Tottenham, 2012). Children continuously exposed to maternal depression likewise show larger amygdala volume than those without such exposure (Gilliam et al., 2015). The amygdala and prefrontal cortex, as well as their interconnections, are implicated in emotional regulation (Wager, 2008), impulsivity (Tsukayama, 2012), reactive aggression (Crowe et al., 2008), and internalization of problems (Tottenham, 2012).

Complex Trauma and Children's Regulated Stress Response System

Not surprisingly, given the close interplay between the care they receive and their brain development, children suffering from abuse and neglect may regulate their stress systems to extremes: their systems are either chronically elevated or chronically suppressed (Gunnar et al., 2006). Although these extremes exemplify dysregulation of normal stress response systems, each may have an adaptive function in certain poor caregiving environments. Studies with adults suggest that chronically elevated levels of cortisol are associated with marked anxiety and fearfulness. Similarly, elevated cortisol could help the child to prepare, or at least to be ready, for further threats in their environment. On the other hand, this anxious vigilance and readiness becomes unhelpful, and even harmful, if the child moves to a safer and more stable environment. It may lead them to misinterpret nurturing behavior as anxiety-provoking or threatening. A chronically suppressed cortisol level in response to early maltreatment is thought to prepare the child for functioning as well as they can in a continually adverse environment. If the child were to stay in that setting, it would make little sense for the body to remain in a chronically stressed state, drawing away resources from important biological functions and thereby negatively affecting other areas of development. Of necessity, the child's biology adjusts, suppressing the stress system, but this adjustment to a chronically aversive environment can also trigger antisocial and aggressive behaviors (Van Goozen, 2007).

There is solid evidence, then, that maltreatment affects children's physiology, especially with respect to managing stress, and that it can do so in quite different ways, either increasing or suppressing the usual response to adjust to adversity. While the adjustments make biological sense given the environment, they come at a cost to the child's general well-being. The good news is that there is also increasing evidence that a change to a high-quality and nurturing environment (e.g. foster care programs) can help to stabilize both types of physiological dysregulation (Bernard, 2012; Ha et al., 2016; Raichle, 2003). Such findings clearly identify the biological foundations for suspicious attitudes and defensive behaviors; they also strengthen the theoretical basis that connects adversity and attachment style (Woolgar, 2013, p. 578). We can conclude that evidence-based interventions that improve the child's environment can also alter—with the goal of normalizing—the physiological development of maltreated children.

The brain responds to experience in specific ways during specific life-cycle phases. To this time, it is believed that prenatal brain development, because of its location in gene expression and interaction between the brain's developing parts, is the least influenced by experience (Raichle, 2003). This is not to say that the prenatal brain is sheltered from maternal experiences, of course. The neurons that most individuals contain in their brains for life are developed in utero. Most of the neurons that an individual will ever have get their start at this time, moving to precise locations as they connect with other neurons. The developing infant brain is shielded against small changes in the prenatal environment, but is nonetheless affected by factors such as maternal nutrition, stress, drug or alcohol abuse, and overall condition of health (Schuurmans & Kurrasch, 2013).

As brain science advances, and especially as imaging devices become more sophisticated, we are better able to align specific brain "sensitivities" with specific ages of development in childhood. Research in the past decade concludes the earliest development stage (birth–18 months), the crucial period for attachment, as an especially vulnerable period. A child's production of high levels of stress hormones during this time has neurobiological repercussions as the brain's priority is self-defense against threat or perceived threat. Again, this specific outcome has evolutionary benefits by increasing the child's chances of survival and reproduction under dangerous conditions. But such an advantage does little good, and much harm, in situations that are not threatening, and encourages a range of physical and psychiatric disorders (Twadosz & Lutzker, 2010). Toddlers (18–24 months) exposed to risk usually experience conditions of insecure attachment. This is evidenced in their ambivalence toward the caregiver (or other adult), confusing their potential for both danger and solace, and therefore both approaching and avoiding them. Studies have found high cortisol levels in affected toddlers, demonstrating that maltreatment may bring about dysregulation. Examination of infants and toddlers in risky home settings indicates that early life dysregulation of the hypothalamic-pituitary-adrenal (HPA) system due to maltreatment causes changes in the brain that can have lifelong consequences.

Among children living outside their families, as in orphanages and foster care placements, research evidence bolsters this conclusion. By measuring salivary cortisol in their wards, studies carried out in

Russian and Romanian orphanages confirmed the dysregulation of the HPA system early in life. These children living in precarious and consequently high-stress conditions lacked the characteristic diurnal fluctuation in cortisol levels of cortisol that children reared in non-threatening situations—in loving families—commonly exhibited: a gradual decrease after an early morning peak. The findings are found to reverse somewhat in children who leave the orphanage to live with adoptive caregivers. Although the specific case of Russian and Romanian orphans may be considered to render atypical results, other cases examining cortisol levels in more typical childhood situations—for example, among young children adjusting to new foster care placements, and even those managed by indifferent child care staff—produce similar results (Teicher et al., 2003). The orphans' situation of extreme deprivation and neglect does not allow for the modicum of environmental stimulation necessary to support basic human development, suggesting that such conditions in childhood likewise adversely affect brain systems that support other fundamental human sensory and motor functions (Perego, 2016). If sense organs do not function adequately during distinct childhood phases of brain development, the process can't proceed in the expected fashion, stunting the child's ability to move about and handle objects (Ponton, 2006).

A closer look at the hippocampus, the seat of memory and learning and among the most stress-sensitive parts of the brain, will demonstrate how it is measurably affected by the child's experiences at specific stages of brain development. The hippocampus plays a key role in regulating the HPA system in response to external stresses, ultimately increasing the release of cortisol, the so-called stress hormone (Bernard, 2012; Gunnar et al., 2006). Early life adversity reduces the number of hippocampal neurons, impairing modulation of the HPA axis, which leads to hyper or hypo-responsiveness (McEwen et al., 1995) even when mild stressors are introduced into the child's environment (McCrory, 2015). Elevated cortisol levels are definite outcomes of high stressors such as physical and sexual abuse (Sapolsky, 2003; Hendricx-Riem, 2015). It is important to note, however, that the repercussions of childhood maltreatment do not necessarily bring about immediate hippocampal changes. These may be delayed and take form much later, even long after the stressor is eliminated (Woon et al., 2008; Teicher et al., 2013; Andersen & Teicher, 2004).

It might be expected that the most profound neurobiological consequences of maltreatment would be discovered in early childhood and/or adolescence, life stages associated with unique brain development, hence hippocampal sensitivity. Research, however, supports the view that maltreatment in middle childhood does the most damage to brain structures, hence later mental health (Hendricx-Riem, 2015). Sexually victimized women, for example, had significantly smaller hippocampal volumes than depressed women without that history of abuse before age 14. Experiences of multiple types of maltreatment before age 12 were also related to smaller left hippocampal volume (Vythilingam, 2002; Whittle, 2013). It must be noted nonetheless that several studies found no significant association between childhood maltreatment and hippocampal abnormalities in adulthood (Carrion, 2001; Lenze, 2008; Korgaonkar, 2013).

In sum, the direct link between early adversity and immediate hippocampal damage has yet to be irrefutably established. It is evident nonetheless that the hippocampus responds to adverse events with the progressive loss of synapses (Oh, 2013). What existing evidence cannot yet answer is the important question as to *when* hippocampal abnormalities make their appearance. If they occur after maltreatment, psychological intervention is called for. But what if atypical hippocampal development predisposes certain children to trauma in response to adverse childhood experiences, and so to later mental health issues? Treatment, obviously, can only address presenting symptoms.

Developmental Traumatology and Neuroscience

As a relatively new and rapidly expanding field, developmental traumatology aims to define the biological, neurological, physical, and psychological effects of child maltreatment. Researchers examine such key family and social factors as socioeconomic disadvantage, caregiver mental illness, poor caregiving, and domestic and community violence. Each of these is considered in relation to its influence on brain function in children, and any corresponding changes in their individual biological and developmental progress (De Bellis, 2002). Developmental traumatologists face the continuing challenge of identifying distinctive biological and neurological differences while organizing the main forms of psychological and social environmental factors; they must also identify critical childhood incidents of both vulnerability and resilience in response to maltreatment within specific developmental stages (Cicchetti et al., 1991).

The premise of developmental traumatology research is that a finite number of traumatic stressors can inflict infinite amounts of subjective stress in a child, in turn allowing a finite number of possible brain and body responses (DeBellis, 2002). The most effective treatment, therefore, begins at the center point of these responses. Based on my own research, I contend that specialized interventions to target specific behaviors and symptoms must differentiate the beginning, middle, and final stages of treatment. The most specialized interventions are achieved when tools are designed and held constant by fixed response perimeters. Only then can the content be adequately informed and achieve specificity. Increases in neuroendocrine and autonomic stress responsiveness create failures in critical circuit networks when these are forced to compensate for abnormal amounts of stress. The alteration in circuitry results in oversensitivity to stress and a reduction in stress level thresholds in maltreated children (Heim et al., 2008). The major and most frequently studied biological stress systems in the body are the catecholamine system, the locus ceruleus-norepinephrine (NE) sympathetic nervous system (SNS), and the hypothalamic-pituitary-adrenal (HPA) axis (Ali et al., 2012; Martinson et al., 2016).

An abundance of research findings on the detrimental effects of maltreatment on the physical health of children and adolescents has recently become available. In a longitudinal analysis, Gilbert (2009) linked childhood maltreatment to increased health care intervention for asthma, cardio-respiratory, and non-sexually transmitted infections in a large sample of low-income youth. Another longitudinal study, reporting data from a large clinical and community sample of maltreated children, uncovered evidence of long-lasting generalized health problems, increased weight, and compromised stress response/immune systems across adolescence and throughout young adulthood (Clark, 2010). Also notable are the links between obesity, anxiety, early alcohol consumption, signs of liver disease, and increased risk of smoking (Knutson et al., 2010; Clark, 2010; Mersky et al., 2010). Risky sexual behavior is also reported among adolescents who were sexually abused as children (Wilson, 2013; Negriff, 2010; Briggs-Gowan, 2010).

The links between exposure to violence and preschoolers' physical and emotional ailments were notable even when controlling for other key factors, including economic disadvantage and caregiver mood and anxiety symptoms (Briggs-Gowan, 2010, p. 1132). Violence exposure was also significantly associated with symptoms of depression, Seasonal Affective Disorder (SAD), PTSD, and Attention Deficit Hyperactivity Disorder (ADHD). Abuse and neglect are inarguably detrimental to the developing systems of children, resulting in lower developmental attainment and suggesting "difficulties along multiple developmental lines" (Briggs-Gowan, 2010, p. 1138; Leeson & Nixon, 2011).

The terms "poly-victimization" and "complex trauma" refer to the group of children and adolescents who have suffered multiple forms of psychological trauma by means of chronic abuse and neglect rather than an isolated event. This subgroup is at the highest risk for psychiatric and behavioral problems (Turner, 2017; Finkelhor, 2007). Poly-victimized adolescents, for example, have double the risk of depression, triple the risk of PTSD, a 3–5-times increased risk of SUDs, and a 5–8-times increased risk of comorbid disorders compared to adolescents with trauma histories but who were not poly-victimized (Ford, 2010). These adolescents also took part in more delinquent acts, alone or with peers, even controlling for gender, ethnicity, and psychiatric morbidity (Ford, 2013). Similarly, personality disorders in children and in adults maltreated as children found increased risk for antisocial, borderline, dependent, depressive, narcissistic, paranoid, and passive-aggressive personality disorders and dissociative symptoms (Wildschut, 2014). Intergenerational transmission of abuse is also more likely when problematic caregiver-child interactions and domestic abuse and alcohol abuse are present (Sheridan, 1995). Harsh caregiving is likewise linked to intergenerational transferal of clinical anxiety by means of highly critical or punitive relations with their children that distort their error processing capabilities (Fonzo, 2016).

Since age at the time of maltreatment influences later mental and physical health developments, how does gender function to differentiate responses to childhood incidents as well as their effects on the brain? The question is complicated because distinguishing between the shaping elements of environment and biology is itself so complicated. To what extent, if it is even measurable, is gender a social construction? To what extent is it innate? How do gender differences manifest in symptoms and rates of psychological disorders? Findings indicate that adolescent female delinquents, for example, show significantly higher rates of psychopathology, maltreatment history, and familial risk factors than do their male peers (McCabe, 2002; Hendricx-Riem, 2015; Teicher et al., 2003). Functional imaging studies of biological stress systems have identified sex gender differences in the brain's response to fear stimuli (Schienle, 2005; Felmington, 2010). Accordingly, female rhesus monkeys repeatedly separated from their mothers between the ages of 3–6 months exhibited increased cortisol responses to subsequent separation and flattened basal cortisol cycles at later ages. These changes were not observed in male monkeys (Sanchez, 2005).

The interaction of three specific factors might provide clues to gendered distinctions in the emergence of some disorders. Bipolar Disorder (BPD), in which women predominate significantly, is the most studied subject to date. These factors are: gender differences in the actual type of adverse early experience; the sexually dimorphic effects of early experience on brain development; and gender differences in brain laterality and hormonal conditions.

Girls, for example, are more at risk for sexual abuse by a male non-caretaker, a major risk for BPD onset (Hendricx-Riem, 2015). Concerning sexually dimorphic effects, the second factor, sexual abuse has been linked to diminished corpus callosum size in girls, a development that in boys is associated with neglect. Finally, in the third factor category, there are significant gender-specific differences in brain laterality and hormonal milieu. Researchers posit that the reduced hemispheric dominance in women allows for switching between right and left hemispheres, perhaps pointing to greater female capacity for affective instability and the "splitting" characteristic of BPD. In maltreated men, predominant left hemisphere specialization, along with the reduced corpus callosum, may divide thought and affect, supporting their denial of symptoms and rejection of diagnoses (alexithymia), thereby undermining both self- and social awareness and heightening the potential for antisocial personality disorders to develop. Briefly and simply, estrogen affects limbic structures, especially in those already sensitized, predisposing women to BPD and other psychiatric manifestations of maltreatment. Progesterone and testosterone contribute substantially to male depression. Male and female hormonal differences as they develop through childhood and adolescence can have significant—and gender-defined—neurobiological effects on the type of mental health symptoms that result from early maltreatment.

From a behavioral perspective, De Bellis (2002) concluded that hyperarousal of the stress system in childhood may prompt secondary behavioral manifestations of restlessness, learning difficulties, and deficits in memory. Masten (2008) established that childhood abuse can also be associated with a change in children's perceptual preferences in facial recognition practices. Specifically, as Heim (2008) recently reported, "abused children showed a preference for the recognition of angry faces and were more likely to categorize ambiguous faces as angry when compared with controls" (p. 700). These results may lend support to Caspi and Moffitt's (2004) first gene-by-environment study. It examined Monoamine Oxidase-A (MAOA) levels in adults maltreated as children and discovered that adults with lower-acting levels of MAOA are more likely to display increases in violent behavior. Furthermore, adults with lower levels of MAOA were also more likely to develop symptoms of conduct disorder and antisocial personality disorder. In adults who were maltreated as children but produced higher-acting levels of MAOA, the likelihood of all symptoms was reduced (Chu et al., 2010). Studies support the theory that maltreating caregivers are unlawfully burdening, and thus compromising their child's stress response system and future capacity for coping with stress.

In 2010, Panuzio and colleagues conducted a longitudinal study on the effects of child maltreatment histories on newlywed couples. Results established that early maltreatment damages the individual's capacity for creating and sustaining satisfactory relationships with intimate partners. Their precise conclusion warrants emphasis:

> The impact of childhood trauma can be accounted for by the dynamics of betrayal, traumatic sexualization, stigmatization and powerlessness which are said to alter children's cognitive orientation to the world, and create trauma by distorting children's self-concept, world view and affective capacities.
>
> (Finkelhor et al., 1985, p. 531)

In sum, the trauma literature confirms that, when left unresolved from childhood, adult disorders such as major depression, borderline personality disorder, generalized anxiety disorder, dissociative disorders, and post-traumatic stress responses are common outcomes (Kaya Tezel, 2015; Boysan, 2009; Briere, 1990; Briere, 1988; Finzi-Dottan & Harel, 2014).

Research findings on how childhood trauma affects the adult brain are varied and at times contradictory. As discussed, a substantial number of studies conclude that hippocampal volume is more adversely affected in younger than in older children; others suggest that the hippocampal volume of children who were older when maltreated is diminished more than in those abused in earlier ages (Teicher et al., 2013; Rao, 2010). The complicating factor is that hippocampal changes can be delayed and consequently might not be evident at the time of measurement. They appear to surface most clearly during the transition from adolescence to adulthood, so the timing of measurement is critical. Also complicating is how the severity of the maltreatment impacts the brain: most particularly, how the combination of multiple types of abuse deleteriously affects hippocampal volume. What is important here is that research conducted to date demonstrates that childhood maltreatment effects hippocampal changes, and that these changes, in turn, often manifest in adult mental health disorders. (Andersen & Teicher, 2004).

Another key question about the relationship between childhood maltreatment and the brain is whether hippocampal changes are treatable and ultimately reversible. Pharmacotherapy appears to effectively reduce hippocampal abnormalities in PTSD sufferers, including that related to childhood abuse; in particular, the class of antidepressants known as selective serotonin reuptake inhibitors (SSRIs), used long-term, has successfully promoted hippocampal neurogenesis (Schnell, 2014). The anticonvulsant phenytoin, commonly used to treat epilepsy, has helped to recover hippocampal volume in adults with PTSD related to a variety of traumas (Bremner, 2005). These neuroimaging findings are specific to PTSD, and it remains to be established whether pharmacotherapy or psychotherapy—or some combination—can "fix" reverses in hippocampal changes in victims of childhood abuse who are not diagnosed with PTSD (Nanni, 2012; Teicher et al., 2013). Ultimately, adult mental and addictive disorders have a strong neurodevelopmental component, however much their development is influenced by such environmental and experiential elements as stress, exposure to substance abuse, social attachments, internal self-representations, and nature and degree of early nurturing, as well as traumatic experiences at varying ages of brain development (Grossman, 2003).

The conceptualization of "mentalizing" came out of a series of experiments with chimpanzees intended to provide insight into whether their minds function in similar fashion to those of humans: do chimpanzees, in other words, begin with the human assumption that their own wants, views, and beliefs determine how others behave toward them? In short, do they assume that the "real" corresponds to their own "ideal"? The term "mentalizing" (theory of mind)—reflecting the individual's ability to process the mental states of others—is now common usage (Frith, 2003). In children, the capacity to mentalize corresponds to their developmental stage, with particular advances made between the ages of 5–6, when mentalizing becomes more refined: children can now understand how others may behave falsely. This research brings to light much necessary information about what is going on in children's minds and brains. But it does not illuminate or necessarily even apply to the other element of mentalizing that is fundamental to working with trauma-affected children and adult survivors: the crucial connection between children's formulation of false beliefs about themselves based on the behavior of others.

The brain's mentalizing system is probably functioning from about 18 months of age, allowing implicit attribution of intentions and other mental states. As noted, explicit mentalizing becomes possible between the ages of 4–6 years. From this age, children are able to explain how misleading reasons have given rise to their false belief of others. In theory and evidence, the ITTM draws the critical distinction between the brain's ability to intuit the false beliefs of others and the brain's ability, between the ages of 4–6, to detect the falsity of negative self-beliefs. Fundamental to the ITTM, therefore, is understanding and deconstructing the brain's production of false negative self-beliefs to detach the child's mental states from the child's reality. Once accomplished, new construction of healthy belief structures becomes realizable.

Recent studies, briefly summarized here, have also focused on the higher order cognitive processes (HOC) to explore the connections between personality disorders and their social causes. HOC is generally conceived of as working to optimize neural resources and initiating pathways between processing systems. The process can be conceptualized in several ways: as reflecting functioning, mentalizing, social cognition, metacognition, or mindfulness. What is vital to know is that "the core distinguishing feature of these hypothetical constructs is that they relate to brain structure as a hierarchy of layers of abstraction and assume a top-down influence on lower orders of this neural pyramid" (Fonagy et al., 2016, p. 59). The brain, accordingly, operates as an information processing system, interpreting code, while the HOC constructs are developed (Fonagy et al., 2016, p. 59). Where children are concerned, studies indicate that theory of mind problems (the inability to identify errors in thoughts, feelings, and behaviors of others) in early childhood (ages 4–5) may predict bipolar disorder in adolescence, while adolescent hypermentalizing in those already diagnosed often negatively impacts their treatment outcomes. Increasing caregiver punishment in childhood also increasingly undermined the ability to mentalize (Fonagy et al., 2016, p. 62). Childhood trauma may culminate in mentalizing processes so undermined as to seriously attack childhood resilience, in turn leading to the onset of mental health problems, if not in childhood then at later life stages. What signifies most in this process is the social context that encourages a child's psychological withdrawal. In short, the important link in trauma diagnosis—and treatment—is that between punishment, heightened anxiety, and compromised mentalizing (Fonagy et al., 2016, p. 62).

Neuroscience findings resemble those of attachment research, in that both suggest that the patterns of attachment insecurity are the child's defensive adaptations to the quality of their caregiving environment (Fonagy & Target, 1997). So, for example, the insecure-avoidant attachment pattern may develop as a strategy to cope with an intrusive caregiver, while an inconsistent caregiver may incite the insecure-ambivalent pattern. Both insecure attachment styles are immediate responses that work in the face of impaired caregiver sensitivity during infancy. Their future consequences might negatively affect well-being (Cohn, 1979).

Most significant at this point in the research trajectory is the development and application of interventions to strengthen mentalizing. This capacity was thoroughly researched among socially deprived mothers, for example, to show that, in this cohort, a high maternal capacity to mentalize will result in a high capacity to mentalize—a secure attachment—in their children, however deprived. Among the 17 mothers with low mentalizing capacity who had experienced insecure attachment themselves and had not received treatment, only one was found to be securely attached (Siegel, 2015).

Even where the social environment is one of deprivation, maternal mentalizing leads to resilience in children. An example of how this function involves a familiar scenario: a mentalizing caregiver, facing their screaming child, will say something like, "You're tired. It's been such a long day. You need a nap, and then you'll feel better." They presuppose a reason for the screaming based on how they assess the motivation for the child's distress. A caregiver lacking this kind of mentalizing skill will more likely respond with an admonition or threat such as "You're screaming. Shut up. You're only screaming to annoy me/get attention." They are not able to "see" the child's inner life. Consistent caregiver responses in this manner will succeed in making the child believe that they do not have an inner life beyond that ascribed to them by their caregiver(s). And if the caregiver is sufficiently bad, the child will disavow the caregiver's mind, psychologically blocking and hence protecting themselves from the reality that, say, the caregiver harbors malignant thoughts toward the child. The child's response, in effect, is "I don't want to know, so I'm not going to know, what's happening in their minds." (Fonagy & Target, 1997).

The child's identity is initially derived from the image of themselves that they perceive to be in the mind of their caregiver. The caregiver has formed an image of the child, and as that child grows up, that image—which is the adult's perspective and does not necessarily reflect the real child—becomes more "visible" to the child. Absorbing that experience of him or herself in the caregiver's mind, an intelligent child struggles to comprehend what "good" the caregiver sees in them. The caregiver's distorted image becomes the core of a self that is created around that image as the child perceives it. Any evil that caregivers project onto the child, consequently, is central to their developing identity as it becomes exactly *what they believe about themselves.*

Un-mentalized children are unprepared to understand themselves and others, leading to "small-t trauma." If this develops as early as infancy, a "big-T trauma" happens because the child has not had the experience necessary to develop resilience and has few inner resources to cope. Even turning to others is a compromising experience for children who mentalize poorly. They don't expect that others can understand them. In childhood and again in adulthood, what provokes extreme repeated stress and undermines the capacity to regulate that stress is this affective dysregulation.

To reiterate—and re-emphasize—a long-held psychological assessment, children are critically dependent on good caregiving during the first years of life. Caregivers who do not meet these needs have children who are predisposed to heightened psychological reactivity to stresses and who lack an effective organized behavioral strategy for seeking comfort from attachment figures in the face of such arousal. Carefully guided toward healthy mentalization, traumatized children will have choices beyond unhealthy and ineffectual automatic behaviors—and consequently the necessary basis to develop true resilience.

Conclusion

The research surveyed in this chapter underlines the merit of practical applications derived from current neuroscience: understanding the brain provides the only clear entry into therapeutic methods that can demonstrably influence children's biology. Neuroscience has made remarkable inroads into the biology of childhood maltreatment; current findings have demonstrated the efficacy of evidence-based treatment. Its success is witnessed in the positive, tangible, measurable changes brought about in such crucial indices as those of behavior, attachment, coping skills, and overall mental health and well-being in maltreated children and formerly traumatized adults. In the ITTM, I have attempted—and continue to attempt, as more evidence is compiled—to integrate these findings in the interests of a unique and beneficial evidence-based intervention designed specifically to resolve the seemingly intractable issues of complex trauma in childhood.

However obvious it may appear, these results support the idea that positive child-caregiver behaviors *do not* affect brain development or individual responses in the same manner that maltreatment and consequent negative self-belief systems (NSBS) do. I highlight this to suggest that, whether it construes a negative or a positive general/self-deduction, the brain applies the same requisites of reason for structuring either, and does not test whether the conclusions are valid. Positive self-deductions are not what initiates a referral for mental health treatment. As recent neuroimaging research indicates, positive messages and experiences don't appear to adhere to the brain in the discernible manner that negative impacts do (Fonzo, 2016).

In the end, current research confirms the depth and breadth of the negative effects, for both adults and children, associated with their maltreatment in childhood, as well as the ongoing potential for intergenerational transmission. Effective treatment methods that include the deconstruction and reconstruction of negative self-beliefs in adults and children, as evidenced in research and practice outcome-based models such as the ITTM, will go far to address the past trauma that so undermines the present and is too frequently transmitted to the future and to subsequent generations. The following chapter focuses on childhood brain development in relation to the conceptualization of false negative self-beliefs.

Note

1. British children's author Michael Morpurgo, cited in "What is an ideal childhood?", *The Guardian*, 15 October 2015, www.theguardian.com/lifeandstyle/2015/oct/17/what-is-an-ideal-childhood/. New York, NY: Guilford Press.

References

Alcantara, A. (1993). Developmental regulation of Fos and Fos-related antigens in cerebral cortex, striatum, hippocampus, and cerebellum of the rat. *The Journal of Comparative Neurology* 334:1, pp. 75–85.

Ali, N. A., et al. (2012). The salivary alpha amylase over cortisol ratio as a marker to assess dysregulations of the stress systems. *Physiology & Behavior* 106:1, pp. 65–72.

Allen, R. & Oliver, J. M. (1982). The effects of child maltreatment on language development. *Child Abuse and Neglect* 6:3, pp. 299–305.

Andersen, S. A. & Teicher, M. H. (2004). Delayed effects of early stress on hippocampal development. *Neuropsychopharmacology* 29:11, pp. 1988–1993.

Andersen, S. T., et al. (2008). Stress, sensitive periods and maturational events in adolescent depression. *Trends in Neuroscience* 31, pp. 183–191.

Bernard, K. D.-M. (2012). Enhancing attachment organization among maltreated children: Results of a randomized clinical trial. *Child Development* 83:2, pp. 623–636.

Boysan, M. G. (2009). Relations among anxiety, depression, and dissociative symptoms: The influence of abuse subtype. *Journal of Trauma Dissociation* 10, pp. 83–101.

Bremner, J. M. (2005). Effects of phenytoin on memory, cognition and brain structure in post-traumatic stress disorder: A pilot study. *Journal of Psychopharmacology* 19:2, pp. 159–165.

Briere, J. R. (1988). Multivariate correlates of childhood psychological and physical maltreatment among university women. *Child Abuse & Neglect* 12, pp. 331–341.

Briere, J. R. (1990). Differential adult symptomatology associated with three types of child abuse histories. *Child Abuse & Neglect* 14, pp. 357–364.

Briere, J. S. & Scott, C. (2015). Complex trauma in adolescents and adults: Effects and treatment. *The Psychiatric Clinics of North America* 38:3, p. 515.

Briggs-Gowan, M. C. (2010). Exposure to potentially traumatic events in early childhood: Differential links to emergent psychopathology. *Journal of Child Psychology and Psychiatry* 51, pp. 1132–1140.

Carrion, V. W. (2001). Attenuation of frontal asymmetry in pediatric posttraumatic stress disorder. *Biological Psychiatry* 50:12, pp. 943–951.

Caspi, A. M. & Moffitt, T. E. (2004). Maternal expressed emotion predicts children's antisocial behavior problems. *Developmental Psychology* 40:2, pp. 149–161.

Chu, A. T., et al. (2010). Clinical implications of traumatic stress from birth to age five. *The Annual Review of Clinical Psychology* 6, pp. 469–494.

Cicchetti, D. & Lynch, M. (1993). Toward an ecological/transactional model of community violence and child maltreatment: Consequences for children's development. *Psychiatry* 56, pp. 96–118.

Cicchetti, D. B., et al. (1991). Attachment organization in maltreated preschoolers. *Development and Psychopathology* 3:4, pp. 397–411.

Clark, D. T. (2010). Child abuse and other traumatic experiences, alcohol use disorders, and health problems in adolescence and young adulthood. *Journal of Pediatric Psychology* 35:5, pp. 449–510.

Cohn, A. (1979). An evaluation of three demonstrations child abuse and neglect treatment programs. *Journal of the American Academy of Child Psychiatry* 18:2, pp. 283–291.

Cook, A. S., Spinazzola, J., & Ford, J. (2005). Complex trauma. *Pediatrics, Psychiatric Annals* 35:5, pp. 1–9.

Copping, V. W., et al. (2001). A child trauma treatment pilot study. *Journal of Child and Family Studies* 10:4, pp. 467–475.

Craighead, W. & Nemeroff, C. B. (2005). The impact of early trauma on response to psychotherapy. *Clinical Neuroscience Research* 4:5, pp. 405–411.

Crowe, S. B., et al. (2008). The development of anti-social behavior: What can we learn from functional neuroimaging studies? *Developmental Psychopathology* 20, pp. 1145–1159.

Davies, P. C., et al. (1994). Marital conflict and child adjustment: An emotional security hypothesis. *Psychological Bulletin* 116:3, pp. 387–411.

De Bellis, M. (2002). Developmental traumatology: The psycho-biological development of maltreated children and its implications for research, treatment and policy. *Development and Psychopathology* 13, pp. 539–564.

Felitti, V. A., et al. (1998, May). Relationship of childhood abuse and household dysfunction to many of the leading causes of death in adults, the Adverse Childhood Experiences (ACE) Study. *American Journal of Preventive Medicine* 14:4, p. 245.

Felmington, K. W. (2010). Neural responses to masked fear faces. *Journal of Abnormal Psychology* 119:1, pp. 241–247.

Finkelhor, D., et al. (1985). The traumatic impact of child sexual abuse: A conceptualization. *Journal of Orthopsychiatry* 55:4, pp. 530–541.

Finkelhor, D. O. (2007). Poly-victimization: A neglected component in child victimization. *Child Abuse & Neglect* 31:1, pp. 7–26.

Finzi-Dottan, R. & Harel, G. (2014). Parents' potential for child abuse: An intergenerational perspective. *Journal of Family Violence* 29:4, pp. 397–408.

Fishbane, M. (2007). Wired to connect: Neuroscience, relationships, and therapy. *Family Process* 46:3, pp. 395–412.

Fletcher, A. N., et al. (2003). Structured leisure activities in middle childhood: Links to well-being. *Journal of Community Psychology* 31:6, pp. 641–659.

Fonagy, P. & Target, M. (1997). Attachment and reflective function: Their role in self-organization. *Development and Psychopathology* 9:4, pp. 679–700.

Fonagy, P. B., et al. (2016). Adversity, attachment and mentalizing. *Comprehensive Psychiatry* 64, pp. 59–66.

Fonzo, G. R. (2016). Early life stress and the anxious brain: Evidence for a neural mechanism linking childhood emotional maltreatment to anxiety in adulthood. *Psychological Medicine* 46, pp. 1037–1054.

Ford, J. D. (2010). Poly-victimization and risk of posttraumatic, depressive and substance use disorders and involvement in delinquency in a national sample of adolescents. *Journal of Adolescent Health* 46:6, pp. 545–552.

Ford, J. D. (2013). Systemic self-regulation: A framework for trauma-informed services in residential juvenile justice programs. *Journal of Family Violence* 28:7, pp. 665–677.

Ford, J. D., et al. (2015). *Posttraumatic Stress Disorder: Scientific and Professional Dimensions*. Academic Press.

Francis, D. C., et al. (1999). Maternal care, gene expression, and the development of individual differences in stress reactivity. *Annals of the New York Academy of Sciences* 896:1, pp. 66–84.

Frith, U. (2003). Development and neurophysiology of mentalizing. *Philosophical Transactions of the Royal Society of London* 358, pp. 453–479.

Giedd, J. S. (2010). Anatomic magnetic resonance imaging of the developing child and adolescent brain and effects of genetic variation. *Neuropsychology Review* 20:4, pp. 349–361.

Gilbert, R. K. (2009). Recognising and responding to child maltreatment. *The Lancet* 373:9658, p. 167.

Gilliam, M. F., et al. (2015). Maternal depression in childhood and aggression in young adulthood: Evidence for mediation by offspring amygdala-hippocampal volume ratio. *Journal of Child Psychology and Psychiatry* 56:10, pp. 1083–1091.

Goodman, S. H., et al. (1999). Risk for psychopathology in the children of depressed mothers: A developmental model for understanding mechanisms of transmission. *Psychological Review* 106:3, pp. 458–490.

Greenough, W. B. (1987). Experience and brain development. *Child Development* 58:3, p. 539.
Grossman, R. Y. (2003). Dexamethasone suppression test findings in subjects with personality disorders: Associations with posttraumatic stress disorder and major depression. *American Journal of Psychiatry* 160:7, pp. 1291–1298.
Gunnar, M. F., et al. (2006). Bringing basic research on early experience and stress neurobiology to bear on preventative interventions for neglected and maltreated children. *Development and Psychopathology* 18:3, pp. 651–677.
Ha, T. A., et al. (2016). Family relations, stress, and vulnerability: Biobehavioral implications for prevention and practice. *Family Relations* 65:1, pp. 9–23.
Hammer, M. (2002). Potential role of the anterior cingulate cortex in PTSD: Review and hypothesis. *Depression & Anxiety* 9, pp. 1–14.
Heim, C. E., et al. (2008). The link between childhood trauma and insights from HPA axis studies in humans. *Psychoneuroendocrinology* 33, pp. 693–710.
Hendricx-Riem, M. E. (2015). Beating the brain about abuse: Empirical and meta-analytic studies of the association between maltreatment and hippocampal volume across childhood and adolescence. *Development and Psychopathology* 27, 507–520.
Herringa, R. J. (2013). Childhood and adult trauma both correlate with dorsal anterior cingulate activation to threat in combat veterans. *Psychological Medicine* 43:7, p. 1533.
Hughes, A. E., et al. (2012). A developmental neuroscience of borderline pathology: Emotion dysregulation and social baseline theory. *Journal of Abnormal Child Psychology* 40:1, pp. 21–33.
Hutchings, J. A., et al. (2002). Evaluation of two treatments for children with severe behavior problems: Child behavior and maternal health outcomes. *Behavioral and Cognitive Psychotherapy* 30:3, p. 279.
Imbierowicz, K. E. & Egle, U. T. (2003). Childhood adversities in patients with fibromyalgia and somatoform pain disorder. *European Journal of Pain* 7:2, pp. 113–119.
Ione, A. (2015). Review of *Neuroscience: A Historical Introduction* by Mitchell Glickstein. *Leonardo* 48:3, pp. 312–314.
Kaya Tezel, F. T. (2015). Relationships between childhood traumatic experiences, maladaptive schemas and interpersonal styles. *Archives of Neuropsychiatry* 52, pp. 26–232.
Kennedy, D. & Adolphs, R. (2012). The social brain in psychiatric and neurological disorders. *Trends in Cognitive Sciences* 16:11, pp. 559–572.
Kirke-Smith, M., et al. (2016). The effect of maltreatment type on adolescent executive functioning and inner speech. *Infant and Child Development* 25:6, pp. 516–532.
Knutson, J. T.-L., et al. (2010). The role of care neglect and supervisory neglect in childhood obesity in a disadvantaged sample. *Journal of Pediatric Psychology* 35:5, pp. 523–532.
Korgaonkar, M. A. (2013). Early exposure to traumatic stressors impairs emotional brain circuitry. *PLoS One* 8:9, p. e75524.
Lee, Y.-R. (2010). Fibromyalgia and childhood abuse: Exploration of stress reactivity as a developmental mediator. *Developmental Review* 30:3, pp. 294–307.
Leeson, F., et al. (2011). The role of children's appraisals on adjustment following psychological maltreatment: A pilot study. *Journal of Abnormal Child Psychology* 39:5, p. 759.
Lenze, S. X. (2008). Childhood adversity predicts earlier onset of major depression but not reduced hippocampal volume. *Psychiatry Research: Neuroimaging* 162:1, pp. 39–49.
Leserman, J. D. (2007). Relationship of abuse history to functional gastrointestinal disorders and symptoms. *Trauma, Violence & Abuse,* 8:3, pp. 331–343.
Levine, S., et al. (2005). Developmental determinants of sensitivity and resistance to stress. *Psychoneuroendocrinology* 30:10, pp. 939–946.
Lev-Wiesel, R. (2006). Intergenerational transmission of sexual abuse? Motherhood in the shadow of incest. *Journal of Child Sexual Abuse* 15:2, pp. 75–101.
Maguire, S. A., Williams, B., Naughton, A. M., Cowley, L. E., Tempest, V., Mann, M. K., Teague, M., & Kemp, A. M. (2015). A systematic review of the emotional, behavioral and cognitive features exhibited by school-aged children experiencing neglect or emotional abuse. *Child: Care Health Development* 41, pp. 641–653.
Martinson, A. C., et al. (2016). Differences in HPA axis reactivity to intimacy in women with and without histories of sexual trauma. *Psychoeuroendocrinology* 65, pp. 118–126.
Masten, C. L. (2008). Recognition of facial emotions among maltreated children with high rates of post-traumatic stress disorder. *Child Abuse & Neglect* 32:1, pp. 139–153.
McCabe, K. L. (2002). Gender differences in psychopathology, functional impairment, and familial risk factors among adjudicated deliquents. *Journal of the American Academy of Child and Adolescent Psychiatry* 41:7, pp. 860–867.
McCrory, C. D. (2015). The lasting legacy of childhood adversity for disease risk in later life. *Health Psychology* 34:7, pp. 687–696.
McEwen, B., et al. (1995). Stress and cognitive function. *Current Opinion in Neurobiology* 5:2, pp. 205–216.

Mersky, J. S., et al. (2010). Comparing early adult outcomes of maltreated and non-maltreated children: A prospective longitudinal investigation. *Children and Youth Services Review* 32:8, pp. 108–1096.

Merzenich, M. (2001). Award for distinguished scientific contributions. *American Psychologist* 56:11, pp. 878–881.

Morpurgo, M. (2015, October 17). What is an ideal childhood? *The Guardian*, p. 11.

Nader, K. O. (1998). Violence: Effects of parent's previous trauma on currently traumatized children. In Y. Danielie (Ed.), *International Handbook of Multigenerational Legacies of Trauma*. New York: Pelum Press.

Nanni, V. U. (2012). Childhood maltreatment predicts unfavorable course of illness and treatment outcome in depression: A meta-analysis. *The American Journal of Psychiatry* 69:2, p. 141.

Negriff, S. N. (2010). Associations between nonverbal behaviors and subsequent sexual attitudes and behaviors of sexually abused and comparison girls. *Child Maltreatment* 15:2, pp. 180–189.

Oh, J.-E. C. (2013). Differential gene body methylation and reduced expression of cell adhesion and neurotransmitter receptor genes in adverse maternal environment. *Translational Psychiatry* 3, p. e218.

Panuzio, J. A. (2010). Physical, psychological, and sexual intimate partner aggression among newlywed couples: Longitudinal prediction of marital satisfaction. *Journal of Family Violence* 25:7, pp. 689–699.

Pechtel, P. L.-R. (2014). Sensitive periods of amygdala development: The role of maltreatment in preadolescence. *Neuroimage* 97, pp. 236–244.

Perego, G. C. (2016). Neurobiological correlates of psychosocial deprivation in children: A systematic review of neuroscientific contributions. *Child & Youth Care Forum* 45:3, pp. 329–352.

Pfefferbaum, B. (1997). Post-traumatic stress disorder in children: A review of the last ten years. *Journal of the American Academy of Child and Adolescent Psychiatry* 36, pp. 1503–1511.

Ponton, C. (2006). Critical periods for human cortical development: An ERP study in children with cochlear implant. In S. Lomber & J. Eggermont (Eds.), *Reprogramming the Cerebral Cortex: Plasticity Following Central and Peripheral Lesions* (pp. 213–228). New York: Oxford University Press.

Raichle, M. E. (2003). Functional brain imaging and human brain function. *The Journal of Neuroscience* 23:10, p. 3959.

Rao, U. C.-A. (2010). Hippocampal changes associated with early-life adversity and vulnerability to depression. *Biological Psychiatry* 67:4, pp. 357–364.

Rutter, M. (2006). Critical notice: Attachment from infancy to adulthood: The major longitudinal studies. *Journal of Child Psychology and Psychiatry* 47:9, p. 974.

Sanchez, M. M. (2005). Alterations in diurnal cortisol rhythm and acoustic startle response in nonhuman primates with adverse rearing. *Biological Psychiatry* 57, pp. 373–381.

Sapolsky, R. (2003). Biology and human behavior: The neurological origin of individuality. *The American Biology Teacher* 65, pp. 468–468.

Scannapieco, M. & Connell-Carrick, K. (2005). Focus on the first years: Correlates of substantiation of child maltreatment for families. *Children and Youth Services Review* 27:12, pp. 1307–1323.

Schienle, A. S. (2005). Relationship between disgust sensitivity, trait anxiety and brain activity during disgust induction. *Neuropsychobiology* 51:2, pp. 86–92.

Schnell, E. L. (2014). Neuroligin-1 knockdown reduces survival of adult-generated newborn hippocampal neurons. *Frontiers in Neuroscience* 8, p. 71.

Schuurmans, C. & Kurrasch, D. M. (2013). Neurodevelopmental consequences of maternal distress: What do we really know? *Clinical Genetics* 83:2, pp. 108–117.

Scott, K. & Copping, V. (2008). Promising directions for the treatment of complex childhood trauma: The intergenerational trauma treatment model. *The Journal of Behavior Analysis-Offender and Victim: Treatment and Prevention* 1:13, pp. 273–283.

Sheridan, M. (1995). A proposed intergenerational model of substance abuse, family functioning, and abuse/neglect. *Child Abuse & Neglect* 19:5, pp. 519–530.

Siegel, D. (2015). *The Developing Mind: How Relationships and the Brain Interact to Shape Who We Are* (2nd ed.). New York, NY: The Guilford Press.

Simons, R. K., et al. (2015). Invited address: "The times they are A-changin'" gene expression, neuroplasticity, and developmental research. *Journal of Youth and Adolescence* 44, pp. 573–580.

Szczepanski, S. M., et al. (2014). Insights into human behavior from lesions to the prefrontal cortex. *Neuron* 83:5, pp. 1002–1018.

Teicher, M. A., et al. (2003). The neurobiological consequences of early stress and childhood maltreatment. *Neuroscience and Biobehavioral Reviews* 27:1, pp. 33–44.

Teicher, M. A., et al. (2012). Childhood maltreatment is associated with reduced voume in the hippocampal subfields CA3, dentate gyrus, and subiculum. *Proceedings of the National Academy of Sciences,* 109: 9, pp. E563–E572.

Teicher, M. A., et al. (2013). Childhood maltreatment and psychopathology: A case for ecophenotypic variants as clinically and neurobiologically distinct subtypes. *American Journal of Psychiatry* 170:10, pp. 1114–1133.

Tottenham, N. (2012). Human amygdala development in the absence of species-expected caregiving. *Developmental Psychobiology* 54:6, pp. 598–611.

Tsukayama, E. D. (2012). Resisting everything except temptation: Evidence and an explanation for domain-specific impulsivity. *European Journal of Personality* 26, pp. 318–334.

Turner, H. A. (2017). Effects of poly-victimization on adolescent social support, self-concept, and psychological distress. *Journal of Interpersonal Violence* 32:5, pp. 755–780.

Twadosz, S. & Lutzker, J. R. (2010). Child maltreatment and the developing brain: A review of neuroscience perspectives. *Aggression and Violent Behavior* 15:1, pp. 59–68.

Van der Kolk, B. (2016). Commentary: The devastating effects of ignoring child maltreatment in psychiatry. *Journal of Child Psychology and Psychiatry* 57:3, pp. 267–270.

Van Goozen, S. H. (2007). The evidence for a neurobiological model of antisocial behavior. *Psychological Bulletin* 133:1, pp. 149–182.

Vythilingam, M. H. (2002). Childhood trauma associated with smaller hippocampal volume in women with major depression. *American Journal of Psychiatry* 159:12, pp. 2072–2080.

Wager, T. D. (2008). Prefrontal-subcortical pathways mediating successful emotion regulation. *Neuron* 59:6, pp. 1037–1050.

Whittle, S. D. (2013). Childhood maltreatment and psychopathology affect brain development during adolescence. *Journal of the American Academy of Child and Adolescent Psychiatry* 52:9, pp. 940–952.

Widom, C. M., et al. (2006). Childhood victimization and illicit drug use in middle adulthood. *Psychology of Addictive Behaviors* 20, pp. 394–403.

Wildschut, M. L. (2014). Survivors of early childhood trauma: Evaluating a two-dimensional diagnostic model of the impact of trauma and neglect. *European Journal of Psychotraumatology* 5:1, pp. 218–248.

Wilson, H. E. (2013). History of sexual abuse and development of sexual risk behavior in low-income, urban African American girls seeking mental health treatment. *Women & Health* 53:4, pp. 384–404.

Wilson, K. (2011). The traumatic stress response in child maltreatment and resultant neuropsychological effects. *Aggression and Violent Behavior* 16:2, pp. 87–97.

Woolgar, M. (2013). The practical implications of the emerging findings in the neurobiology of maltreatment for looked after and adopted children: Recognizing the diversity of outcomes. *Adoption & Fostering* 37:3, pp. 237–252.

Woon, F. H., et al. (2008). Hippocampal and amygdala volumes in children and adults with childhood maltreatment-related post-traumatic stress disorder: A meta-analysis. *Hippocampus* 18:8, pp. 729–736.

Chapter 3

Reconstructing Negative Self-Beliefs: The ITTM's Early Childhood Deductive Reasoning Theory

> Children are not so limited in ability to reason deductively as Piaget—and others—have claimed. This ability shows itself most markedly in some aspects of their spontaneous behavior—and we have seen that it reveals itself with great clarity in the comments they make while listening to stories . . . . at least from age four, then, we must again acknowledge that the supposed gap between children and adults is less than many people have claimed.
>
> (Donaldson, 2006, pp. 55–56)

In 1957, pioneering psychologist Margaret Donaldson was pursuing graduate studies at Geneva University under the direction of Jean Piaget, one of the modern "greats" in child psychology. When Donaldson left his laboratory, she was intrigued, but not entirely won over by his theory that children under the age of 7 years are fundamentally limited in their capacity for reason, hence logical deduction. Based on sequential biological-developmental stages, Piaget's theory posited that seven years is the threshold to "operational" thinking, the point at which the child is able to shift their egocentric viewpoint to consider others, and consequently to make deductive inferences. After about the age of 11, children become capable of thinking about abstract concepts and judging hypotheses logically (McLeod, 2015; Piaget, 1952; Piaget & Inhelder, 1958).

Donaldson's inaugural study, *Children's Minds* (2006), laid out her counter-argument,[1] based on years of intensive study of children in her own laboratory nursery school at the University of Edinburgh. Taking on Piaget's central concepts of "egocentrism" and "decentering," her test results challenged his conclusion that children live "in the moment" without comprehending "the relation of one state to those which come before or after it" (Donaldson, 2006, pp. 12–13). Her principal finding, cited previously, is that preschool children are not nearly as limited in the crucial ability to decenter or take in other perspectives than their own as had been understood to that time (Donaldson, 2006, p. 12). It appeared, rather, that the child "first makes sense of situations (and perhaps especially those involving human intention) and then uses this *kind* of understanding to help him to make sense of what is said to him" (Donaldson, 2006, p. 55; her italics). Distinguishing between "embedded" thinking, which takes place within the familiar contexts of existing knowledge or beliefs, and "disembedded" thinking, which lacks the supportive context of meaningful events or objectives, Donaldson argued that children as young as 3 or 4 are capable of such reasoning (Hughes, 2001).

Donaldson's research was a significant forward step in child development theory. Since her time, despite further advances in the field, in attachment theory, and in neuroscience, the complex questions of how and when the human brain develops the capacity to reason have yet to be definitively answered.

This chapter considers the developmental limitations of the brain in early childhood to demonstrate how these contribute to the formation of self-beliefs, and also deter children from developing self-applied methods to recognize and correct false negative self-beliefs. Negative self-deductions influence everyone, to greater or lesser disadvantageous degrees, throughout our lives. I contend that the primary negative self-belief formulation, at around the age of 5, is likely to be the one that is reinforced most frequently and consistently over time. When traumatic events and/or unacceptable living conditions in childhood are regularly layered upon each other over the first such instance of a negative self-belief, the brain's automatic pattern-seeking process is constantly re-engaged. It is difficult to see how such self-belief patterns could avoid forming deeper and wider pathways in the brain when it is exposed to complex trauma living conditions every day. Until at least the age of 5, a child experiences the behaviors and responses of their caregiver(s) as definitive representations of themselves. The logical and most effective starting point in treating childhood complex trauma, then, is at the point of the primary negative self-belief formulations of children and caregivers both.

The ITTM's approach to understanding the processes of reasoning, and then to reconstructing the negative self-beliefs in adults who refer their child/teenager for treatment, is rooted in the dual-processing theories of higher cognition. Evans (2008) noted that "So many authors have appealed to dual processes in so many different ways," that even providing an overview is "a complex and challenging task" (p. 256). For cognitive theorists, higher order cognitive processes are unconscious, fast, and automatic, and occur within System 1; social psychologists, on the other hand, maintain that higher cognitive processes are slow, deliberative, and conscious, occurring within System 2 (Evans, 2008, p. 255). Nonetheless, Evans identifies a consistent finding: the dual processes (System 1 and System 2) develop in sequence (p. 259).

The charts below summarize Evans's key conclusions concerning the attributes of each system:[2]

TABLE 3.1 Higher Cognitive Processes: System 1 and System 2

Understanding System 1, Cognitive Unconsciousness	*Understanding System 2, Cognitive Consciousness*
• The automatic and unconscious in human behavior. • A concrete and/or domain-specific process that rapidly contextualizes problematic issues with prior knowledge and beliefs. • Complex information processing that is conducted without conscious awareness. • A working memory system that includes "a rapid, one trial learning" (Evans, 2008, p. 260) related to specific episodes. • System 1 evolved in animals (including humans) before System 2. • Belief-based reasoning occurs in System 1, but the components of System 2 can be used to resolve maladaptive self-beliefs.	• Clear and controlled, not implicit and automatic. • Abstract within domain-general contexts. • Slow, step-by-step, and limited by capacity. • Language-reflective. • Capacity for hypothetical thoughts and thinking about the future. • Ability to consider and integrate counter-factual information. • Opposed by a number of psychologists who maintain that System 1 controls human behavior without our awareness and System 2 is a conscious reasoning process primarily used to justify our sense-making of our *behaviors*.

The two-system account of dual reasoning processes informs the theoretical underpinnings of the ITTM and offers a concise framework for describing its principles and practices. The ITTM formulates interventions based on the assumptions of System 1, while operationalizing aspects and capacities of System 2. This combination works to reconstruct and resolve the unconscious primary negative self-beliefs in adults, caregivers, and children who have experienced complex trauma in childhood. In line with Evans's (2008) idea to end the long debate by considering System 1 and System 2 as one process, the ITTM accesses and applies methodology and techniques from both systems throughout the 21 sessions of its phase-based treatment.

Also relevant to illustrate the interplay between the two types and processes of higher cognitive functioning is Epstein's **Cognitive-Experiential Theory (C-ET)** (2014). Particularly important to the ITTM is Epstein's scientific articulation of Rogers's (1951) self-concept theory as "an organized implicit theory about the self that had been automatically acquired from lived experience, and is necessary for adapting to everyday life" (Epstein, 2014, p. xiii). As such, Epstein's theory provides an **Integrated Theory of Personality** that further supports the theoretical framework and scientific articulation goals of the ITTM. For example, Epstein (2014) describes implicit beliefs (System 1) as automatically derived from experiences that inform our thoughts, feelings, and behaviors and bias our conscious thinking (System 2). His recognition of the "ubiquitous influence of unconscious processing" (System 1) is the specific aspect of psychoanalytic theory with which the ITTM develops methods for resolution as applied in practice. One of the ITTM's explicit questions, informed by higher cognitive theory, is: how can the unconscious System 1 processing of negative self-beliefs generated from childhood complex trauma be most clearly articulated and effectively reconstructed with children and adults to allow the authentic self to emerge?

The ITTM's **Early Childhood Deductive Reasoning Theory (EC-DRT)** is similar to C-ET in its integration of a number of Epstein's concepts. Both EC-DRT and C-ET:

- Integrate Self-Theory, which maintains that people's beliefs (System 1) significantly contribute to their interpretation of events, thoughts, feelings, and actions (System 2).
- Go beyond Self-Theory to include the beliefs we have about others and the interactions between both (System 2).
- Integrate Learning Theory, which contends that the content of experiences is automatically acquired through associative learning (unconscious) that then contribute to the content (conscious) of implicit beliefs.
- Focus on the elements of schema construction, where Learning Theory focuses primarily on describing how individuals learn their behavioral responses.

Finally, both EC-DRT and C-ET integrate psychoanalytic theory through its adaptations to unconscious processing psycho-dynamics (System 1) and transference (System 2).

Within the conceptual framework of dual processes of higher cognition (Evans, 2008) and Epstein's (2014) Cognitive-Experiential Theory (C-ET), the ITTM's Early Childhood Deductive Reasoning Theory (EC-DRT) considers how the brain's unconscious processing during early childhood principally influences the formation of negative self-beliefs, and how those processes automatically deter children and adults from consciously (System 2) recognizing and correcting false negative self-beliefs. Negative self-deductions influence everyone, to greater or lesser disadvantageous degrees, depending on the frequency and intensity of complex trauma conditions and stressors in childhood and adulthood. Left unacknowledged and unaddressed, they persist as the primary negative self-belief system throughout the course of our lives.

Wang (2014) cites research that shows the average age of earliest memory recall is 3.5 years, signifying the end of the childhood amnesia period (p. 1680). Childhood amnesia refers to the phenomenon of having very little ability to recall the earliest experiences of our lives. The ITTM is guided by its central observation: most often, the earliest recalled negative experiences of childhood occur around the fifth year of age. Perhaps, as Wang explains, "some early memories may remain accessible as children get older, but they may be postdated when recalled at later time points" (p. 1680). It is also possible that, since older children are able to recall their memories of later ages, "the boundary of childhood amnesia increases with age until it reaches the adult level" (p. 1680). The influence of negative experiences in childhood, however, has not been studied as a potential contributing factor once the childhood amnesia period is surpassed. EC-DRT supposes negative experiences as the most important element when treating child and adult victims of CT. In sum, EC-DRT raises questions about 3.5 years as the age when childhood amnesia ends; future research to uncover the components of negative-experience recall in teenagers and adults who have experienced childhood complex trauma are critical to trauma treatment.

The ITTM constitutes a practice method for accurately extrapolating the most impactful experiences in early childhood in children, teens, adults, and parents. The method combines System 1 and 2 reasoning processes, and then applies other methods to deconstruct and reconstruct invalid, logical-sounding, negative self-beliefs into positive and valid self-beliefs. My own charted experiences, and those of ITTM-trained clinicians, demonstrate its potential to identify the earliest recalled negative self-belief and work toward significant and sustainable reductions in symptoms and behaviors (Copping, 2001). In this manner, the ITTM provides a promising trauma treatment. Its methods are adapted to suit the age and individual capacity of each individual. It demonstrates equally effective results when applied with clients of all ages (above 4 years old) who have suffered some of the most chronic and severe traumatic experiences and conditions.

Children in the care of welfare agencies, for example, are usually removed from their families of origin due to abandonment, neglect, or abuse, and not infrequently go back and forth between foster and family homes. For these children, the frequency and intensity of negative self-belief reinforcement over time is much more intense and enduring than most, with a wide range of psychological, emotional, cognitive, and physiological repercussions. Certainly, separating the child from complex trauma living conditions at home is important. Within this group, however, there is a subset of children and youth who struggle across multiple domains whether placed with foster parents, or relatives, or returned to biological parents. The ITTM's accumulated practice-based evidence suggests that all negative self-generalizations, when left unaddressed and unresolved, continue to guide and influence thoughts, feelings, and behaviors in a number of predictable and deleterious ways.

The Brain's Inherent Capacity to Reason

Alongside the work of Margaret Donaldson and others, my research disputes Piaget's theory about the limited capacity for reason and logical deducation of children under the age of 7 years (Piaget, 1952; Piaget & Inhelder, 1958; McLeod, 2015). For her part, Donaldson conceptualizes deductive inference as a process that involves three closely related but separate categories: compatibility, possibility, and necessity; she argues that the compatibility factor is the most important of all (Donaldson, 2006, p. 40). This factor refers to how a child learns (consciously and unconsciously) which aspects of the world are compatible, and which are not, when they make deductive inferences. For example, the brain's unconscious development of the capacity to reason in order to function in the world seems to prevent a young child's brain from consciously concluding that "if the moon came out last night and if the tree is blowing in the wind today, then that must mean we will go swimming today." Deductive inference, as Donaldson points out, is a simple matter involving

> the drawing of the conclusion that if something is true, something else must be true. The truth of the first two statements—the premises—makes the truth of the third statement—the conclusion—necessary. If the first two are true, then nothing else is possible other than that the third is also true. The truth of the first two statements is not compatible with the falsehood of the third.
>
> (Donaldson, 2006, p. 40)

Deductive inference (System 1, reasoning processes) , especially in 4–5-year-olds, makes it possible to know some things without having to prove (System 2 reasoning processes) that the conclusion is necessarily true. Although various experiments have attempted to demonstrate a child's ability to make deductive inferences at 3 years of age or younger, none has succeeded (Donaldson, 2006, p. 59).

The ITTM approach observes that children, at around the age of 3 or 4, begin to develop the capacity to recall and verbalize *general* conclusions about the world around them (System 2 reasoning processes). For example, 4-year-old Lucy deduces that "if the sky was blue yesterday, and the sky is blue today, then that means the sky will be blue tomorrow, right Mommy?" Although this deduction sounds logical to the child, it is invalid. In the case of general deductions, real-life examples (System 2 reasoning processes) of the sky's unpredicatability over time will correct the conclusion (System 2). The inability of the child under the age of 5 to consciously challenge unconscious, automatic conclusions, however, is an altogether separate component of the reasoning process that warrants explicit attention. At the very least, the automatic reasoning process of forming negative and invalid self-beliefs places children at risk for mistakingly assuming at least one negative conclusion about themself is true without requiring proof that it is actually true. The lack of lived experience and apparent limitations of conscious cognitive capacity, especially at the age initially formulated, opens up the possibility that these childhood negative self-beliefs will be carried unconsciously, played out in future experiences—despite their baselessness. The ITTM represents my long-term commitment to understanding why current methods often fail to resolve the over-personalization effect of negative self-belief constructions and to developing an effective method that works to effectively and sustainably deconstruct and reconstruct the earliest recalled, negative, self-belief deduction.

Reasoning patterns established in childhood become integrated into the individual's procedural knowledge, thereby operating as a faulty set of instructions for daily life, the "how to" of the individual's existence (Lawson, 2004). The EC-DRT method incorporated into the ITTM offers this interpretation: the requisites of reason posit that, once there are two premises (two pieces of concrete evidence) that share a common category, a conclusion that *seems* "natural" and "inevitable" is formed. Yet conclusions generated in childhood are often false, as exemplified in the general deduction that Lucy makes: "if the sky was blue yesterday and the sky is blue today, then that means the sky will be blue tomorrow." As Mercier (2011) contends, "premises are seen as providing *reasons* to accept the conclusions" (p. 57). The child at this age and developmental stage believes it is true—a belief based on the brain's evident "satisfaction" that the "rules" on which such initial deductions are determined have been fulfilled, and that all required conditions to generate a general conclusion have been met. A negative self-belief system constructed by 6-year-old Bobby is based on his direct experiences and the child-brain's processing of that experience: "If Mommy hit me, and if Daddy hit me, that must mean I deserve to be hit." Bobby has formed a conclusion based on two pieces of concrete experience that fulfill the first and second requisites of reason, which, again, may "seem" logical, but is nonetheless invalid. The point of error is obvious to an adult. The ITTM method applies some basic mathematical principles to disprove and thus depersonalize the first-recalled negative childhood self-beliefs across all age groups.

During the stage of early childhood, Lucy (in the first example) does not have the benefit of enough real-life experience of observing the sky to know that her conclusion is false. In Bobby's case, the hitting continues, and his negative self-belief is thereby reinforced and sustained as "true." The child's automatic and inherent unconscious construction of the self-deduction (System 1) comes into being because the brain, at this age and stage, does not automatically discern whether the conclusion is false or whether its impact on the child is negative, in the short or long term. The conclusion is formulated because the concrete evidence (proof) gives the brain what is required to meet the first (selection), the second (accomodation), and the third (assimilation and integration of the concept "I") requisites of reason. The negative self-belief can now be represented in one of the most elementary and universally accepted mathematical equations: **1 + 2 = 3**.

The **1 + 2 = 3** elemental equation evolved from Aristotle's study of the brain's logical reasoning or sense-making process. Applying the brain's most basic mathematical reasoning equation to disprove the validity of faulty self-deductions is a straightforward and effective method to deconstruct these negative self or "I" (most inherently personal) deductions, as further discussed in the next chapter. The brain's capacity to formulate logical (but not valid) deductions in early childhood can be attributed, fundamentally, to the prolonged social evolution of human beings. Logical thinking, consequently, predates the development of formal logic processes by philosophers and mathematicians—possibly by millions of years (Woods & Grant, 2002). Among historians of philosopy, it is generally agreed that the Greek logician Aristotle (384–322 BC) devised the first general theory of knowledge; his work on the syllogism (1 + 1 = 2) remains unmatched in its influence on Western thought (Woods & Grant, 2002; Smith, 2017).[3] Aristotle described the syllogism as focusing not on **what is stated** (the content) but on the **structure** (form) of the argument and the validity of the inference drawn from the **premises** (things supposed) of the argument. He recognized how the brain stops short of testing the truth or falsity of conclusions, no matter how logical they sound. He termed this process "deductive inference"; put simply, "if something is true, something else must also—*of necessity*—be true" (Donaldson, 2006, p. 40). This, in short, is a general definition of the "logical argument."

According to the rules of deductive inference:

The Structure of a Syllogism

- All conclusions must flow naturally from the premises.
  and
- The premises must be based on **valid actual** evidence (truth).

Consequently, "*XX* results of necessity from *YY* and *ZZ*, if it would be impossible for *XX* to be false when *YY* and *ZZ* are true."

(Smith, 2017)

The first two statements—the premises—when true make the conclusion appear necessarily true, in that no other conclusion than the third truth could be possible (Donaldson, 2006, p. 40). Although many of the components of Aristotle's Syllogism Theory complement the theoretical principles of the ITTM, the ITTM's **1 + 2 = 3** EC-Deductive Reasoning Theory differs in one distinct way: in the latter, each premise is comprised of *two* separate concrete experiences (**1 + 2**). In Aristotelian theory, the second premise must provide direct support to the first premise (**1 + 1**).

The healthy brain in early childhood will *always and only* select concrete knowledge/experience as the content for premises (Woods & Grant, 2002). Philip Johnson-Laird (1999, 1996; Johnson-Laird & Byrne, 1993) theorized that in order to demonstrate deductive competence before they are able to comprehend formal rules for valid reasoning, children have to be capable of constructing "models" of their childhood world. In his view, this is accomplished "either directly by perception or indirectly by understanding language," and they must also demonstrate a certain capacity "to search for alternative models." Children assume this model-making capacity more readily than they acquire conscious formal rules of reasoning (System 2) before they attain logic. Even adults are often obliged to infer from scanty information from which they cannot make valid deductions (Chao et al., 2000; Johnson-Laird & Byrne, 1993, p. 332).

After early childhood, the child's stockpile of experiences expands with the accumulation of life events. Expanding alongside are the brain's capacity for accessing two concrete experiences, its ability to accommodate those experiences providing they share a common category, and its capacity to assimilate information to form and generate logical-sounding conclusions. The ITTM does not focus on how the brain's mechanisms develop an increasing capacity, over time, to reason. The model concentrates instead on the period of early childhood, when the brain is not yet equipped with the capacity or accumulated life experience to recognize or correct its construction of logical-sounding but invalid negative self-beliefs. Research has demonstrated that, by the age of 8 years, children are capable of reason within certain contexts, such as choosing between something that is equal to or greater than another thing (Donaldson, 2006).

The ITTM emphasizes how, in children under 6 years, the brain does not test automatically the truth or falsity of general and self-deductions prior to their formulation. If this "gap" in brain function goes unrecognized, important immediate, short-, and long-term consequences in children and adults also remain unacknowledged. Consequently, even years later and in adulthood, those affected in early childhood often still do not automatically understand the need to test the truth or falsity of general and self-deductions, formed at the time of their earliest recollection, that provide their content. Often the result is "epistemic distortions and poor decisions" (Mercier et al., 2011, p. 57). Moreover, in the early and especially vulnerable phases of child life, the ability to seek counter-examples to prove the falsity of the deduction requires formal operational reasoning abilities that usually do not exist in children under 6 (Chao et al.; Girotto et al., 1988).

Ongoing research increasingly demonstrates how negative beliefs about the self heighten the risk for persistent, and worsening, psychological symptoms and outcomes across the lifespan (Wesley et al., 2015; Kaya Tezel, 2015; Thimm, 2010). The negative beliefs created by children around the age of 5 years almost always go undetected and unresolved, despite the fact that these are the ones that commonly generate the most long-running harmful implications. Is it not time to rethink the functions and mechanisms of reasoning especially as they occur in early childhood (Mercier et al., 2011; Grant, 2nd ed. 2007; Copping, 2001)?

The Brain and the Requisites of Reason

In keeping with System 1 higher cognitive reasoning theory, the ITTM sees the reasoning process just as inherent and autonomic to the brain as beating is to our hearts and equally as impersonal. The brain is an organ: it doesn't care about the nature of our self-conclusions, whether or not they are good for our self-esteem, whether they will work for or against us, or even whether they are true or false. The short and long-term negative outcomes or problematic symptoms and/or behaviors are of no concern to the brain.

System 1's reasoning processes include the unconscious function of ignoring certain sights and sounds and focusing on others. The ITTM defines this delineation process as **selection**. Selection is one of the fundamental rules of deductive processes. If we were not able to select certain aspects of life and ignore others, our minds would become overwhelmed with information and stimulus and we would not be able to function or survive (Woods & Grant, 2002; Donaldson, 2006). This is even more the case with children: they are not mentally, physically, or emotionally equipped to survive on their own, and are therefore at much greater risk of not surviving if not under the care of adults. Since health and well-being increase the likelihood of survival, it is not surprising that positive self-deductions are readily experienced by the brain to that end. But many positive self-deductions in childhood may also prove false when tested, because neither is the brain partial to, nor specifically wired to formulate, valid positive self-deductions. Positive self-deductions, however, even if false, don't tend to result in referrals for treatment. The ITTM's EC-DRT theory proposes that the individual will likely develop symptoms and negative behaviors, if the negative self-belief goes undetected, because the stockpile of a young child's tangible experiences is built on the behavioral and emotional responses of caregivers. Thus, the primary negative self-deduction is based on the child's factual knowledge about the caregivers and is not a valid conclusion about *the child's individual self.*

In trying to reject self-beliefs that the brain recognizes do not match up with the "true" authentic self, and to return the individual system to a state of homeostasis, symptoms and behaviors may be the human organism's best attempt and only option to alert the individual that help is needed to correct the falsity in order to establish or return to its optimum functioning level. In other words, the brain's inherent and impersonal ability to reason can be seen to increase the individual's opportunities for survival. Johen van Benthem (2008) aptly captures the purpose and potential of the ITTM's early childhood brain-based method in arguing that, "The key issue is not the static notion of correctedness, but the dynamic one of correction." It is not the ability to be "right" at all times that is important so much as the ability to reorder beliefs, plans, or actions that may have gone awry (van Benthem, 2008, p. 70).

The brain is a pattern-seeking and pattern-repeating organ that appears to adhere to certain "rules" that ensure its capacity to formulate reasoning pattern pathways. The first breath drawn by a newborn baby signals the brain to begin to select certain sounds and to discount others. Although individual selections differ, each selection of one sound or behavior and not another protects the child from being overwhelmed by the world's infinite number of abstractions all at once (Grant, 2007). It may be that, as soon as the infant's basic survival is secured, the higher cognitive reasoning development begins, a hypothesis that requires further study at this point (Demetriou, 2011). Because children require looking after to ensure their basic needs for survival are met until they are old enough to survive independently, the behavioral responses of caregivers, siblings, and other family members are usually the first source of content used by System 1's process of reason to construct general and initial "I" deductions. The selection of negative or positive behavioral responses of caregivers is irrelevant because, as long as there are caregiver responses, System 1 appears to find criteria to meet what the ITTM describes as selection requisites. Only concrete or witnessed truths satisfy the brain's requirements for acquiring two premises to increase the brain's capacity to generate conclusions.

The ITTM's Method for Understanding, Explaining, Diagramming, Deconstructing, and Reconstructing Early Childhood Negative Self-Beliefs

Case History: Sarah's Negative Self-Belief System (at 4 Years Old)

Selection

If Auntie (Sarah's foster mother) promised me she would wake me up from my nap (even if I had a bad cold) when my Mommy came for her once-a-month visit to see me and my sisters

1

Another Premise

+

If Auntie (and Mommy) didn't wake me up when my Mommy came

2

Accommodation

Once a child's brain has selected two premises, the brain attempts to satisfy the second requisite of reason. The accommodation (+) can only be achieved if the two premises share a common category. If they do, the brain will accommodate both premises (**1 + 2**). In this example the brain will accommodate both premises because they share a common group: Auntie.

Assimilation and Integration of the "I" at the Start of the Concluding Statement

If a reasoning equation has advanced to a **1 + 2** position, then the brain proceeds to attempt to achieve Requisite 3.

Assimilation can be understood to mean the equation: the brain is well on its way to formulating a rule-abiding, self-deductive, reasoning equation. The brain assimilates the equation by inserting an = sign.

If 1 and (+) if 2, then that must mean (=)

The brain is assimilating **1 + 2** towards its conclusion with the insertion of the = sign

1 + 2 = 3

Integration of the "I" occurs always immediately after the assimilation (=) sign and before the rest of the deduction/conclusion is put in.

If

If (1) Auntie promised me she would wake me up from my nap (even if I had a bad cold) when my Mommy came for her once-a-month visit to see me and my sisters

AND (+)

If

If (2) Auntie didn't wake me up when my Mommy came

Then that must mean =

1 + 2 = 3

I can't trust what people say.

The brain's drive to satisfy the basic rudiments of logic occurs regardless of negative or positive impacts or implications to individuals such as a child believing they can't trust what people say. The deductive reasoning equation is a requisite-led, System 1, unconscious reasoning process of the brain.

The ITTM first moves through a step-by-step process to accurately reveal and identify the client's primary negative self-belief(s) in early childhood. The client is taught how and when and why the brain is automatically driven to establish the capacity to reason; according to System 1 processes, by ensuring the child-brain's ability to formulate general and self-deductions (if the human species is to survive). The ITTM then applies a step-by-step method to deconstruct the negative self-belief(s) by applying the rules of propositional calculus, to test negative self-beliefs for truth or falsity (using System 2 processes). Not only is the mathematical equation the brain has applied incorrect, the deduction in the example is invalid.

To have the 1 + 2 = 3 equation be true, the deduction would have to conclude as follows:

(1) If Auntie promised me she would wake me up from my nap (even if I had a bad cold) when my Mommy came for her once-a-month visit and (+)

If (2), Auntie (and Mommy) didn't wake me up when my Mommy came then that must mean (=)

(3) My Auntie chose to not keep her word.

This example demonstrates that the brain is designed to produce logical-sounding patterns of reasoning, but is not concerned with whether the conclusions constructed are true.

The invalid mathematical illustration of Sarah's early childhood deductive reasoning process would look like this:

$$\mathbf{1 + 2 = 4}$$

The child's brain automatically links "I"—the entity of the self—to the Auntie's actions and integrates "I" as the subject instead of Auntie. In the language of propositional calculus, the "I" is outside of or separate from the mutually exclusive (**1 + 2 = 3**) set (which would include Mommy, not "I"). Articulating and illustrating the reasoning process using a universal, mathematical equation is an effective method for depersonalizing the over-personalization of "I" and for seeing and understanding that the **1 + 2 ≠ 4** equation is false. Furthermore, according to mathematical principles, an odd and an even number will never equal an even number. If ever it did, the conclusion is *100% false*. For these reasons, whenever *"I"* has been substituted for the true subject named in the premises, *the negative self-belief will be irrefutably false*, even when general beliefs about the world and nature can be expected to be rectified naturally through life experience over time.

Children, adolescents, and adults are unlikely to recognize the falsity of early childhood negative self-beliefs *on their own*:

The ITTM's Early Childhood Deductive Reasoning Theory (EC-DRT) Process

1. The brain integrates the *"I"* at the beginning of the conclusion, automatically and outside of the child's awareness and the limited scope of caregivers and/or other significant others' behaviors.
2. The self-belief *sounds* logical, and therefore will be interpreted by most humans (who are not trained logicians or mathematicians) as true. Although children do sometimes question whether the negative self-belief is *really* true or not, the brain patterns back to the two most recent (or impactful) experiences (premises), which are required to be true in accordance with the brain's automatic adherence to the first requisite of reason (selection).
3. Although children sometimes take action to test whether they can generate different or positive responses from caregivers (i.e. being extra good), applying the ITTM has shown that, by 14 years and up, many more ongoing examples of caregivers' behavior or complex trauma living conditions over the years have transformed the slightly hopeful "am I" questions into "I am" statements.

The child-brain predisposes all of us to incorporate the "I" as representing ourselves into our meaning-making of most impactful, negative self-related childhood experiences; this is, especially the case in early childhood, when the years of life experience have not accumulated to form a reasonably solid store of practical, real-life, experience-based evidence to fall back on. The brain's essential drive and its mechanisms for ensuring everyone's capacity to reason makes it impossible *not* to personalize negative self-beliefs when the self, the "I," is automatically integrated at the conclusion's starting point. The early childhood brain, at the very least, is not circuited to construct valid conclusions.

While all this is happening in the child's brain, the child is not conscious of an "I" (themselves), but this discernment will slowly come to them as an integral part of the developmental process. Perhaps it is at this very point that they begin to "see" a separate "I" because of the brain's integration of the "I." When traumatic events or unacceptable living conditions continue throughout childhood, into adolescence and young adulthood and beyond, the negative self-belief will again be constantly reinforced. Most importantly, they are now personalized because numerous life experiences in the growing up process are used to "prove" their validity. After reviewing the research, Mercier, et al. (2011) concluded that "there is considerable evidence that when reasoning is applied to the conclusions of intuitive inference, it tends to rationalize them rather than to correct them" (p. 59).

The most important aspect of the integration of the "I" is the impossibility of *not* personalizing the "I"—or what follows. This is essential to the ITTM's effectual functioning: it works with clients, children, or adults *to correct their belief systems*, an extremely challenging objective for clinicians and clients alike. Once the child-brain has integrated the "I" into their language, and after many years of personalizing the "I" that they have accepted as self-representational, that "self,"—even if wholly negative and "lacking"—is a familiar one that the client struggles to relinquish. It becomes difficult to reconstruct the "false self" to reflect a more positive or accurate reality—even when there is tangible history of opposing evidence. Making a list of alternate proofs to refute the client's primary negative self-belief is not effective because doing so may not go far enough to deconstruct or depersonalize the original automatic negative self-belief made by System 1 processes in the brain. Not surprisingly, then, there are few existing treatments that have developed a method to successfully attack these ingrained negative self-beliefs.

To reiterate, the human brain reasons because the human brain is pre-wired to reason, an automatic, inherent process that demonstrates the brain's primary goal of increasing the chances of survival. Reason allows for healthy functioning. System 1 of higher cognitive processes is **not** designed to be concerned about whether the conclusions people draw about themselves or the world are true or false, positive or problematic, regardless what short- and long-term negative effects might ensue. In terms of basic survival, if the brain were unable to reason itself in relation to the world and the billions of other humans in it, we would be incapable of separating one element in the world from the next, as well as incapable of distinguishing our own self from that of others.

Our conscious thinking process and the constant demands on our attention in the present appear to keep us from being able or needing to be conscious of what is going on in the brain "behind the scenes." Our physical, emotional, and mental energy and attention are engaged in remaining alert and focused on what is going on around us, again, to increase the likelihood of survival. When it comes to the brain's inherent drive to develop our capacity to reason, however, the challenges should not distract clinicians or researchers from the benefits of raising our awareness about our brain's automatic functions, as well as the understanding of the unconscious and conscious higher cognitive reasoning processes and systems of developing or practicing methods that are designed to work in conjunction and alongside both systems, rather than with one or none.

The ITTM's Early Childhood Deductive Reasoning Theory (EC-DRT)

As explained, the necessary computations for effectively applying the steps to deconstruct NFBS with clients are based on the principles of propositional calculus, which mirror the brain's reasoning process. Propositional calculus and all mathematics can and may be framed in the brain, but are not automatic brain processes, unlike the brain's pre-established drive to secure its higher cognitive reasoning processes. Mathematics, formal logic, and deductive reasoning arose from the realization that the brain is not wired to produce only valid conclusions, no matter how logical they sound (Krantz, 2010).

Current theories focus on understanding the formulation and disputation of deductions by observing individual processes as these occur (Johnson-Laird & Byrne, 1993). There are three principal approaches to explaining the mind's deductive methods: through factual knowledge, through the application of formal rules, or through mental models (Johnson-Laird, 1999). Formal logic theorists develop inference rules to test the development and validity of arguments and conclusions, and deductive reasoning logicians devise mental models to explain adult processes of generating deductions. The mental model theory assumes a three-stage process at work in deduction: comprehension (constructing an initial mental model), description (formulating a tight description of the models that have been constructed), and validation (searching for alternative models that show the presumed conclusion to be false) (Johnson-Laird & Byrne, 1993, p. 362). Recent research on mental models and reasoning suggests that human beings are rational in principle regardless of the choices they make, and the outcomes, in practice.

Dialectical method theory also lends much support to the ITTM's brain-based method for deconstructing invalid and reconstructing valid self-deductions with clients. The method brings the conclusion back to the beginning: the first point of its construction: the process point of selection (abstraction). This means a return to the factual knowledge that the brain automatically selects to formulate premises, which then serve as tangible evidence for arriving at a logical-sounding conclusion. Referring to previous examples, this is indicated by the equations 1 + 2 = 3 or "if my mother . . . (1) and (+) if my mother . . . (2), then that must mean (=) I deserve to be hit (3)." The habitual repetition of these thought processes takes place without most people being remotely aware of them, despite the fact that no human action could take place in their absence (Woods & Grant, 2002, p. 79; Goel, 2005).

The early childhood brain automatically attributes the proof of caregiver actions as true representations of themselves. If a child's brain were able to "take in" the fact that the caregiver's maltreatment would continue, and if the child were capable of separating the self—which has not yet established the sense of "I"—confronting their primary caregiver could potentially increase the risks to the child's safety or survival. Most importantly, if a child's brain were equipped to be aware of a caregiver's inadequacies to meet the child's needs for safety and nurture, their own ability to adapt their needs or behaviors to correspond to their circumstances is not likely to be possible. A 5-year-old is not capable of taking the necessary steps to pack their bags and find another primary caregiver who will be their lifeline. Thus, as noted, as far as the child's brain is concerned, the whole truth of the world is transmitted through the lens of the primary caregiver's behavioral responses. Unless there is external intervention, the child is usually trapped in the complex trauma environment until they are reasonably capable of independence, when they are able to leave. As young adolescents/adults, their negative self-beliefs and the lived experience of being unable or failing to alter their caregiver(s)' behavior are carried with them into the outside world, and usually into their attachments to intimate partners. For these reasons, the ITTM examines the brain's inherent structuring process, in constructing deductive reasoning equations, to inform and guide the development, implementation, and evaluation of methods that sustainably deconstruct and reconstruct negative self-beliefs formulated in early childhood.

A caregiver request for a child's mental health treatment typically occurs when the child begins to act out or otherwise demonstrate symptoms. "Acting out" is the language of a child and their system as a whole, trying to tell the world that "all is not well." I always praise acting out behaviors for the fact that we otherwise might not become alerted to the situation of children who are not getting their needs met, at times where even their most basic needs, such as food, clothing, and shelter are being met. The children who are "internalizers" pose a greater risk because they hide their true situations, making unacceptable living conditions and subsequent impact even more likely to go unnoticed. Consider the child who is acting out in response to a caregiver who spends most or all of the day lying on the couch. To treat the child individually and not address the caregiver's evident depression, or more importantly, their own primary negative self-beliefs that feed and worsen depression over time, is counter-productive for both, and destroys hope for the child (Ford, 2015). The child or teen, believing that they are the problem, faces an increased likelihood of traumatic impact, the intergenerational transmission of negative self-belief system development, and the to-be-expected symptoms and behaviors associated with it.

Moreover, when the primary negative pathway of the brain is re-activated by either continuous or individual traumatic events in childhood or adulthood, the earliest and most impactful negative self-deduction, with its associated thoughts, feelings, actions at whatever age the individual then was, are reignited and reinforced. The re-activated pathway in the brain is deepened and strengthened by varying degrees of stress, along with reduced stress tolerance capacity. As can be expected, the deeper the pathway, the more likely the brain is to re-fire into this established pathway and the most frequent reinforced responses. The individual, consequently, is likely to re-experience and display the same emotional age level and intensity of powerlessness, paralysis, numbing, dissociation, fear, and reduced cognitive capacity as they actually were when their first most impactful experience occurred, whether 5 years old, 10 years old, or 16 years old. Many adults under stress experience emotions typical to that of a much younger child. Caregivers, too, often describe how their 13-year-old reverts to or is acting like a 5-year-old child.

When conscientious clinicians, working with their adult/child clients, formulate a list of contraindicated, real-life examples of the client's successes, they believe the "tracking" will go a long way toward dismantling the negative self-belief. But usually, the client's short-term relief and understanding of their own situation is short-lived. An adult client will often comment that, while they understand the clinician's approach of providing counter-evidenced examples of the negative belief systems opposite, and agree that their personal successes and achievements to that point are legitimate, they stop short by adding that, "although I can see the list of real-life examples are true, I still for some unknown reason believe and feel that my negative, self-belief is true." If the listing of counter-examples to prove the falsity of negative self-beliefs fails, the client often feels even more unhelpable and hopeless: "Even getting myself to the point of coming to get treatment from someone who is trained to help, can't help me."

So we return to the matter of the brain's role in this process. A list of concrete successes (evidence) may work to introduce new thoughts, but belief systems, as discussed, are formulated by the brain, based on two pieces of solid evidence, very early in life. By the time that most children/adults are referred to treatment, the pattern-seeking function of the brain has re-embedded the negative self-deductions—likely hundreds of times since the moment that the "I" was integrated into those self-beliefs. In doing so, the brain secures the breadth and depth of the pathway.

One way to work through the client's dilemma is to acknowledge that, since belief systems inform thoughts, attempts to affect or change personal thinking will often be futile or just serve as a short-term Band-Aid when and if the client is burdened by an unresolved, negative self-belief. To address the belief system effectively, an explanation on the brain's inherent function of establishing each human's capacity to reason (System 1), and on how the brain begins, at around age 5, to integrate and assimilate "I" at the beginning of conclusions to ensure each individual's capacity to establish the existence of the self, as separate from everything and everyone else, is essential. In other words, negative self-deductions such as, "I deserve to be punished" become recognized for what they are: automatic reasoning processes of the brain. Knowledge about the brain's inherent process for ensuring each individual's capacity to reason the self and the world around them provides each client with an alternate, brain-based, depersonalized explanation for the unavoidable over-personalization and reinforcement of negative self-beliefs.

Propositional calculus, at this point, provides an invariable and irrefutable method to test the reasoning equation (the negative self-belief deduction) for validity, and the client will see and comprehend that it is demonstrably false. This final step allows the individual, likely for the first time ever, to realize that the brain's integration of the "I" *was never personal*: it did not originate from a place of truth despite sounding logical based on two concrete examples of evidence (premises). Arriving at this critical point obviously requires a systematic method for the clinician to follow in deconstructing and then reconstructing the client's beliefs within the brain—constructing a new pathway in the brain while cutting off the invalid self-deduction. The ITTM's three phases outline the steps to be undertaken, and also presents a tracking method to ensure the sustainability of the new pathway and corrected belief system in the client's brain.

Of course, the process raises the question for the client: if the "I" is not who they think or have generated subsequent thoughts, feelings, actions, and reactions are, then who are they? The ITTM's advanced CBT diagrammatic methods capture the invalid "I" of the past (based on the caregiver's behavioral responses, not the child's) by means of a simple drawing. For the present, two are required: the "PAST" Diagram of a "bad day" is shown to mostly mirror the past. The other, a "PRESENT" Diagram for a "very good day," reflects the true unencumbered self. This is the necessary starting point for developing the fully realized self, based on the child's realistic goal of discovering their own authentic self and reaching their own individual potential (not caregiver-defined), as represented in the "FUTURE" Diagram. Establishing raw scores and reviewing, tracking, and achieving goal numbers within each diagram demonstrates changes in outcomes as well as necessarily increases the client's daily action-taking.

A mechanistic analogy perhaps best describes the approach. Any car owner understands that when their car breaks down, repairs will need to be made by a mechanic experienced with its operating system. The mechanic may not get very far if they start the work by accessing the owner's feelings or negative behavioral responses regarding their car's need for a new engine. Although a compassionate approach, it will not result in the desired outcome: to make the car once again roadworthy. Affect-based treatments may unintentionally strengthen the negative effects of the "I" and the personal involvement, self-responsibility, and self-blame associated with the "I" instead of disputing—and most certainly instead of disproving—the false, negative self-belief. The most obvious treatment goal is to deliver a full-proof method that affords the client absolutely no other option *but* to depersonalize and irrefutably extract the "I" out of the negative self-belief equation; "*I* deserve to be hurt." Clinical application of the ITTM's brain-based method has repeatedly proven that describing how the brain's pre-established drive to establish its capacity to reason in early childhood, and applying the mathematical equation that the brain utilizes to construct negative self-beliefs, sustainably depersonalizes and extracts the "I" from that negative belief system.

Identifying, understanding and modifying an individual's schemas is recognized as an essential aspect of cognitive therapy for treating personality disorders. Thimm (2010) emphasized that cognitive schema "constitutes the central pathway to psychological functioning and adaptation" (p. 219). Schema Therapy focuses on the therapist connecting with and guiding a client through their trauma-related emotions, within a positive and supportive structure, the goal being to improve their capacity for revising their emotionally regulated responses (Young, 2003). The positive reconfiguration of the client's traumatic impact is used to assist the client in challenging and changing their negative self-schemata (Young, 2003). As previously mentioned, affect-focused treatments have dominated the schema field for the past 30 years, yet stability levels of self-schemata have remained largely unchanged (Wang, 2010; Beck, 2004). Unlike Schema Therapy and Cognitive Behavioral Theory (CBT), the ITTM begins with the premise that self-beliefs (whether positive or negative) are first formulated outside of our awareness and it is these self-belief constructions that then inform our thoughts, feelings, and actions.

Conclusion

The ITTM is a brain-based method that is most effective with clients because it offers a non-negotiable, completely impersonal, mathematical option for disproving and depersonalizing primary negative self-beliefs. Mathematics is the closest we can get to exacting and proving truth and falsity in the real world, where the rules and numbers are clearly removed from the individual from the start. No effort will succeed in permitting the human to personalize how the rules of propositional calculus apply to truth and falsity. The ITTM and its EC-DRT methods respond to one of the most long-standing clinical challenges in child and adult mental health education, training, and practice.

Highlighting the objectivity and impersonality of the brain as an organ offers an alternative method to retrieval and/or re-experience of past or currently associated affect. This chapter has outlined the conceptual framework underlying the ITTM's methods. The next three chapters provide a sampling of the model in its practice of its three-phase-based application with caregivers, adults, and children who have been referred or self-refer to the ITTM program.

Notes

1. Donaldson was not the first to dispute Piaget's findings; see, for example, D. M. Jeffree, R. McConkey, and S. Hewson (1977), who challenged Piaget's famous test outcomes, arguing that the tools he used to measure children's capacity were inadequate.
2. See Evans (2008) *Table 2: Clusters of attributes associated with dual systems of thinking*, p. 237, for a complete listing of System 1 and System 2 attributes.
3. Robin Smith, "Aristotle's logic," in *The Stanford Encyclopedia of Philosophy* (Spring 2017 Edition), Edward N. Zalta (ed.), forthcoming, https://plato.stanford.edu/archives/spr2017/entries/aristotle-logic/.

References

Beck, A. (2004). *Cognitive Therapy of Personality Disorders* (2nd ed.). New York: Guilford Press.

Chao, S.-J. A., et al. (2000). The emergence of inferential rules. *Cognitive Development* 15:1, pp. 39–62.

Copping, V. W. (2001). A child trauma treatment pilot study. *Journal of Child and Family Studies* 10:4, pp. 467–475.

Demetriou, A. M. (2011). Educating the developing mind: Towards an overarching paradigm. *Educational Psychology Review* 23:4, pp. 601–663.

Donaldson, M. (2006). *Children's Minds*. London: Harper Perennial.

Epstein, S. (2014). *Cognitive Experiential Theory: An Integrative Theory of Personality.* New York: Oxford University Press.

Evans, J. (2008). Dual-processing accounts of reasoning, judgement, and social cognition. *Annual Review of Psychology* 59, pp. 255–278.

Ford, J. D. (2015). *Posttraumatic Stress Disorder: Scientific and Professional Dimensions* (2nd ed.). Cambridge, MA: Academic Press.

Girotto, V. L., et al. (1988). Pragmatic schemas and conditional reasoning in children. *The Quarterly Journal of Experimental Psychology* 40:3, pp. 469–482.

Goel, V. (2005). Cognitive neuroscience of deductive reasoning. In *The Cambridge Handbook of Thinking and Reasoning*. Eds. K. Holyoak & R. Morrison. Cambridge University Press. pp. 2-38.

Grant, A. (2007). *Reason in Revolt: Marxist Philosophy and Modern Science.* New York: Well Read Publications.

Hughes, C. D. (2001). "I got some words and you're dead!": Violent fantasy, antisocial behavior, friendship, and moral sensibility in young children. *Child Development* 72:2, pp. 491–505.

Jeffree, D. M., McConkey, R., & Hewson, S. (1977). *Let Me Play*. London: Condor Books.

Johnson-Laird, P. N. & Byrne, R. M. J. (1993). Precis of deduction. *Behavioral and Brain Sciences* 16, pp. 232–380.

Johnson-Laird, P. N. (1996, 3rd Printing 1995). Mental models, deductive reasoning, and the brain. In M. Gazzaniga (Ed.), *The Cognitive Neurosciences* (Ch. 65). Cambridge, MA/London: The MIT Press.

Johnson-Laird, P. N. (1999). Deductive Reasoning. *Annual Review Psychology,* 50, pp. 109–35.

Kaya Tezel, F. T. (2015). Relationships between childhood traumatic experiences, maladaptive schemas and interpersonal styles. *Archives of Neuropsychiatry* 52, pp. 226–232.

Krantz, S. G. (2010). *An Episodic History of Mathematics: Mathematical Culture through Problem Solving*. Washington, DC: The Mathematical Association of America.

Lawson, A. (2004). The nature and development of scientific reasoning: A synthetic view. *International Journal of Science and Mathematics Education*, Vol 2(3), pp. 307–338.

McLeod, S. A. (2015). *Jean Piaget*. Retrieved from www.simplypsychology.org/piaget.html.

Mercier, H., et al. (2011). Why do humans reason? Arguments for an argumentative theory. *Behavioral and Brain Sciences* 34, pp. 7–111.

Piaget, J. (1952). *The Origin of Intelligence in Children*. New York: International University.

Piaget, J. & Inhelder, B. (1958). *The Growth of Logical Thinking from Childhood to Adolescence*. New York, NY: Basic Books.

Smith, R. "Aristotle's logic," in *The Stanford Encyclopedia of Philosophy* (Spring 2017 Edition), Edward N. Zalta (ed.), forthcoming, https://plato.stanford.edu/archives/spr2017/entries/aristotle-logic/.

Thimm, J. C. (2010). Relationships between early maladaptive schemas and psychological developmental task resolution. *Clinical Psychology and Psychotherapy* 17, pp. 219–230.

Van Benthem, J. (2008). Logic and reasoning: Do the facts matter? *Studia Logica* 88, pp. 67–84.

Wang, C. (2010). Stability of dysfunctional attitudes and early maladaptive schemas: A 9-year follow-up study of clinically depressed subjects. *Journal of Behavior Therapy and Experimental Psychiatry* 41, pp. 389–396.

Wang, Q. (2014). Your earliest memory may be earlier than you think: Prospective studies of children's dating of earliest childhood memories. *Developmental Psychology* 50:6, pp. 1680–1686.

Wesley, M., et al. (2015). Early maladaptive schemas and early trauma experiences in depressed and non-depressed individuals: An Indian study. *Journal of Psychosocial Research* 10:1, p. 125.

Woods, A. & Grant, T. (2002). Reason in revolt. In *Dialectical Philosophy and Modern Science, 1*. New York: Algora Publishing.

Young, J. K. (2003). *Schema Therapy: A Practitioner's Guide*. New York, NY: Guilford Press.

Part 2

Practice

Chapter 4

Phase A: How the Model Works—Caregivers and Children

As discussed in Part 1 of this book, most clinicians recognize that children's mental health outcomes improve when caregivers are involved in treatment along with them. An analysis of the relationship between such caregiver participation and its outcomes found that combined caregiver-child/family therapy, or even caregiver-only treatment groups, were more effective than child treatment alone (Dowell, 2010). So important is the caregiver in the treatment equation, that, for certain childhood problems, caregiver treatment alone is as effective as treating the child (Thienemann, 2006). Results such as these have long emphasized (and continue to do so) the value of formulating treatment programs that emphasize caregiver involvement in children's treatments (e.g. American Psychiatric Association, 1994). This chapter focuses primarily on the ITTM's first stage, or Phase A, in relation to the other two stages, and within the "larger picture" of trauma impact treatment that is its structure.

The long-term cross-generational benefits of helping adults understand that they are not to blame for their own maltreatment or neglect by caregivers during childhood is also well documented (McCormack & Thomson, 2017; Hughes, 2016; McWey et al., 2013; Bailey, 2009). My own studies found that caregiver depression improved when psycho-educational sessions about trauma impact on children and caregivers were followed by individual caregiver treatment sessions *prior* to seeing the child. The objective in both cases is the same: to reconstruct primary negative self-deductions formulated in response to traumatic events or living conditions in childhood (Copping et al., 2001). Definitions of caregiver involvement, however, vary across studies. Most treatment programs involve caregivers in their own parallel sessions to learn about the impact of trauma while their child is in a separate room with a therapist (Stallard, 2007). In others, caregiver involvement signifies training in behavioral management skills, as well as education about the child's meaning-making and adults' key role in that process.

The ITTM emphasizes the principle—sustained by my empirical research and therapeutic practice—that caregiver involvement in their children's therapy must deal above all with patterns of intergenerational trauma transmission. Treatment for caregivers to address their trauma-related symptoms of depression, anxiety, hyperarousal, and traumatic re-experiencing, among others, is emphatically *the cornerstone* of the child's treatment. McWey and colleagues examined the value of specific attention to the "interrelationship between patterns, beliefs, and behaviors" in adults with complex trauma histories (McWey et al., 2013, p. 133). They identified both a "universal theme of childhood maltreatment" and three additional components: patterns, beliefs, and behaviors. Study participants disclosed distrust of, lack of communication with, and alienation from their own caregivers. A majority (63%) recognized intergenerational patterns and 75% divulged their strong desire to raise children differently than they were raised. Yet a striking 71% confessed to practices that were "destructive," and all (100%) were classified by social agencies as "at-risk" for removal of their children. The researchers concluded succinctly that:

> differences in parental awareness of intergenerational patterns of abuse, participant desires to parent differently in relation to their own experience of being parented, and the degree to which their behavior is congruent with the abusive behavior of their own parents, have implications for clinical interventions with at-risk parents.
>
> (McWey et al., 2013, p. 142)

Resolving adults' symptoms is obviously beneficial for them, but it is also important because it enables them to help the child cope adaptively with trauma-related distress. Improvement in the caregiver's emotional functioning will also enhance their emotional attunement with the child, as well as their overall empathy. This, in turn, encourages improvements in the child's health and well-being. The ITTM's multigenerational approach motivates, informs, and instructs the caregiver about the most efficacious ways to help their child cope with traumatic impact in manageable steps that are readily put into practice.

The Three Phases

Every healthy baby arrives bearing their own operating system and individual potential that, in a healthy environment, can be realized over the course of that child's lifespan. Failing to extricate and disprove the primary negative self-beliefs (constructed in childhood) in adults, caregivers, and children who have experienced complex trauma distort the individual's perception of their authentic self throughout their lifespan. Because that self-perception misrepresents the authentic self, the individual cannot recognize and thereby reach their full potential. The ITTM is designed to accurately define, deconstruct, and reconstruct these primary negative self-constructions in adults, caregivers, and children in 15–21 60-minute sessions. It can be applied in diverse situations, and requires a relatively brief training period for students and clinicians to learn and for adults, caregivers, and children to receive. Its sequential delivery provides a viable framework for the implementation of advanced Cognitive Behavioral Therapy (CBT) diagrammatic structures specifically designed to interrupt intergenerational transmissions of trauma impact. Cognitive behavioral approaches are commonly and successfully employed to reduce the frequency of specific child behaviors, such as hitting peers and siblings, for example. Despite their known value, however, standard CBT interventions are not designed to identify, treat, or resolve the radices of behavioral issues on their own. The ITTM fills in this important therapeutic gap.

In **Phase A**, ITTM clinicians deliver six 90-minute, accessible Trauma Information Sessions (TIS) in a course setting. The recommended size is 15–30 caregivers per group. The six sessions are psychoeducational in nature and provide continuously updated information about the effects of trauma on children, adults, and families. Advanced CBT diagrams are the primary clinical skills method. The diagrammatic structures integrate principles of trauma, attachment, and CBT theories. The principle approaches of each phase are summarized in Table 4.1 below.

Phase A—Trauma Information Session's Goals

The TIS Material Is Intended

- To sensitize caregivers to the child's experience of trauma.
- To strengthen caregivers' ability to respond effectively to the traumatized child.
- To challenge caregivers' interpretations of the child's behavior as oppositional.
- To disengage caregivers from conflict with the child.

TABLE 4.1 Major Therapeutic Activities of Phases A, B, & C

Treatment Phase	*Therapeutic Strategies*
Phase A **Six group-based sessions attended by children's caregivers**	Psycho-education on a broad spectrum of trauma-related literature. Cognitive behavioral framework introduced for understanding behavior and to promote metacognition and self-reflection. Caregiver monitoring of self-regulation and of their own position. Promotion of self-efficacy through daily monitoring of change.
Phase B **Average of eight individual sessions with children's caregiver(s)**	Cognitive behavioral processing of traumatic or impactful experience in caregiver's childhood: identification of trauma theme, deconstruction and disputation of the primary faulty belief system, attribution of faulty belief to childhood experiences. Implementation of the one-on-one program between caregiver and child (minimum of two hours a week). Co-development (caregiver and clinician) of hypothesis on the faulty belief(s) system developed in child because of impact from trauma.
Phase C **Average of seven sessions for the child with caregiver present**	Directed Sand Tray stories and diagrams to address the child's relational bond with primary caregivers and to expose and allow reconstruction of traumatic experience(s). Cognitive behavioral processing of the child's traumatic experience; identification of dominant trauma theme; disputation of the resulting faulty belief/dilemma for the child; countering of self-blame. Active involvement of the caregiver as an observer and co-director of the therapy process. As necessary, attachment re-creation intervention to address the security of the relational bond between caregiver and child.

In **Phase B**, one chosen caregiver (if two participated in the Phase A) takes part in seven individualized sessions. Clinicians are trained in advanced CBT's formal logic-based methods to rapidly and sustainably reconstruct negative self-deductions rooted in the caregiver's own childhood. Everyone has at least one, so at least one can be located whether or not they have a history of unresolved trauma from childhood.

In **Phase C**, caregiver and child participate in four assessment and treatment sessions. Directed Sand Tray methods are employed to gather information about the child's experience of trauma, their relationship with the caregiver, and their belief systems. Having addressed their own issues in the two previous phases, the caregiver is now prepared to participate as "co-therapist" in the child's treatment. Therapy along with the child resolves impact related to the attachment relationship with the caregiver, the loss of significant relationship(s) in the child's life, shame or guilt for the history of problematic behaviors, and ultimately the impact from the traumatic event itself.

Phase A (TIS) is consciously structured to reduce current wait lists and open up access to treatment (15–30 participants). Caregivers are immediately provided with a course start date or a variety of course start dates to select from at intake. In this manner, the ITTM offers an alternative to traditional treatment for children and their caregivers in a service system overburdened by the high numbers of children and adults affected by trauma and waiting months or years for treatment.

The Role of Metacognition in the ITTM

Metacognition has been described simply as "thinking about thinking." A more inclusive description would add that it is composed of cognitive processes and involves answering whether a cognitive goal has been met. John Flavell, one of its major theorists, contends that metacognitive knowledge is divided into three categories: knowledge of person variables, knowledge of task variables, and knowledge of strategy variables (Flavell, 1979, 1987; Livingston, 1996). All the sessions in Phase A draw upon metacognition principles by linking thoughts to feelings and thoughts to feelings to actions. Time is taken to process and compare conscious thinking to unconscious thinking to increase the caregiver's awareness of what they do and do not know in reference to their particular situation (Posen, 1997).

Knowledge of person variables applies to the process of how humans learn, as well as their own awareness of their learning processes and styles. Phase A of the ITTM looks extensively at the learning process in a clearly outlined pattern. Person variables are at the root of teaching (and learning) about the ramifications of trauma, its impact on the child and the child's family, the effects of a history of traumatic impact, and the process of looking and thinking about relationships. Specifically, diagrams enable the group to express, think about, and chart and choose their best learning mode through an incorporation of visual, auditory, and tactile experiences. The trauma information group sessions focus on auditory learning. Visual learning techniques through diagramming shine new light on children's behavior. The anger release program, along with the charting process, focuses on tactile learning experiences.

Task variables involve knowledge of tasks and the types of processing demands placed on the individual. The charting of behavioral loops and PAST, PRESENT, and FUTURE Diagrams is integral to the daily practice of "homework assignments" in each treatment phase. In this manner, the individual considers and directly experiences how behavior change operates. The ITTM program is task-oriented because the instrument of change and remediation is personal engagement, making the personalized homework essential to the goal of redirecting the thought process and constructing new pathways in the brain as the first step to sustained behavioral changes.

Strategy variables include knowledge about cognitive and metacognitive strategies as well as knowledge about when and where it is appropriate to utilize such strategies. Creating an improved life plan is one of the model's principal purposes. The revised and more effective plan must begin with strategies to strengthen the emotional attunement level between caregiver and child within the safety and containment of the family. To ensure that cognitive changes and goals are reached, sequential processes that regulate and monitor the learning process are applied. The practice of consistently assigning homework throughout each session, whether with adults or children; the discussion and review of the homework; and the re-assignment of the previous week's homework or further homework is a sequential process that regulates, monitors, and contains clients. This process of containment through diagrams and homework assignment includes a strong component of participant self-questioning.

Self-questioning is a metacognitive comprehension strategy and a necessary element of engagement and treatment throughout the ITTM process. Focal points include the individual's role within the family of origin and the immediate family, self-perception of self, and personal capacity to learn and initiate positive changes. Strategizing incorporates the knowledge acquired in Phase A and charted and acted upon throughout each phase of treatment. The Membrane Diagram in Phase B is a clear example of "strategy at work." The diagram requires concerted thought and effort to shift behavioral responses of the self, to the self, and towards others. Individuals need to grasp the validity and expected outcomes of their choices within and between the **permeable, non-permeable and semi-permeable membrane** response options, the appropriateness of each choice, and the subtle and not-so-subtle distinctions between each state.

Simply processing knowledge of personal cognitive strengths or weaknesses with a client and reviewing what is required to bring about positive changes, without also actively engaging the client in actual techniques to aid them in doing so, *is not metacognitive.* Clients need to learn real practices for integrating and reiterating new information, reflecting and reviewing the changing process of their thoughts and feelings, and involving themselves in tracking their own progress—or lack of it—on a daily, even hourly, basis. These actions prepare the client with information about their own state of being while also allowing them to provide detailed feedback to the clinician. At that point, the clinician and client are equally informed about the latter's state; the clinician can build on the client's new awareness to teach further practices to their ongoing benefit. Metacognition equates with the "deep learning" and internalization of concepts. Consequently, the assignment for daily completion and the weekly review of homework are diligently attended to with each client through each phase of treatment. Cognitive strategy instruction teaches individuals how to better regulate their cognitive activities. The Behavior Choice Program (BCP) intoduced in Phase B is an example of such an approach. The program teaches children to make conscious choices of their own, decreases the role of caregivers as enforcers, and increases self-responsibility-taking, impulse control, self-initiated behaviors, and self-esteem.

Phase A: The Trauma Information Sessions (TIS)

As noted, the six 90-minute opening sessions are psycho-educational in nature. Principles of trauma, attachment, and cognitive behavioral therapy are presented. Caregivers receive relevant articles, diagrams, charts, and homework assignments after each session. A portion of ITTM training involves teaching clinicians how to design and capture the salient features of each client's complex trauma experiences, their effects, outcomes, and resolution, by using diagrammatic structures. Where caregivers are concerned, the ITTM interprets their extrinsically motivated referral of children to treatment as a vital one-time opportunity to develop and strengthen their existing levels of intrinsic motivation prior to beginning individual treatment with them (Phase B) and the conjoint treatment of caregivers and children (Phase C).

The elements of Phase A, briefly outlined ahead, indicate the specific strategies and tools that work to increase the degree of self-determination in adults as characterized by competency, inter-relatedness, and autonomy (Deci & Ryan, 2000). The stronger the self-determination, the higher the level of intrinsic motivation will be. In turn, a heightened sense of intrinsic motivation will increase the level of the hope that is the basis of all self-improvement efforts.

KEY: Competence—**C**; Inter-relatedness—**I-R**; Autonomy—**A**; Structure—**S**:

Referral:

- Caregivers who meet the criteria for their child to participate in the ITTM program are immediately enrolled in the six-week, 1.5-hour per week psycho-educational Trauma Information Sessions (**C, I-R, A**).
- The caregivers' extrinsic motivation in referring their child to treatment is utilized to engage their participation in Phase A, along with up to 50 other caregivers, as a pre-requisite for continued treatment (with their child).

Trauma Information Sessions:

- These are designed to inform adults and caregivers about the most up-to-date information available about trauma impact on caregivers and children (**C, I-R**).
- This education works to increase their base of knowledge and competency (**C**).
- Advanced Cognitive Behavioral Therapy (CBT) diagrams are the primary clinical skills method. The diagrammatic structures integrate principles of trauma, attachment, and CBT.
- The objectives are to develop caregiver empathy for the child's experience (**C, I-R**), to reposition caregivers to better provide their child with security and containment (**C, I-R**), to improve caregiver

self-regulation and disengage the caregiver from conflicted interactions with the child (**C, I-R, A**), and to encourage hope, self-efficacy, and motivation for change (**C, I-R, A**).

Information sources:

- The psycho-educational material has been carefully designed to capture common trauma themes, symptoms, and behaviors of adults who have experienced trauma in childhood. Although the child (not the caregiver) has been referred for treatment, the course is designed to ensure that caregivers begin to apply to themselves what is learned by means of the information sessions and their related homework. The idea is to lead them to think of themselves as the former child or adolescent who has experienced trauma impact (**C, I-R**).
- The positive outcomes generated in caregivers' exploration and re-connection with their own childhood trauma reinforces their self-empathy, as well as empathy for their children (**C, I-R**).
- They become increasingly more motivated as they begin to realize the importance (and the child's need) for the caregiver to be the first active agent of change in their lives: that is, the caregiver starts to appreciate the value of being the clinician's informant, as well as assistant, in resolving the child's trauma impact (**C, I-R, A**).

Attendance:

- Caregivers must participate each week. Because of the treatment's sequential operation, those who miss even one week will be unable to catch up to the rest of the participants (**S**).
- Caregivers who miss sessions are given the choice—and encouraged—to re-enroll in a future course (**A**).

Topics:

- These include such basics as a caregiver's choices for continuing or stopping treatment (**A**);
- why the caregiver is beginning treatment before the child (**C, A**);
- the need for containment (**C**);
- homework requirements in the course (**C**);
- the caregivers' importance to children's response to trauma;
- what is trauma (**C**);
- emotional attunement (**C, I-R**);
- the differences between trauma in adulthood and trauma in childhood (**C, I-R, A**);
- the stress and chaos map (**C, I-R**);
- the support map (**A**);
- time commitment requirements for each phase of treatment (**C, A**);
- confidentiality amongst members of the course (**I-R, A**);
- information on the behaviors and symptoms of children and adults who have experienced trauma (**C, I-R, A**);
- the pathway positions of caregivers and adjusting that pathway position (**C, A**);
- emotions/anger (**C**);
- faulty belief systems (**C, A**);
- self-defeating behavioral loops and how to interrupt them (**C, A**);
- brain development (**C**);
- reviews of articles and homework (**C, I-R**); and
- preparing for individual adult trauma treatment sessions in Phase B (**A**).

Homework:

- Caregivers receive articles to read, diagrams to fill, and charts to complete each week (**C**).
- Homework is designed and paced to ensure successful completion by the caregiver. In this way, caregivers are set up for success at the start and are likely to commit to continued success (**C**).
- Caregivers are also supported in their choice to stop the program at any time and choose to continue to fail themselves and ultimately their child if they so choose (**A**). The program identifies this as a caregiver's prerogative, and supports their ability to choose what they need at any point and time, ideal or not (**A**).
- On the other hand, caregivers invested in continual failure and unhappiness are unlikely to have chosen to attend the course (**C**).
- Step-by-step instructions and support and encouragement for completing assignments are provided. Caregivers are informed from the start that if the diagrams and charting exercises are not completed by the following week or at least by the close of the Trauma Information Sessions, they will be unable to proceed to the Phase B core material sessions (**A**).

Phase B:

- Phase A material is reviewed in Phase B, but it is *not* re-delivered in one-on-one sessions with clients. Hence, if a client has been unable to complete more than three of the homework assignments in Phase A, they will be encouraged to re-enroll in Phase A (**A**).
- The amount of homework, which is meant to support integration of course material at home and in everyday life, increases incrementally each week (**C, A**). The homework tasks require application of the material to the self, increasing the self-awareness level of the caregiver (**I-R**). The diagrams provided to the caregivers for homework completion initiate the process of change in the caregiver and in the home prior to and in preparation for clinician involvement (**C, A**).
- The caregiver will gradually apply more cognitive, emotional, and behavioral resources to themselves and their child (**C, I-R, A**).
- This active process begins, and continues to, effect changes in both caregiver and child; the caregiver becomes increasingly aware of how much the changes can be attributed to their own efforts rather than those of the clinician "expert" (**C, I-R, A**).

Containment and self-regulation:

- Each session is specifically designed to contain caregiver affect and develop caregiver self-regulation (**C, I-R**).
- The risk of emotional dysregulation in caregivers is controlled for by: a) the large group numbers (**I-R**), b) restricting opportunities for personal story-telling, c) co-regulation of caregivers' affect by the ITTM director (**C**), and d) the use of diagrams.

In Phase B, the clinician personalizes the treatment steps for each caregiver, in order to make them aware of their individual pacing and processing needs, and the time-frames required for integrating treatment gains. Caregivers complete a personalized diagram with the clinician's guidance. Metacognitive techniques awaken their consciousness of how their own efforts and interaction with the clinician are integral to fulfilling this requirement. As a result, they are increasingly encouraged to work toward the successful completion of the more individualized aspects of charting and awareness, which, again, raises their confidence, hope, and motivation.

In addition, these diagrams become the clinician's basis for assessment and treatment to the point of resolution prior to progressing to Phase C. The clinician also evaluates the caregiver's ability to implement the four main goals of the Trauma Information Sessions undertaken in Phase A, as well as assessing the caregiver's perception of the child at this point. The latter appraisal allows identification of the nature and degree of distortion of that perception due to the caregiver's personal trauma history. The clinician is then equipped to make a fair judgment of the caregiver's ability to contain the impact of their own childhood or adult experiences, their level of empathy for the child, and their capacity to provide containment for the child's traumatic experience(s) and symptoms. If more than seven sessions with the caregiver are deemed essential at any point during Phase B, due, for example, to their substance abuse or symptoms of dissociation, the clinician refers them to an adult individual treatment center. The family's treatment process is put on hold until the caregiver's issues have been addressed and a treatment plan for those issues has been implemented. Although current behavioral interventions are designed to change caregivers' behavioral responses regarding their children, they are not used to assess, address, or resolve the adults' primary negative self-beliefs at the core of those responses and interactions. This is an essential part of the ITTM approach.

Using Advanced CBT Diagrammatic Structures

Diagrams provide an external structure and a visual target for the caregiver as they carry out the requirements of Phase B. They are specifically used to contain the affect associated with unresolved traumatic impact and negative self-beliefs (NSBS). The introduction of diagrammatic structures in the first and every session of Phase B ensures that they will witness consistent evidence of their ability to contain their own affect week after week. The positive and direct experience of contained affect, as demonstrated in each session, allows them to create new, and more importantly, effective, self-regulation practices for themselves. During each session, the clinician and caregiver work together to produce the most accurate yet simplified diagrammatic representation of one specific aspect of their primary treatment goal. The jointly produced diagram is copied and taken home after each treatment session for the client to scrutinize, evaluate, and adapt to more accurately reflect their ongoing transformation and development of new thoughts, feelings, and actions. This important process introduces clients to a technique for learning, practicing, and benefiting from slowing themselves down to permit the core's self-emergence. At the same time, it provides specific evidence of the caregiver's growing competency, autonomy, and ability to self-determine. Well-illustrated, highly simplified diagrams instill a new level of hope in adults. What has often long been internalized as an unmanageable, even overwhelming, indication of personal inadequacy is reconstructed to confirm the manageability and resolvability of the problem(s). The diagrams also permit visual tracking of changes specific to the caregiver's unique processing and current capacity to take action. Upon completion, each session's diagram is attached to a chart that "maps" every day of the week to follow. The caregiver goes home to chart the number of instances in which they have experienced being in one or more of the PAST, PRESENT, or FUTURE Diagram positions. This is done three times daily, every day. At the beginning of each subsequent session, the caregiver totals their position frequency numbers, and they and the clinician agree on new frequency totals to be reached prior to the next session.

As cave drawings suggest, externalizations of thought in the form of drawings—more properly diagrams—are ancient (Donald, 1991; Kirsh, 2010; Norman, 1994; Tversky, 1995, 2001). All manner of thought, concrete and abstract, spatial and non-spatial, can readily be mapped to the page. Moreover, such pages can be infinitely reviewed and modified by their creator and others. Thought visualization does more than clarify meaning, important as that is. The process also encourages the use of everyday spatial reasoning skills regarding distance, direction, size, shape, position, connectedness, inclusion, and more—for abstract as well as spatial reasoning. In addition to their most common, literal, spatial applications—for example, to estimate distances and determine routes—they are also useful for psychological evaluations of behavior and functionality (Nickerson, 2013, pp. 254–6).

Expression, whether to "articulate" ideas (in every sense) for the self or for others, is clearly a core human objective. Cognitive tools provide expressive media: the thought and the tool together represent situations that are at once external to and a joint product of the thought and the tool. As cognitive tools, both the page and language occasion thought expression. Where words "cannot be found," which is often the case for trauma victims, and especially for children who may also lack the necessary vocabulary for vocal expression, the page is often the best means of representation: they tell their story on the page, a diagram that helps them to order their thoughts and memories while permitting otherwise challenging access to these by clinicians. "Getting it down" on paper often further encourages self-awareness and self-interpretation. The process itself is dialectical: once thoughts are "shaped" on the page, their very shaping affects the internal version. What goes on the page affects what is inside the head, and the design itself affects further mapping as thoughts are refined, solidified, recalled more explicitly, and so on (Nickerson, 2013, pp. 256, 270). Cognitive tools "both effect and affect thought" (Nickerson, 2013, p. 270; Ross, 2017; Novick, 2000).

In therapy, as in design, the utility of diagrams is ultimately determined by their specific usage. The ITTM uses diagrams to structure and focus the client's thoughts and their external expression on the page. The clinician applies this "on the page" form of expression to contain the effects associated with negative self-schemata. Diagrams capture abstract concepts in a tangible, visible manner which assists in normalizing a large range of traumatic experiences and outcomes. The charting schedules accompanying each ITTM diagram are the instruments that establish and generate achievable and successful targets only. Clinicians are trained on how to define realistic target goals, with the client's input and endorsement, and then lower these slightly below the client's assessed capacity. This ensures successful total charting outcomes that not infrequently better the initial targets. By setting and achieving targets in manageable, practical, realizable ways that quickly produce successful results, this process demonstrates unequivocal evidence of a caregiver's increased competency and increased relatedness with the self. Friendly et al. (2008) describe how structures create the levels of stability required by individuals to construct reasonable expectations about their environments and how to master them. Areas of personal life that lack structure indicate that a personal sense of competency in that area is also lacking. The competency construct subsists within every life context; it reinforces the argument for every individual's need for a structure in which a series of small and larger successes are actualized. Target goals that are diagrammed and charted present measurable, ongoing, gratifying self-representations of progress. The diagrams provide visual and trackable tools for daily positive affirmation, daily observation, reinforcement, and self-regulating monitoring opportunities.

Large diagrams purposely emphasize the differences between the universal effects of trauma on individuals and between natural human tendencies to over-personalize the negative effects of trauma impact. When the experience is adequately depersonalized, differences between the event and the caregiver's perception and experience of its impact can be more clearly understood for what they are: distinctive elements of the larger picture of complex trauma. The caregiver can interact more openly with a neutralized diagram that depicts a specific aspect of the effects of trauma without the associated negative or overwhelming affect. They begin by charting their current position on the diagram and targeting where they want to be by the end of treatment. Charting targets increase each time the client progresses one step, or an established set of charting numbers, toward the goal. Within six weeks of charting, the clinician is usually following the target charting goals and listening to the client's weekly insights on their own change and self-related processes. The caregiver proceeds to demonstrate and transfer their competency, increased energy for inter-relatedness, and improved autonomy with their child, weeks prior to the child commencing treatment with them in Phase C.

The rules for establishing reliable and replicable research outcomes are used to determine the effectiveness of diagrammatic interventions: these tools should only be considered reliable when psychiatric history, age, gender, geographical, and cultural differences *do not* interfere with the intervention's capacity to generate desired outcomes consistently. The ITTM's logic-centered diagrammatic tool appears to rapidly facilitate the successful reconstruction of negative self-beliefs in chronically distressed, traumatized, and psychiatrically disordered adults, children, and teens.

The "dandelion" diagram (Figures 4.1, 4.2) is used, for example, to raise the caregiver's awareness of the roots of their own issues as well as their child's, and to support redirection of the caregiver's focus on the child's behavioral responses and symptoms to the root issues bringing about negative symptoms and behaviors in the caregiver and child.

The flower of the dandelion represents the individual symptoms and negative manifestations of the caregiver's unresolved trauma history. The root represents the primary negative self-belief system that they formulated in response to traumatic childhood events. As in metaphor, running a lawn mower over the dandelion and the stem that carries the toxicity up into the flower does not eliminate the dandelion's root. Within days, the dandelion stem will rise again. Furthermore, if the flower is left unattended long enough, it eventually turns to seed that will successfully spread its negative effects into the larger environment beyond itself but still related to its individual self (and neighbors' yards). The client is asked

FIGURE 4.1 The Dandelion Diagram

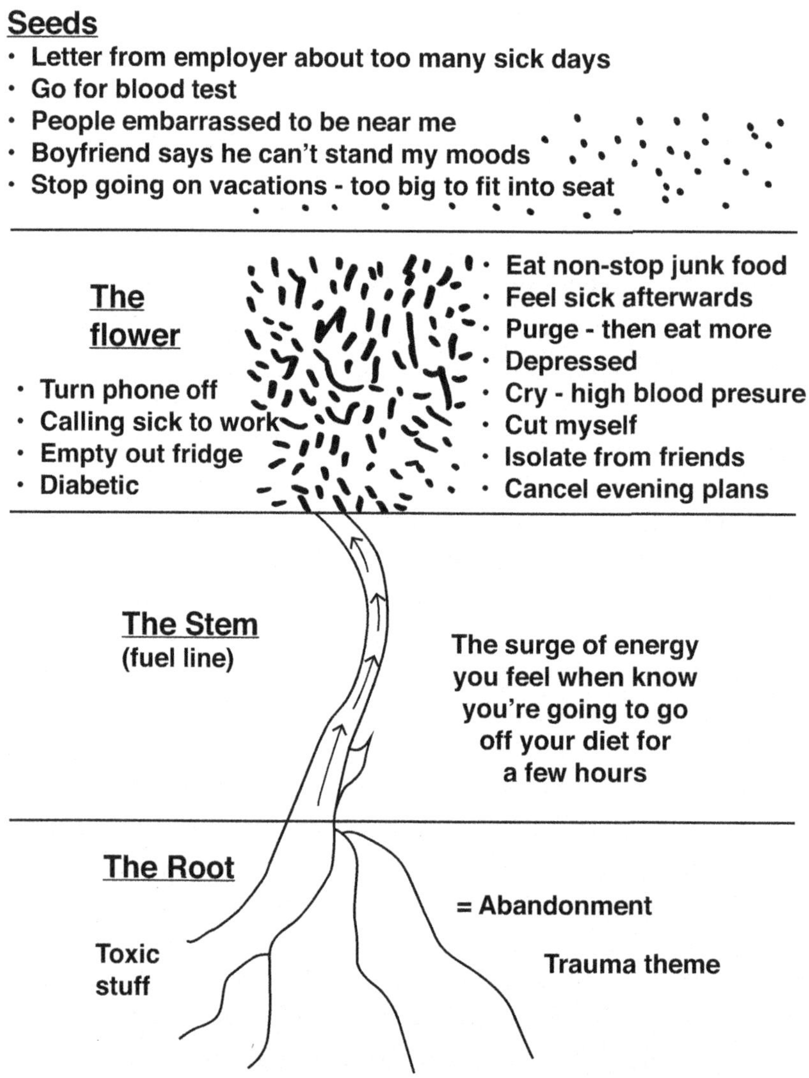

FIGURE 4.2 Charting the Dandelion Diagram

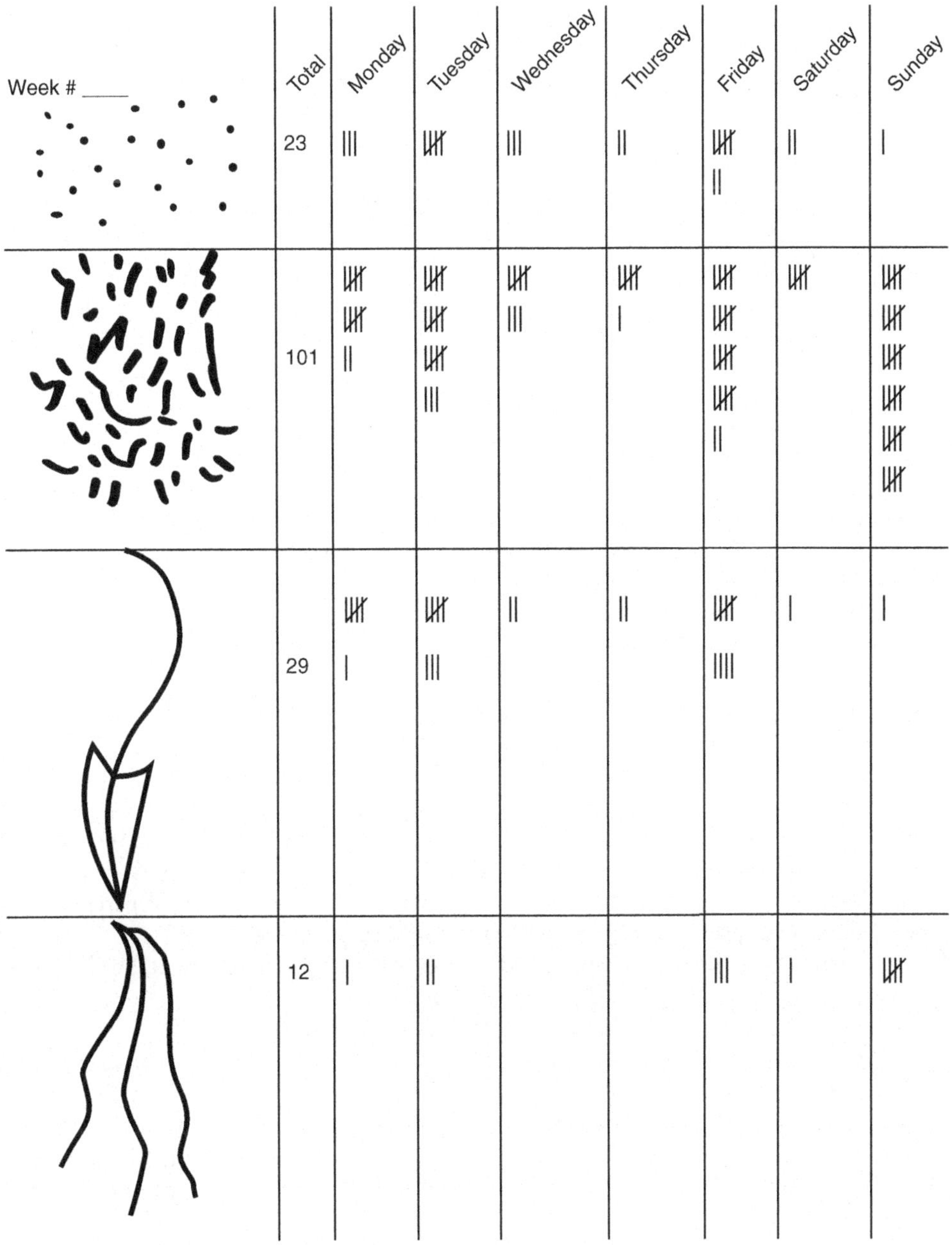

to tally the number of times they find themselves within each portion of the diagram, at three clearly established times each day, for the next week and up until the next scheduled appointment. Whatever the treatment method, the overarching purpose of all psychological treatment is inarguably to achieve lasting change in the client's often debilitating and destructive negative symptomology and resulting behaviors.

Conclusion

This chapter has discussed how diagrammatic structures employed in the first and every session of ITTM treatment aim to demonstrate the client's ability to contain their own affect. The client's resulting positive and direct experience of contained affect *in each session* helps them to adapt their experience of self-mastery through the feelings and cognitions associated with successful self-regulation practices. During each session, the clinician and client work together to produce the most accurate yet simple diagrammatic representation of one specific aspect of the client's primary treatment goal. This jointly created diagram is copied and taken home as proof of the client's growing competency, autonomy, and ability to self-determine. Simple and comprehensible diagrams instill a new level of hope in adults. What has often long been internalized as an unmanageable and continuous indication of personal inadequacy is reconstructed to demonstrate competency, manageability and resolution. The session's diagram is attached to a charting schedule that includes every day of the week. Diagrams provide an opportunity to track the change process specific to the unique processing and current action-taking ability of the client—which guides the clinician to the client's individually tailored next steps in treatment. The chapter appendices give a clearer sense of the actual session discussions (client feedback and review of the week's charts) and the types of diagrams employed.

References

APA. (1994). *Diagnostic and Statistical Manual of Mental Health Disorders: DSM-V-TR* (5th ed.). Washington, DC: American Psychiatric Association.

Bailey, J. H. (2009). Parenting practices and problem behavior across three generation: Monitoring, harsh discipline, and drug use in the intergenerational transmission of externailizing behavior. *Developmental Psychology* 45, pp. 1214–1226.

Copping, V. W., et al. (2001). A child trauma treatment pilot study. *Journal of Child and Family Studies* 10:4, pp. 467–475.

Donald, M. (1991). *Origins of the Modern Mind: Three Stages in the Evolution of Culture and Cognition*. Cambridge, MA: Harvard University Press.

Dowell, K. O. (2010). The effects of parent participation on child psychotherapy outcome: A meta-analytic review. *Journal of Child and Adolescent Psychology* 39:2, pp. 151–162.

Flavell, J. (1979). Metacognition and cognitive monitoring: A new era of cognitive-developmental inquiry. *American Psychologist* 34, pp. 906–911.

Flavell, J. (1987). Speculations about the nature and development of metacognition. In F. E. Weinert & R. H. Klewe (Eds.), *Metacognition, Motivation and Understanding* (pp. 21–29). Hillside, NJ: Lawrence Erlbaum Associates.

Friendly, R. A., et al. (2008). Child adjustment to familial dissolution: An examination of parental factors using a self-determination theory framework. *Journal of Divorce & Remarriage* 50:1, pp. 66–80.

Hughes, K. L. (2016). Relationships between adverse childhood experiences and adult mental well-being: Results from an English national household survey. *BMC Public Health* 16:224, pp. 205–206.

Kirsh, D. (2010). Thinking with external representations. *AI & Society* 25, pp. 441–454.

Livingston, J. (1996). *Effects of Metacognitive Instruction on Strategy Use of College Students*. Buffalo, NY: Unpublished manuscript, State University of New York at Buffalo.

McCormack, L. & Thomson, S. (2017). Complex trauma in childhood, a psychiatric diagnosis in adulthood: Making meaning of a double-edged phenomenon. *Psychological Trauma: Theory, Research, Practice, and Policy* 9:2, pp. 156–165.

McWey, L. P., et al. (2013). Intergenerational patterns of maltreatment in families at risk for foster care. *Journal of Marital & Family Therapy* 39, pp. 133–147.

Nickerson, J. C.-J. (2013). Cognitive tools shape thought: Diagrams in design. *Cognitive Process* 14, pp. 255–272.

Norman, D. A. (1994). The power of representation. In D. Norman, *Things That Make Us Smart: Defending Human Attributes in the Age of the Machine* (pp. 1–21). William Patrick Books.

Novick, L. R. (2000). Spatial diagrams: Key instruments in the toolbox for thought. In L. R. Novick, *Psychology of Learning and Motivation* Vol. 40, pp. 223–278.

Posen, D. (1997). *Always Change a Losing Game: Playing at Life to Be the Best You Can Be*. Richmond Hill, ON: Firefly Books.

Ross, B. H. (2017). *Psychology of Learning and Motivation* (vol. 67). Cambridge, MA: Elsevier.

Stallard, P. (2007). Early maladaptive schemas in children: Stability and differences between a community and a clinical referred sample. *Clinical Psychology and Psychotherapy* 14, pp. 10–18.

Thienemann, M. A. (2006). A parent-only group intervention for children with anxiety disorders: Pilot study. *Journal of the American Academy of Child & Adolescent Psychiatry* 45:1, pp. 37–46.

Tversky, B. (1995). Cognitive origins of graphic productions. In B. Tversky, *Understanding Images* (pp. 29–53). Secaucus, NJ, USA: Springer-Verlag.

Tversky, B. (2001). Spatial schemas in depictions. In M. Gattis (Ed.), *Spatial Schemas and Abstract Thought* (pp. 79–112). Cambridge, MA: MIT Press.

Appendix 4.1

Phase A: Trauma Information Sessions Checklist

The diagrams and explanations provided in this and all other chapters are specific excerpts and examples from the ITTM Training Manual in part, not in whole. Practice of any parts of the ITTM presented in this book are not designed to deliver the outcomes achieved after completing the 50–100-hour ITTM Training program, where the ITTM manual is provided in full alongside detailed instruction and advanced clinical skills training. For more information on training options, visit www.theittm.com

Session 1

- Reasons for the caregiver's attendance and participation.
- Emotional distance created by trauma and the meaning of behaviors and symptoms.
- Caregivers' natural response to trauma.
- Overview of Phases A, B, and C.
- Do's and Don'ts: rules and guidelines regarding attendance, homework, confidentiality, and emergencies.
- Noticing improvement.
- What is trauma? Is the event important? Impact: the cement analogy and how the ITTM addresses trauma.
- Caregiver's trauma and impact of the same (scale).
- Introduction of containment and attunement (scale).
- Homework: read handout materials.

Session 2

- What stood out from last time?
- Trauma impact review.
- Caregiver participation, articles, containment review.
- The difference between trauma in childhood and trauma in adulthood.
- Examples of how a child's experience is different.
- Brain differences.
- What is your child's dilemma?
- Behaviors.

- Development of belief systems in the child.
- Stress and Chaos Map: adult's world, child's world.
- Time commitment for treatment.
- Support map and connections.
- Homework: complete support maps with lines of connections; read handouts.

Session 3

- What stood out from last time?
- Belief systems of children: how they are formed.
- Review of homework: support map, what happens to support when trauma occurs—isolation and the "wounded animal" factor.
- Relationships between caregivers and children: pathways.
- Discussion with groups about pathways; Pathway A places the caregiver in the lead; analogy of tour bus driver.
- Pathway A charting homework.
- Grief and loss (five minutes) from previous week handouts.
- Caregivers acting out emotional trauma; helpful or hurtful ways.
- Homework: diagram tonight's Pathways materials—charting what you observe at least once per day. Hand in support maps with child's first and last name on it.

Session 4

- What stood out from last time?
- Charting pathways homework: What did you observe? Add up numbers: 80%?
- Article on adolescent characteristics—what stood out for you?
- Eight basic emotions.
- Anger.
- Anger and children: "Mad is the hat for sad," anger buckets, and the differences for children and adults.
- The ABCs of Anger: exploding and imploding.
- Behaviors: three components that join and work together to form a behavior.
- Picture of a typical family and the amount of thought, feeling, and action they rely on.
- Self-defeating behaviors create loops.
- Behavioral loops and exercise.
- Homework: two examples of positive imploding and positive exploding (Big As) to hand in for next week.
- Continue charting pathways and hand in next week.
- Complete a behavioral loop of thoughts, feelings, and actions.
- Look at your loop 2–3 times over the week.
- Prizes for the adult and youth with the most components in their loop.
- Bring in your behavioral loop to hand in next week.

Session 5

- What stood out from last time?
- Homework review: examples for imploding and exploding; update on charting pathways; behavioral loops.

- Behavioral loops: who completed, can anyone share, themes, level of difficulty, etc.
- Charting of loops: explanation of PAST, PRESENT, FUTURE.
- Review of the importance of completing homework.
- Positive methods for exploding and imploding.
- Information on the behaviors and symptoms of children.
- Chronological age versus the emotional age of the child.
- ITTM model: top-down approach = treatment, not symptom reducer.
- How caregiver's and child's roles intersect.
- Homework: for those who haven't completed loops to complete them for next session. Review of charting loops—PAST, PRESENT, FUTURE. Continue to chart pathways with the goal of attaining 80% in the A category.

Session 6

- What stood out from last week?
- Homework: review of loop completion.
- Review of loop charting: what did you notice (80% of time)?
- Hand in loops, pathways, and charting for both.
- Interrupting loops.
- Anger loops.
- Homework: do a loop that you get into with your child and chart this loop in the past, present, and future over the next week. Continue charting pathways.
- *The Five Stages of Change* by David Posen (1997).
- Where were you when you began treatment? Where are you now?
- What to expect in Phase B and Phase C in terms of materials covered, homework completed, energy, and major themes.
- Feedback about Phase A. Give each client their first Phase B appointment date and extra charting paper.

Appendix 4.2

Phase A, B, and C Diagram Examples

Phase A Diagrams

A1a: The Intergenerational Trauma Treatment Model (ITTM)

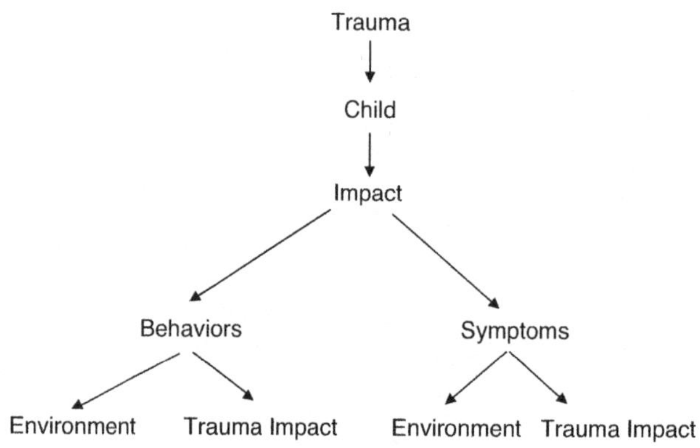

A1b: Medical Model Version of Trauma Treatment

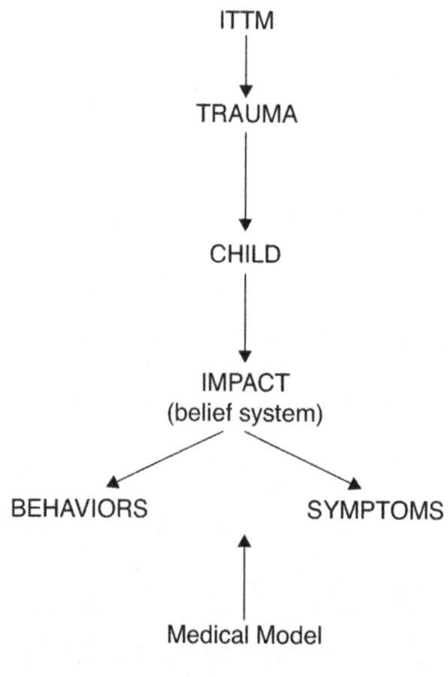

A2: Overview of the ITTM's Three Phases of Treatment (21 Sessions)

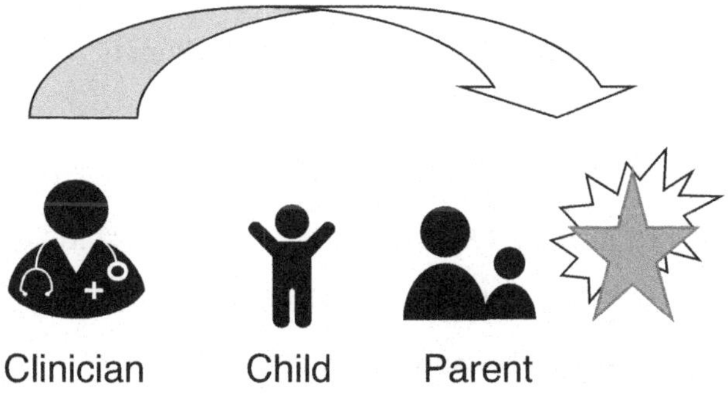

Phase A: Information on the impact of trauma on the child/teen provided to the caregiver—six Trauma Information Sessions

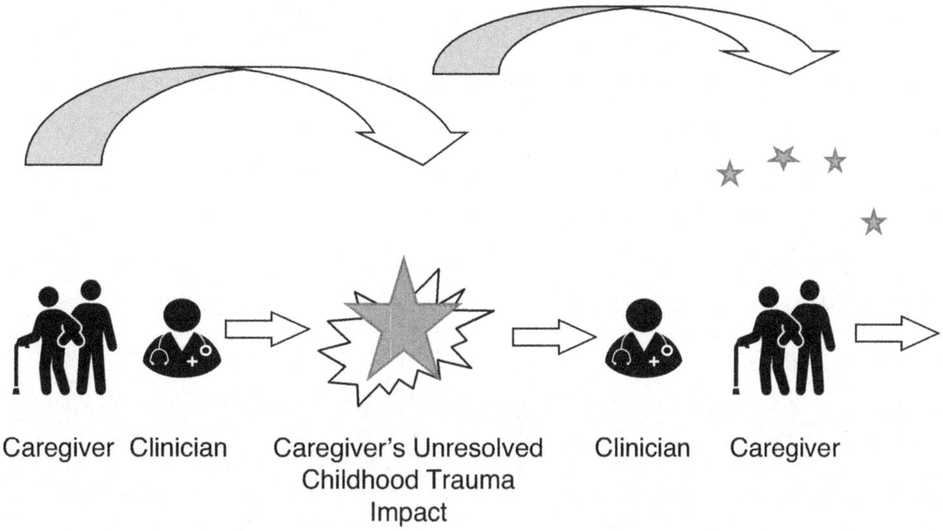

Phase B: The clinician leads the caregiver through the caregiver's childhood trauma impact—eight sessions

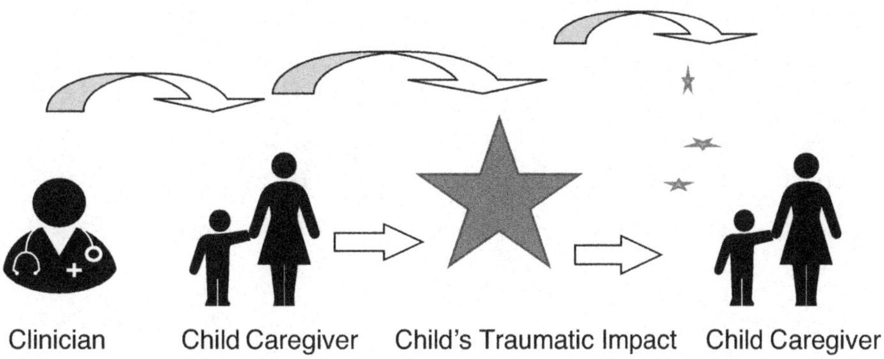

Phase C: The clinician guides the caregiver to be the active agent of change in the child's trauma treatment—seven sessions

A3: What Is Trauma?

Alcohol Abuse Neglect Chronic Illness
Sexual Abuse Custody Battle Genocide
Adoption Excessive Punishment Witnessing Violence
Residential Schools Drug Addicted Caregivers Unexpected Separation from Caregiver
Accidents Multiple Home Placements Financial Hardship
Favoritism of Siblings Separation and Divorce Death
Real or Perceived Threat to Caregiver's Life Inconsistent Access Visits

A4: The Traumatic Event Itself Is Not What Needs to Be Treated

If we are not treating the event, if it is in the past and gone, then what are we treating?

Answer: The individual's primary most negative *impact* of the event(s) and experiences.

Our beliefs inform, influence, and guide each of our thoughts, feelings, and actions. When negative self-beliefs remain unrecognized or unresolved, negative and worrying thoughts, feelings, and actions remain, and frequently worsen across the lifespan.

A5: Wet Cement Analogy

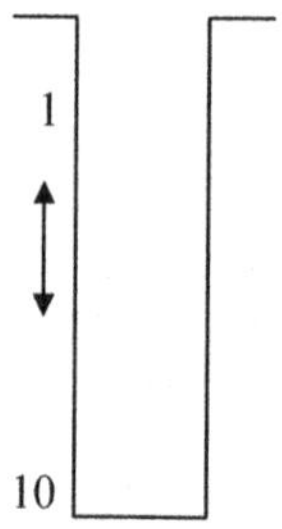

Think of it as walking along a sidewalk of wet cement and you step your foot into it to make an imprint. Each person's step sinks in (or is impacted) to a different degree.

A6

Example: There are three children; these children each experienced the same traumatic event losing a sibling in a car accident, yet:

- Child A is impacted at 10/10, Child B is impacted at 5/10, and Child C is impacted at 3/10.

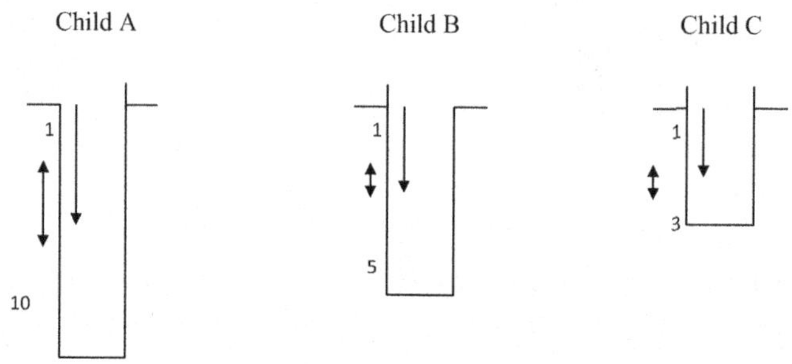

What happens if another stressful and/or traumatic event happens at age 35 and the previous one has not been treated?

A7

As a Child (Draw First) *Then Add, at Age 35*

Answer: Your thoughts, feelings, and actions will fall to the degree you first experienced as impactful in childhood. You will likely feel ONLY as competent as an 11-, 8-, or 6-year-old because it's unresolved and that is the age you were when the first and most impactful trauma occurred.

Appendix 4.3

The Caregiver's Unresolved Childhood Trauma Impact: Group Discussion

Clinician addressing the group session:

I want to ask the adults: how many of you had a traumatic event in childhood?
What was the degree of impact you felt on a scale of 1–10? → Draw this scale and circle the number.

Have the caregivers call out their numbers:

A8: Impact Scale

-10 -9 -8 -7 -6 -5 -4 -3 -2 -1 0 1 2 3 4 5 6 7 8 9 10

- Notice how quickly you could come up with the number: approximately three seconds.
- How many of you raced home and told your caregivers what happened to you? For example, "Mommy and Daddy I'm currently experiencing a 9/10 on the impact scale of what happened to me!"
- How many of you felt your caregiver or caregivers knew without even asking?
- What was going on for you? Did you feel disillusioned or negatively surprised by the event or reactions or lack thereof by others?
- How many of you felt completely understood?

The ITTM treatment program seeks to discover:

→ The degree of impact for your child.
→ At what age it occurred.
→ Then the job of treatment is to bring this degree of impact up to flush. It is then that the behaviors and the symptoms of the child will reduce substantially, and it is then the treatment will be complete.

- Most often children will not express the effects of trauma in words. What do they use? Behaviors.
- Children's and teen's systems will often exhibit behaviors when under stress.
- Kids will not risk disclosure when they do not feel safe (physically or emotionally) or if they are picking up that their caregiver cannot handle the details of the trauma.
- Would you tell your caregiver if something awful or upsetting happened to you?
- What are some of the reasons you would not tell them?

A9: Containment

Introduction of Containment and Attunement

Wall of Containment

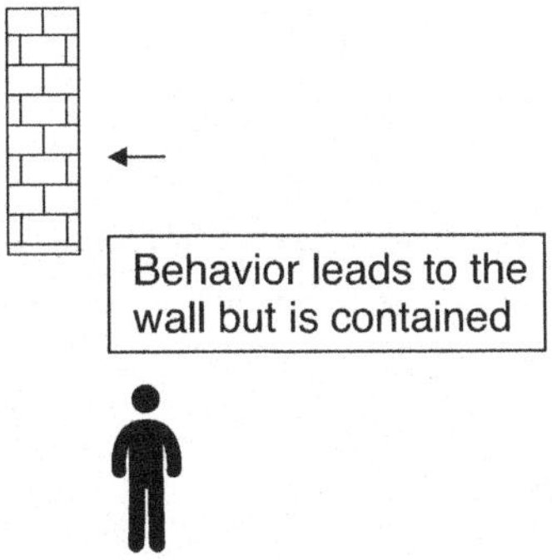

Safety-No Gaps

Gaps in the Wall of Containment

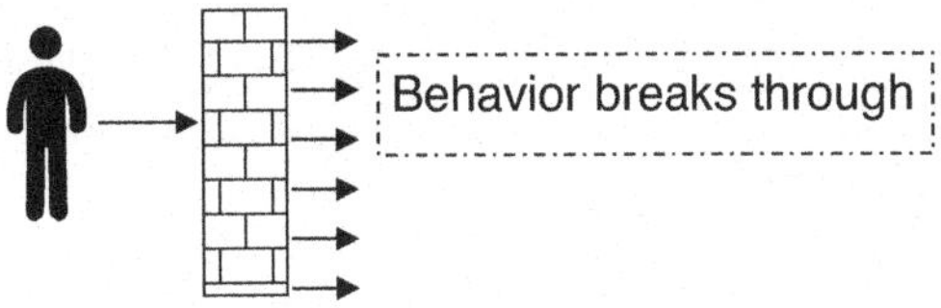

No Safety-Full of Gaps

A10: Another Option

No Gaps → Containment

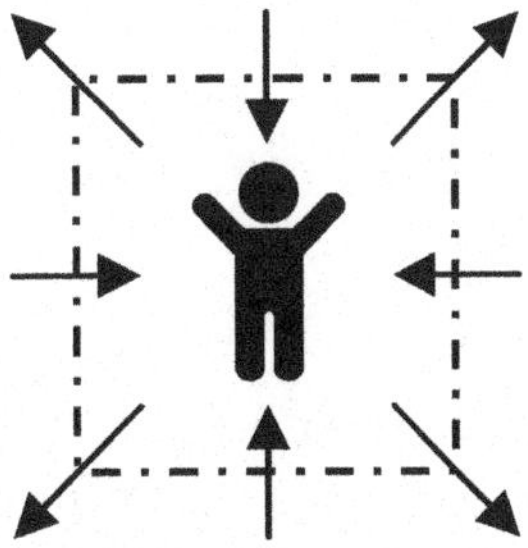

Child can't help but extend much energy to try and work to fill the gaps

→ No containment

A11: Emotional Attunement

- Remember when we talked about emotional distance.

- Attunement can be described as the emotional connection which resonates between the child and caregiver.

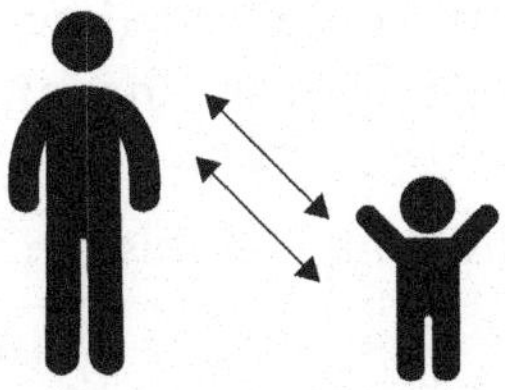

- Emotional attunement enables each person to feel felt by the other.
- In other words, when a caregiver feels they really, truly know, understand, and appreciate their child's little spirit.

Exercise:

- I want you to think back as a child on what your emotional attunement with your own caregiver may have been.
- On a scale of 0–10, 10 being feeling really understood, accepted, and appreciated for who you were, where would you place yourself in terms of your emotional attunement with your own caregiver or caregiver?

-10 -9 -8 -7 -6 -5 -4 -3 -2 -1 0 1 2 3 4 5 6 7 8 9 10

- What would you like to say about the strength of your attunement to your child?

-10 -9 -8 -7 -6 -5 -4 -3 -2 -1 0 1 2 3 4 5 6 7 8 9 10

- Considering one of your children who is not in this room, realistically where would you say it is now?
  → Remember it's not uncommon after a trauma for the emotional attunement to be affected.

-10 -9 -8 -7 -6 -5 -4 -3 -2 -1 0 1 2 3 4 5 6 7 8 9 10

- **When caregivers or kids have different numbers on this scale, we always go with the caregivers' expectation.**

Attunement goal:

- We won't begin treatment in Phase C with the child until you are at an 8 with your child.
- If you as a caregiver are only striving or able to provide your child with a 5, and if all children dream of a 9 or 10, who is going to be the one that tells your child you are limiting dreams for yourself and your child? Not us.
- You can only ever expect the amount of improvement to be as high as the number for emotional attunement that you are striving for with your child. The child will never attempt to or believe that the number can be higher than the number you are showing them through words and behaviors
- You may feel "Hey, I've come a long way from feeling like a -2 to a 6," but who gets to tell your child that this is good enough? Not us! You are doing all this hard work, so we might as well get the best we can for you!
- We are going to show you how to achieve a minimum of a number 8 and help you remain there.

A12: Caregiver Pathways—Phase A

A

ONLY Pathway to be on with your child.
Caregiver is in the LEAD, guiding the child.
Caregiver can see what is ahead/what is coming.
Caregiver can protect and prepare child.
Child can be “a child.”

B

Caregiver and child are equals—“friends.”
“You and me against the world.”
Caregiver manages child issues.
Child manages caregiver issues.

C

Caregiver and child on two separate Paths.
Each doing their own thing.

D

Child in the lead, caregiver following.
Child is in control.
Child has no buffer, no protection, no containment.
There is no connection/weak or no *attunement*.

E

Family & Children’s Service Agency or another individual (or relative) is in the lead.
Someone other than caregiver is making decisions about the child’s life.
Someone other than caregiver is “driving the bus.”

Important Point

Pathways naturally shift during adolescence. This does not necessarily mean you are not on Pathway A.

A13: Charting Caregiving Pathways—Phase A

	Monday	Tuesday	Wednesday	Thursday	Friday	Saturday	Sunday
A 	IIII	II	1	III			I
B 	II	IIII		III		IIII	IIII
C 							
D 	IIII	IIIIIIII	IIIIIIIIII	IIII	II	IIIIIIIIIIII IIIIIIIIIII	IIIIIII IIIIIII
E 							

A14: Understanding Human Behavior

There are three components that join and work together to form one behavior: feeling (F), thought (T), and action (A). One happens first, one second, and one third—with the result being one behavior.

- What order do you think these occur in?
- Who thinks (A, F, T); (T, F, A); (F, T, A); (A, T, F); (F, A, T)?

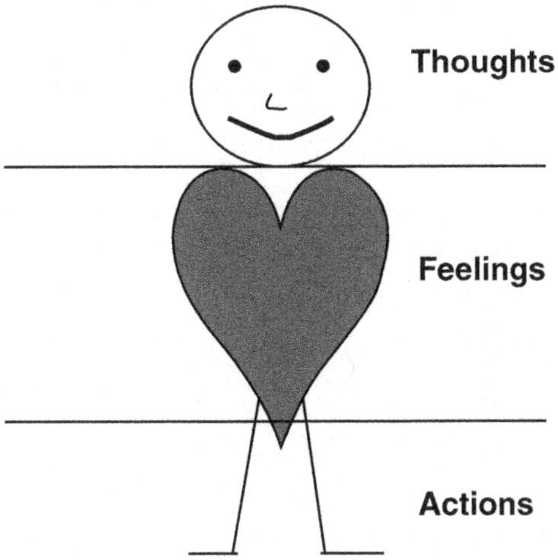

- We each place different percentages of energy and emphasis on the experience and presentation of our Ts, Fs, and As.
- Draw your present family (and/or family of origin) to scale, and place the appropriate percentage number beside the head, heart, and legs that matches the size of each thought, feeling, and action drawn. For example, Dad's might be Ts = 30%, Fs = 10%, and As = 60%, to total 100%.

A15: Family Thought, Feeling, Action With Percentages Assigned

Introduction to behavior change:

- Many of you may be here because you're unhappy with some of your child's behaviors.
- We are going to teach you about what exactly goes on to make a behavior.
- For you to gain a better understanding of behaviors and how to then change behaviors, we are going to bring you through an exercise that will both give you a lot of insight and allow you to first learn how to change one of your own behaviors.
- Only then will you be in a very good position to understand and learn how to help your child change their behaviors.

A16: Self-Defeating Behavioral Loops

- Negative behaviors form patterns that are hard to interrupt because they have been developed over time, often not consciously, to provide emotional safely and security. Also remember that familiar ways of doing things are more comforting even though they may not be the best for you or your family.
- CHANGING BEHAVORS CAN BE SCARY!
- What would be an example of a dysfunctional behavior pattern that is hard to interrupt?
- That is: addiction, abusive relationship patters, procrastination, anger, aloneness, the dieting loop, or the "I must get fit" loop, or the "I should" loop, or the "I'm guilty" loop.

Powerful/Powerless	Violence
Cycle of Abuse	Helpless
Hopelessness	Abandonment
Denial Loop	Argumentative
Shame	Anger
Not Good Enough	Guilt
Victim	Procrastination

- Behavior patterns that start a certain way, that have a predictable middle, and continue to escalate and peak before they end, in a familiar and predictable way each time before they come to an end, are called behavioral loops.
- They are usually coping behaviors that may have been useful at one point but are no longer helpful—that have now turned into self-defeating behavioral loops that take more out of you (to the negative) and drain you of more energy than they might have worked to give you at their start.
- You also always know when a behavioral loop is going on because you will always feel worse about yourself by the end of it, and guilt usually follows.
- You have some more examples of these in your homework package.
- **** Read example to group so they understand what a behavioral loop is.**

Exercise:

- I would like each of you to take time and think about what behavioral loop you have going on in your life.
- It will most often be the one you have wanted to change for a while where you tell yourself, "I must get at that one day" . . . or the one where you say, "Geez, I just did it again."
  1. An event usually happens that gets your loop started (diagram this on the board).
  2. You know you would like to change it or stop doing it because it is exhausting, but you tend to do it again anyway if the opportunity arises.
  3. You have your old familiar run at it anyway until you meet the familiar finish line (until next time).
  4. It always takes more energy than it gives you.
  5. Loops have a beginning, middle, and an end.
  6. You know it so well it's a pattern.

What might your loops be?
Who doesn't think they have a loop?

Homework:

- Complete a behavioral loop of your theme with the basic components of Ts, Fs, As.
- Remember that every action leads to a reaction.
- You may want to leave every other TFA blank so you can fill in more detail later as you go along in the week.
- Fewer than nine pieces is not a loop.
- You need at least 30 pieces.
- You must draw it in a circle to see it as a loop.
- Have a look at your handout for some examples.
- I want you to look at your loop at least 2–3 times during the week.
- Remember, don't leave completing this loop to the minute, or else you will not have a very complete loop outlined, and put in every detail you can into a separate slice.
- Who doesn't understand how to do a loop?
- We have fantastic prizes for the adult and the teen with the most components to their loops. You will need to bring in your loop next week for hand-in.

Behavioral Loop—Example 1—Theme: Lack of Self Care

Although two behavioral loop examples are written here horizontally, behavioral loops must be diagrammed with clients as a loop (diagrammed in Figure 4.18).

T= Thought; F= Feeling; A= Action
T: There are phone messages.
F: I'm too tired and burnt to answer them. (dismay)
A: I ignore them.
T: Maybe somebody needs to talk to me.
F: Resentment.
A: Ignore them more.
T: This is my time off. Don't they realize that?
F: More resentment, anger.
A: Ignore them even harder, light a cigarette.
Husband comes home. "Did you get those phone messages?"
T: He has no understanding of my need for solitude.
F: Hurt, even angrier A. No, "I'LL GET THEM WHEN I'M DAMN GOOD AND READY!"
Husband's response: "You don't need to yell at me!"
T: He REALLY doesn't understand. He has no empathy. I've had a hard day.
F: Sorry for myself, misunderstood, NOT cherished.
A: Light another cigarette. Become withdrawn. Speak only in grunts. Husband, "Is something bothering you?"
T: Can't he see that I'm upset? What's the matter with him?
F: Lonely, more misunderstood, angry at myself for picking someone who can't read my mind.
A: Say "NOTHING" in loud voice. Snarl. Husband: "Are you sure you're OK?"
T: He's going to keep bugging me about this.
F: Picked on.
A: Say "If the damn messages are so important, ANSWER THEM YOURSELF!!!"

Behavioral Loop—Example 2—Theme: Short-Term Gain/Long-Term Pain/Self-Sabotage

T= Thought; F= Feeling; A= Action

Thurs. 3:00 p.m.

T—I want to have a chocolate bar.
F—Yuck, that will only make me fat.
A—Skip the chocolate bar.

Thurs. 6:30 p.m.

T—Oh, I would just love a piece of cake for dessert.
F—Guilt.
A—I'll start my diet next Monday; it's the beginning of a brand-new week.

Thurs. 9:00 p.m.

T—Sure would like some Pringles.
F—Good, I'm starting fresh on Monday.
A—Eat Pringles.

Fri. Dinner

T—Would I ever love to just pig out on some greasy food!
F—Initially guilty, overcome by "Ohh, go ahead"; feeling out of control.
A—Pig out on greasy food.

This cycle repeats itself all weekend long with every guilty thought of junk food being rationalized by "Oh well, I'm starting on Monday . . . this time it's a for-sure thing—good food only starting Monday."

Sunday Night

T—Oh would I love a bedtime snack.
F—You better get it before midnight.
A—Major gorge.

Monday 3:00 p.m.

T—Boy could I ever go for a Kit-Kat.
F—Total confidence: No way, its Monday and I've started a diet—absolutely no snacks allowed.
A—Skip the Kit-Kat.

Monday 6:30 p.m.

T—Oh would I just love a small bowl of that funky, chunky ice cream the kids are having for dessert.
F—Too bad I can't.
A—Skip the ice cream.

Monday 10:00 p.m. (no one is watching)

T—Funky monkey chocolate . . . "mmmmmmm."
F—Compromise: well, maybe just a small bowl wouldn't hurt.
A—Eat ice cream.

Tuesday 3:00 p.m. (sugar is low time)

T—Boy, could I go for a chocolate bar right about now.
F—Well, I guess I've already ruined my super-strict one-snack rule last night anyway.
A—Have the chocolate bar and promise myself that I'll start this diet all over again next Friday; it's the beginning of a new month.

This cycle repeats itself many times over the year. Usually the willpower is a bit stronger at the beginning of each month, lasting a few days before I go off.

Near the end of the year and around Christmas holidays, I rationalize every thought of "snack junk food" by promising to restart the cycle in the next week, month, or year.

A17: Behavioral Loop Example

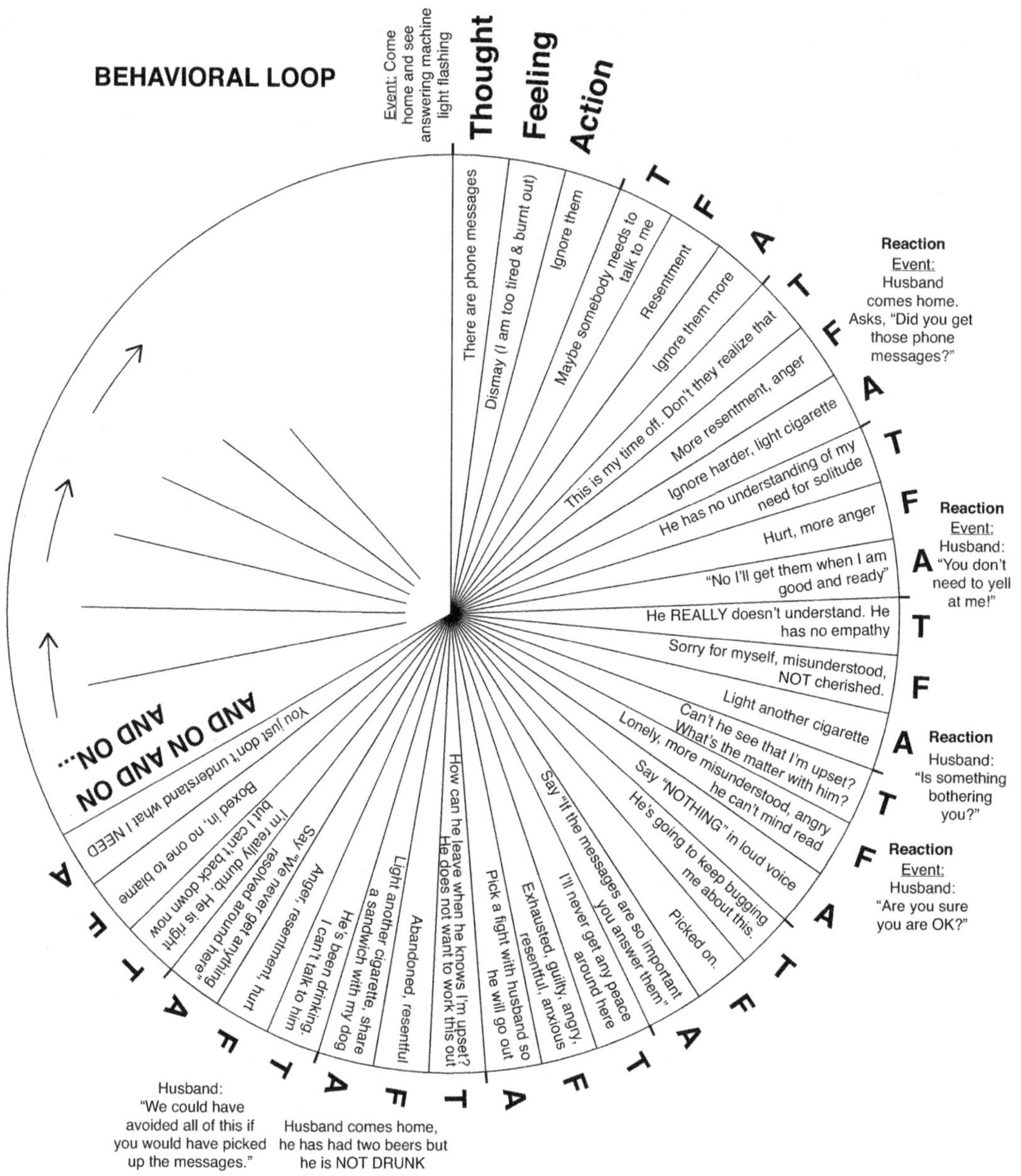

A18: Behavioral Loop Chart

Week# ________

	Monday	Tuesday	Wednesday	Thursday	Friday	Saturday	Sunday
Past  I'm in my loop and / but I don't realize I am in it (till much later)							
Present  I'm in my loop and I know it							
Future 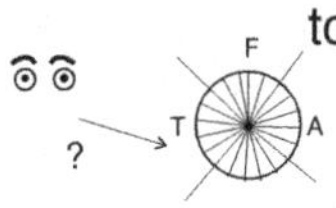 I see the opportunity to go into my loop but I am going to choose to not enter into it!							

Behavioral Loop

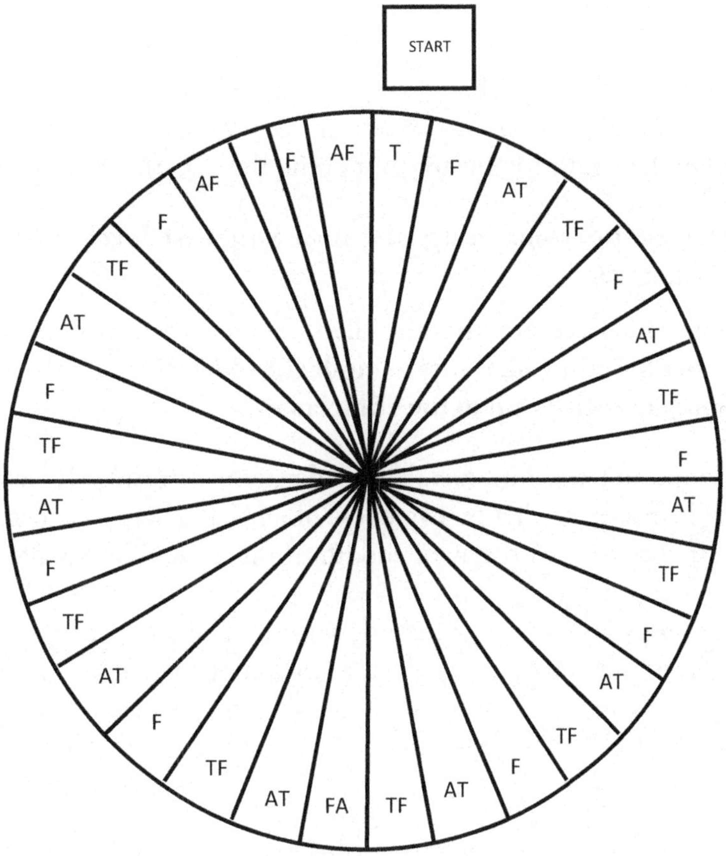

Examples of loops:

- Abandonment.
- Self-defeating cognition (I am bad).
- Cycle of abuse.
- Hopelessness.
- Denial.
- Violence.
- Anger.
- Helplessness.
- Grief.
- Guilt.
- Power.
- Procrastination.
- Hostility.
- Behavioral management.

Thought precedes a feeling:

- You may think that you suddenly have a feeling out of the blue, but if you remember carefully, you will realize that there was a thought that triggered that feeling.
- Loop is a circle—not linear.
- People's behavioral loops intersect with each other and this can affect the whole family.
- Thought, feeling, action.
- Loop has a minimum of 36 pieces—thought-one, feeling-two, action-three, thought-four, etc.
- Chart for at least two weeks how often you are in the past behavior (don't recognize loop), present behavior (aware of loop), or future behavior (not going into loop).

** **Clinician's guide to creating, completing, and reviewing first-level order and second-level order behavioral loops with caregivers.**

*** **Whether a clinician wants to ensure that the client has successfully completed and charted a *first-level order loop* or whether the clinician wants to guide the client through the completion and charting of a *second-level order loop* is entirely up to the clinician.**

- **First-level order loops** and charting first-level order loops is primarily designed and utilized as an effective method to increase the clients' awareness of all that goes in to comprising their own behaviors and to apply straightforward behavior modification techniques to alter the frequency of those behaviors.
- **Second-level order loops** and charting these loops will lead to deeper work at a deeper emotional level for the client. You can sometimes reveal and interrupt the clients' unresolved traumatic impact at a certain level with this additional loop method—which may often end up making your work with PAST, PRESENT, and FUTURE Diagrams (when you get there) smoother and faster for yourself and for the client.

Phase A—completing loops:

- Clients have been asked to identify a self-defeating theme in their life and to complete a behavioral loop on this self-defeating theme.
- Clients have completed a behavioral loop and kept it for charting purposes and/or have handed it in for the clinician's review when they attend Phase B.
- Clients may have charted themselves in relation to their loop for at least two weeks during or since the completion of Phase A. If they haven't completed their loop correctly and/or if they haven't charted their loop, the clinician must attend to helping the client complete and chart their loop.
- Clients who have completed a behavioral loop on their own self-defeating behavior may have gone on to complete a second behavioral loop that describes their thoughts, feelings, and actions as they occur with their child on stressful days. If they have not completed this second loop in relation to their interaction with their child by Phase B first session, then the client should follow up and have the client complete this.

Phase B—reviewing caregiver's loops with caregiver:

- Ask to see client's loop that they have brought in with them that day or pull it out of client's file (review client's loop).
- Check to see if the theme the client identified for their loop reflects what has been described in the loop. **See attached example.
- Check to see that the client has placed thoughts, feelings, actions, and reactions in the right sections of the loop.
- The clinician asks the client if this loop is a full and comprehensive account of their loop, or if the client has since realized since the completion of the group that there may be pieces or chunks of the loop missing. If so, assign the re-doing of the loop to include the missing parts as homework for client.
- If or once the client's loop is accurate, thorough, and complete, ensure the client has charted themselves each week in relation to their loop until they are the FUTURE position of the loop 80% of the time and continue with the client charting for three additional weeks of maintaining the FUTURE position to solidify the change.

Case example:

- In the attached example, the client classified her loop's theme as "Anger Cycle." The loop reveals a cycle that the client enters with her partner that frustrates, hurts, and angers her.
- The clinician needs to personalize the loop for the client and does this by re-naming the loop to be "My Anger Loop."
- The client is strongly encouraged through the clinician's word selection to use language that is designed to enhance the self-responsibility-taking level of their feelings, their behaviors, and their actions.
- **First-level order** themes mean the client has taken an example of an event (e.g. being criticized) and has attached a feeling or a theme to it—titled: "Anger (General Descriptor) Cycle" as the theme.

- Even though we try to make clear to the client in Phase A not to pick a series of externalized events to complete the details of the loop but rather to get at a ROOT (or personal) theme of how the client ends up feeling once the loop has been experienced, many clients will find doing so difficult and will resort to mostly external events to get the details for completing the content of their loop.
- **First-level order** loops could be said to be more externalized events generated, whereas **second-level order** loops could be described as more internalized and personal-trauma-theme generated.
- In this case, however, when the clinician first reads the title of the theme "Anger Cycle" the clinician can immediately notice that this loop has not been personalized to the extent that it needs to be by the client. After reading the entire loop through once, the clinician senses that the "Anger Cycle" theme is a "**first-level order**" theme.
- The clinician senses a **first-level order** theme upon reading the loop (Anger Cycle) . . . and the clinician can sense that there may be a narrower root theme running as a more specific common denominator throughout the body of this loop. That is, a more personalized/individualized feeling theme that appears to be emanating from this client's loop called a **second-level order** theme.
- The **second-level order** theme that could be said to be implicitly revealed in the loop is "lack of self-care-loop," or "I don't deserve to take good care of myself," or "my needs for self care are not important." There may be others that upon reading this client loop you would say are more accurate than the ones I have selected here, for example. The client will accurately identify which one "fits most."
- The clinician hypothesizes possible **second-level order** themes (one or two), but the client is the one that will most accurately select the theme that personally speaks the loudest to them. You can tell the theme is the most accurate one there is when it succeeds at capturing and holding almost all the thoughts, feelings, and actions identified in the client's loop within it. This is how the clinician and client will know that they have got the most accurate, personalized theme for the client.

Specific steps for clinicians:

- To first assess what order level loop the client has completed, the clinician first asks themselves after reading the entire loop over in full once (without correcting anything along the way):

Does the theme the client chose seem to reflect a surface (first-level order) theme or does there appear to be a deeper, ROOT (second-level order) theme beneath the surface as I read the loop over?

- Specifically, when the clinician reads this client loop over, for example, does the clinician feel that *anger* is the predominant feeling that they themselves are left with after reading the client's loop (if they put themselves in the clients shoes), or does there seem to be another deeper ROOT feeling underneath the whole loop description?
- If so, make note of that feeling in the file and simply finish checking the loop for accuracy (or have client correct if completed incorrectly), and then proceed with charting homework

Or proceed to getting into the second-level order work on the loop with the client if you so choose.

Steps for conducting second-level order loop work:

- The clinician will ask the client, "what does this loop leave you feeling like after you have been through it?" If the client says, "it leaves me feeling angry," then you probably have the **second-level order** ROOT theme of the client: "My Anger Loop."

- If the client says (or you can tease out with the client) that "it leaves me feeling as if I am not good enough as I am—for my partner," then "Not Good Enough as I Am" would be the **second-level order** ROOT theme.

Once the client recognizes and personalizes this second-level order theme, ask the client:

- Can you remember other times in your life that you have experienced this theme of "I am not good enough as I am"? Might it have arisen more often during periods of stress?
- Can you then agree with the idea that this is a theme that you carry around within you at times—that is not a result of external conditions, but rather where you might have incorporated that theme into your thinking and feeling over time?
- Would you now like to see what completing a loop on how that theme sometimes gets carried around within you reveals? I believe it will be most helpful and insightful for you. "This process of completing the loop is called a **second-level order** loop. Are you interested in trying it?"

Sometimes, but not always . . . the client's **second-level order ROOT theme will guide you towards their unresolved childhood trauma theme. This will *not* be the case if you leave the client's **first-level order loop** as is.

- Alternatively, you can complete the charting exercise with the client to ensure the client gets into the "future" with their charting (for at least three weeks of charting) and make a case note on what you suspect is the **second-level order** theme underlying this client's loop which you can then use as a hypothetical guide in the completion of the PAST, PRESENT, and FUTURE Diagrams with the client when you get there.
- However, you must never assume as you begin to complete the PAST, PRESENT, and FUTURE Diagrams with the caregiver that the theme from the **second-level order** loop is the traumatic theme that will or should be revealed in completing the PPF diagrams.
- Many clinicians have made this error in the past, as a result of over-enthusiasm, to apply what has been discovered before the timing is right.
- The **second-level order** ROOT theme of the loop however, *is* something to keep in mind as you proceed into the *core* material of Phase B. You can discuss the similarities of the traumatic theme identified in the process of creating the PAST, PRESENT, and FUTURE Diagrams with the **second-level order** theme of their behavioral loop after you complete the PPF diagrams if it is relevant at that time—not before.

There are very specific reasons for this that we can discuss as needed.

Appendix 4.4

Testimonial From a Parent

Separation Anxiety Disorder, Depressive Personality, Attention Deficit Disorder, Learning Disabilities, Post Traumatic Syndrome, Tourette Syndrome, Obsessive-Compulsive Disorder, Child Witnessing and Physically Abused. These are all labels that the medical profession placed on my son.

Difficult, rude, bad, liar, lazy, mouthy, disruptive, slow, A.D.D., trouble maker and different are the labels that the educational profession placed on my son.

Troubled, sad, hurt, sensitive, loving, observant, frustrating, angry and lost are the descriptors that I used to label my son.

Exhausted, overwhelmed, out of my league and terrified pretty much described me... The one in charge!!

This seemed to be my life from 1993 to 1999. That is how long I had been trying to get help for John. It was after yet another psychiatric assessment that we were thankfully referred to this trauma recovery program. It had been recommended by a child psychiatrist that I had sat on a committee with. She did not know a lot about it but had heard that the results were evident and that the type of trauma had no bearing on acceptance into the program.

I should probably fill you in on the events that led us to this program. In 1990, my husband was just recovering from his second nervous breakdown. I had four children; a daughter 5, a son 2 $\frac{1}{2}$ and twin sons 15 months old. On December 23 I drove my children to my parents to exchange Christmas presents, as my plan was to spend Christmas at home. On the way home we were involved in a car accident. I lost control of the van when it hit black ice and we ended up rolling down the highway. When we stopped my daughter informed me that Jimmy (the youngest twin) was not in the van. She told me that "he flew out the window and the wind blew him away." He was pronounced dead at the scene of the accident..John, the child that was referred to this program, was occupying the front seat during the accident. His side was the pivot point for the van rolling and the roof collapsed in towards his head. He was just short enough that the roof just grazed him.

In the time after the accident, John had frequent nightmares. He remembered things that I did not; the radio had been left on, I had not turned the van off, and the worst, that my hand was waving in front of him and he was crying for me but I would not take his hand. I had been hung by my seatbelt and so was unconscious for most of the accident. My husband was not involved in the accident and blamed me for the death of our son.

The marriage eventually ended after my ex. had another nervous breakdown and was diagnosed with manic- depression. John began to act out at this time. His behavior at school was alarming and continued through to this year. Access visits became difficult as their father was hurting the children. Supervised access visits were finally put in place. However John still struggled with schoolwork and had difficulty socializing, as he tended to lash out when angry. He began to revert to what we termed "baby mode".
He spoke in a baby voice and claimed he was three. This carried over into his classrooms and John was known for crawling around the room and talking like a baby when he was unsure or stressed. Resource became the teachers way to time out John. Any time his behavior was unmanageable he was sent down to the resource teacher.

Today we are almost finished the program and our life is relatively peaceful and more manageable. The time commitment for the information piece of this program seemed daunting some days. I would leave the information sessions and wonder if my time had been well spent or wasted. The answer was evident in my child's reaction to the things that I said to him when I got home. After session one, I went home and told John that I met a woman named Valerie that loved kids with behavioral problems because the kids were being honest and letting people know that their world was not O.K. John dragged me into the other room and had me repeat this bit of news to his siblings. He felt very special and not so different that night. After session two I went home and told John that there was nothing he could ever do that would change how I felt about him. I loved him always. He climbed on my lap and cried. He had feared that he was so bad that I would send him away. (During a different program this was raised several times as an alternative to gaining control of things myself). Seeing the impact that these simple things had on my family led me to believe that this was a different program and so far seemed to be working. In the following sessions I began to understand that a lot of the things that John was reacting to were not of his choosing.., adults had made decisions that affected his life. So now it was time for me to take responsibility but not take on the guilt or to blame myself. It was an apparent fact that I would need to look at myself and change how I reacted to life in order to effect a change in the house. The effort was exhausting but so worth the time it took to complete. One of my key issues with John was that he would save his schoolwork to do with me. By the time that I got home from work and finished supper I knew that I was in for three hours of sitting John down and trying to complete his work. This also meant that I would have to ignore the rest of the kids because if I looked away from John he would be off and need to be refocused to continue. Valerie suggested I spend no more than an hour with John each night to complete homework and that the school hold him accountable for any unfinished work.

It seemed like such a small thing to implement but the results were astounding. I actually found time for myself to read at night! The biggest change can be seen with John 's report cards and his marks. For the first time in four years John is progressing well to promotion. Every other year he has been placed into the next grade as his level of competent work was not at grade level. This year, John has won four student of the month awards as well as scoring 100% on several tests. The resource teacher has not seen John at all this year and the school social worker has taken John off of her list of students needing support. All of these positive changes came about because I was willing to look at myself and identify how my actions impacted my children through the behavioral loops.

Creating my own behavioral loop was probably the most illuminating exercise that I completed. Many times I would get caught in my loop and bottom out before stepping back and trying to figure out what was going on. I still end up in my loop but not nearly as often. I can successfully identify my thought pattern and change it before I enter the loop. I can also gauge my parenting skills by the pathways and where we land during conflictual moments. I had struggled with the parent in the lead and the parent and child side by side, as I believed that children's feelings were as important as the adults. I finally understood that the parent in front was not a control freak and the buddy system required the child to make life-altering choices because the parent was incapable. I could allow my children to voice their thoughts on events happening in our lives and still be the one responsible for any decision being made.

I find that every new strategy that is introduced to me is explained, supported with clear manageable steps, and not implemented until I fully understand the reasoning behind the change. The resistance I get from my children when I am introducing new strategies is minimal. They seem to comprehend that this program is different and works. Andrew especially, does not resist being taken to his appointments because he loves the freedom he has to express himself through sand tray play therapy. We relied on John to choose an age he would like to regress to. He chose three and told a story about a three year old. John and I then acted the story out. We brought in our own special props, (a big bucket for John to sit in and pots and pans for him to bang). We improvised with other items available in the playroom. The play was video taped and that night John gathered us and we sat down as a family to watch it. This was a very special treat as I have a rule that there is no TV on school nights!! My youngest son was all aquiver and wanted to know when he could get a chance to act out a play with mom.

The next age that John chose to be was 5. He again told a story through the sand tray and miniatures. John and I then acted out this story and it was videoed as well. John has decided to be eleven next. He will be doing a story in his next session about this age. Since the start of John 's therapy, the baby behavior that we have had to deal with has decreased to the point that we really notice if he does slide into baby mode.

Another significant change introduced in our home, that all three children were invited to do was the anger bag. Each child does one minute on the bag each day. There was lots of resistance when I first introduced this activity but the children now comment on how quick to anger they are when they have not used the bag that day. It has helped the flare-ups that were occurring. I also brought baby bottles back into the house at my youngest son's request. The children were each given a bottle and told that for thirty minutes each night they could be any age they wanted. John was three, Jason was one and Jayne said that she wanted to be fourteen but one week earlier.., before she got grounded. She called us freaks and refused to participate. On the Friday night both the boys filled baby bottles with milk and came looking for me. Amy and I were watching a movie. John climbed on her lap and Jason was on mine. She fed John the bottle. It was great!!! The next night, Jayne filled her own bottle. She used it to spray all of us with the water she had in the bottle. At least she was participating!!!!!

As I enter into the Parent in Training piece I am confident that my parenting skills will not only improve but I will receive on going validation for the great job I have done so far. I believe in this program. After the long lonely battle I had getting help I want to spread the news. My life is so much better after just six information sessions, three parent sessions and five child sessions. Imagine the outcome when we complete this.

P.S. John is going away to camp for three weeks this summer. Last year he could not even go out to dinner with his Godfather because he was so worried about leaving me.

John has provided us with his take on this program.

I hate it. I have a hard time thinking about things. They make me feel all mixed up and sad. After I'm done though I feel so much better. It really does help.

Talking about the accident was the best part for me. It made me feel so awful but I needed to talk about it.

I don't need bottles as much anymore. I can drink from a training cup real good.

The anger bag helped me not freak out as much. I'm more in control. That's a good thing. I'm maturing and need to make good choices.

Appendix 4.5

Our Trauma Treatment

Our Trauma Treatment

I came to the trauma treatment program looking for help for my son, who was then ten years old. He had been diagnosed with Attention Deficit Hyperactivity Disorder, was taking a potent medication, and our step family had just moved from another province. The medication he was on had caused tremendous weight gain, and under the advice of a pediatrician we were lowering the doses, trying to get him off it. The behaviours that were being held in check , I suppose, by the medication, huge angry outbursts that seemed uncontrollable, began to resurface. As we waited for our first session with a therapist, our son experienced a terrible rage, and we ended up admitting him to hospital under the advice of the pediatrician. There he was taken off the medication, and then Ritalin was prescribed.

Our first visits with the therapist began just after our son left the hospital. We were assigned a new psychiatrist, and were seeing him at the same time. I am most thankful that we had that therapist at that time. The psychiatrist, my son's fourth, prescribed two new medications in three months. The second one caused a life-threatening reaction. The therapist was telling me to stop giving my son time-out. I cried with relief. It was the first advice in years that I didn't question, and had no difficulty following. The psychiatrist offered us a place in a children's home for our son. The therapist recommended a new program. It was called a Trauma Treatment program. We stopped seeing the psychiatrist. That gifted therapist helped guide me while we waited for the program to begin.

My son's trauma centred around divorce. He was just about three years old when I left his Dad. The divorce meant being separated from me for long periods of time, hours or overnight, to visit Dad, living separately from his Dad, going back and forth between two very different homes, and changes in the ways I interacted with my son. These circumstances all contributed to his trauma. He showed us something was wrong by his behaviour - spitting at people, hyperactivity, impulsiveness, angry outbursts. As the years passed, the behaviours increased and worsened. By grade two, he started refusing to go to school. During his third to tenth years of life, I took my son to a total of seven mental health professionals , four of whom were child psychiatrists. The diagnosis of ADHD was either suggested or confirmed by each of them.

As our son got older and the acting-out behaviours became worse, the psychiatrist told us to use time-out. I was told I was the custodial parent, I had to do it. I now know how much harm these time-outs did to my son, and that they are part of his trauma. I also know how much damage they did to our relationship. The first psychologist had also recommended time-outs. After I read the book she recommended on giving time-outs, I gave her an article from a well-known parenting magazine on why time-outs are not good. I wish I had kept that faith in my own ability to know what was right for my child.

As we began the trauma treatment program, I was learning to replace my "knowledge" of ADHD with knowledge of trauma. I had no realization at first of what was happening to my thinking, but I slowly began to "get it". I had to let go of all my thoughts related to my son's behaviour, and re-program my thinking. I replaced thoughts like "He's hyper" with thoughts of "he's stressed", "he needs a consequence" with "he needs me", "he needs time-out" with "he needs time-in", "he's driving me crazy" with "I am too stressed right now, I need to calm myself" .

After talking with our therapist about containment, I had an immediate opportunity to practise it. My son was having a difficult evening and began kicking a door, swearing and screaming. My first reaction thought was "he needs me to contain him" and I knew what to do. I calmly approached him to let him know I was there for him, and I said I was afraid he might hurt himself. He became somewhat calmer, briefly, then began to escalate the acting out behaviours. I remember wondering if he was expecting a time-out, although we hadn't imposed it for some time. I waited for the right moment, knowing I was in tune with him, then put my hand on him. My son ended up in my arms, crying. I fought back my own tears as I held him and gently rocked him. I felt I was healing him.

The information on thoughts, feeling and actions, and examining loops of thinking and interacting, really helped me to understand how to change my reactions to my child's behaviours. To fully appreciate that my thoughts led to my feelings and then actions, and that of course the same was true for my child, was truly enlightening. I had not spent much time wondering what we was thinking when he spat on someone, or swore at me, because in my belief that he had ADHD, he was acting impulsively without thinking. I was so focused on his behaviour, the action , that I neglected his thoughts and feelings, I now realize. When I started replacing my own thoughts, my reactions changed, and the loops between him and myself ended.

Another extremely helpful exercise for myself coincided with the awareness of my thoughts leading to my feeling s and actions. I had felt stressed for years, and now that things were starting to change, I became very aware of stress reduction. Learning to take a few minutes every day to calm myself, to empty my yucky bucket, became a necessary "good mother" activity. I caught myself often at first, thinking some stressed thought, feeling tense or angry in accordance with that thought, and starting to yell. I have learned to empty my "yucky bucket" on a daily basis, to avoid letting it fill up and spill over. I did not want my children to ever feel that my love bucket was empty.

The other enlightening exercise was the punching bag. I had asked often for advice on trying to help our son deal with feelings of anger. I did not realize the anger as a core he carried around, like a half-full yucky bucket. The punching bag was used every day, at a particular time, as an anger release management practice. So much safer and more effective than the medication, risperidone. Over time, one of the noticeable side-effects from this prescribed activity, was that my child became much calmer. So much safer and more effective than Ritalin.

During our treatment program, the therapist and I worked out a past, present and future diagram of my son's thoughts , feelings and actions. When we did this, I had such great hope for his future. It was encouraging to see, in his present, that his thought, feelings and actions were getting better. When we were nearing the end of our program, I looked back at this diagram. It was with tremendous joy that I realized that the hope and goals for my son's future thoughts, feelings and actions had become his new present - what a beautiful gift!

Our child is healed. Our step family is healed. We cannot say enough good things about the Trauma Treatment Program. It is brilliant.

Our journey began with a gifted therapist who knew what we needed. We received the program with a wonderful person who gave us more through her wisdom, patience and grace than I would have thought possible. To the person who wrote the Trauma Treatment Program, and to these two therapists, I thank you with all my heart for our healing.

I stopped listening to a favourite song years ago, because it represented everything I wanted our step family to be, and I had failed to reach that goal. I can now listen to our song with renewed hope and joy. We are a family of four persons, and I think one of our strengths is being supportive of each other. The song is called "Helplessly Hoping " by Crosby, Stills, Nash and Young, and the words that reflect our present are:

They are 1 person
They are 2 together
They are 3 alone
They are 4 each other.

Appendix 4.6

ITTM Implementation

Kirk Donald, January 2017
Clinical Director, Pathways for Children and Youth, Kingston, Ontario

Bringing a new program like ITTM into an organization is a significant change. The need for the new program, the rationale for selecting ITTM, and the implementation process all impacted how well ITTM was eventually accepted and integrated into the service spectrum.

The need for a different treatment approach for children and youth who had experienced complex traumatic events became evident when treatment outcome data was analyzed. Prior to ITTM, significant service hours were typically invested over an extended period of time, often several years, without achieving the desired outcomes. The data demonstrating this was shared with staff, and it resonated with their subjective experience. The result was that both the staff and management of the organization were eager to find a more efficient and effective treatment approach for these children.

A Trauma Workgroup was established to review the current trauma literature and to recommend alternative treatment approaches that the agency should consider. The committee was comprised of frontline staff and managers. The final committee report with the rationale for adopting ITTM was circulated to all staff and was also presented at an all-staff meeting. The uniqueness of the ITTM program's structured phases, the active involvement and treatment of the caregivers, and its approach to reconstructing the child's negative self-deductions were important factors in the selection of this model.

Although ITTM was delivered by a relatively small group of staff, all staff received initial training in ITTM. Their familiarity with the program helped ensure appropriate referrals to ITTM, both from new and existing clients. The ITTM Team was mostly comprised of staff who had a strong desire to participate in the program following the initial training. One senior staff was appointed to become the in-house ITTM resource person to other staff, and one manager was appointed to organize and manage the program.

The ITTM Team received additional training and then held regular bi-weekly meetings as the team members took their first clients through all three phases of ITTM treatment. The meetings provided a forum for communal learning and support as each member developed their skills in implementing each phase of the model. Every second meeting included a phone consultation with ITTM author Dr. Valerie Copping where issues were discussed and resolved, and nuances within the three phases were explained.

As team members gained experience with the model, the phone consultations were ended and time between team meetings was extended.

The ITTM senior resource staff person was trained to be an ITTM trainer. This enabled the agency to manage the normal personnel transitions, training and supporting new ITTM Team members as original team members retired or left. This role also helped ensure fidelity to the model. The resource staff person would periodically join other ITTM Team members in a co-therapy capacity, ensuring consistency within each Phase.

Appendix 4.7

Reflections on the Intergenerational Trauma Treatment Model (ITTM)

Erin Rittich-Haber, M.Ed, RP
Reach Out Centre for Kids (ROCK), Burlington, Ontario

Perspective on the Program From the Beginning As a Clinician

Valerie Copping's first overview presentation to all of ROCK clinical staff early in 2001 is a distinct event in my memory.

The ITTM presents a systematic way of assessing and treating behaviors and symptoms in children and youth, with an understanding of how both environmental and relational factors contribute to the presentation of the child and family. As a clinician, the notion of working with trauma felt contained and manageable within the context of the ITTM methodology, given the clear direction built into Trauma Therapy within the model rather than a daunting and potentially open-ended prospect.

Excited to learn more about the model, ITTM training introduced clear methodology of identifying the "negative self-beliefs" from early childhood of the caregiver, in Phase A and B through advanced CBT diagramming techniques. After doing this work with the caregiver, the caregiver and therapist co-develop a working hypothesis of the child's negative self-belief as a function of their understanding of the trauma (and events immediately surrounding the trauma at the time of the event) in preparation for working with the child in the last phase of the ITTM, Phase C.

First, the ITTM clearly externalized traumatic events from the child, looking at not the nature of the trauma itself as the object of treatment, but rather, the *impact* on the child and family and resulting *impact* on the environment of the child/family or caregiver responses to these events. The focus of the ITTM is theoretically rooted in the impact of traumatic events rather than the trauma events per se, and represented a clear departure from specialized models designed to treat types of trauma, such as sexual abuse.

The ITTM shifted in the way the effects of trauma are understood, moving to a view that inherently recognizes that the way in which a person references themselves to the events or series of events in terms of forming a belief system (often negative) about themselves as the most lasting and potentially debilitating effect of sustaining trauma experiences. As such, the model conceptualizes a way of understanding complex trauma or multiple sustained trauma, as in the end, it all comes down to how an individual made sense of and/or made conclusions about themselves in relation to the trauma, forming core beliefs about the self.

With children, not only are we needing to consider their forming beliefs about themselves or resulting trauma impact, but also how those inherently faulty identity conclusions about the self may have inadvertently been reinforced in their environment or primary relationships following trauma. This continuation of negative conclusions about the self may be due to ongoing environmental needs making these behaviors of the child adaptive to survival of the attachment system/relationship, or by the parent unwittingly reinforcing these faulty beliefs through attending to the behaviors and symptoms stemming from trauma impact, rather than understanding and healing the root issue through attuned and contained responses to the child.

As well, a developmental overlay of understanding is contained within the model, as the ITTM elucidates an understanding that the child's ability to make sense of traumatic events is limited by his or her developmental cognitive capacity at the time of traumatic impact. The ITTM thereby provides an understanding of why the impact of trauma is potentially more profound during childhood, given young children (particularly under the age of 12) cannot make sense of traumatic events as a separate occurrence from themselves (given that the capacity for abstract thought is not yet developed).

The child's brain capacity lacks the ability to separate themselves from direct causality with respect to traumatic events, and instead makes sense of the events immediately before, during, and after trauma as somehow a result of actions they took or failed to take during the time of crisis/trauma. At the same time, children are very responsive to trauma treatment, and positive changes in the environment and parent-child relationship are likely to maintain these changes as the child grows and develops. The ITTM presents a model for clearly discovering and identifying the nature of the child's felt self-blame and/or self-assignment of direct responsibility and thereby presents a roadmap for the healing process with both the parent/caregiver and child.

The framework of the ITTM conceptually separates out presenting behaviors and symptoms in the child and postulates that some presenting behaviors and symptoms may relate more to ongoing environmental and relationship issues than from the impact of traumatic event(s). In effect, the ITTM is a brain-based, bio-psycho-social framework of understanding, or lens, that can be used to formulate and re-formulate treatment issues and direction with a child, youth, and their caregiver(s).

Understanding behavior as "language" intuitively felt so right and made so much sense, particularly when considering the limited ability of a child to articulate their internal world. Within the ITTM, children's behaviors are interpreted and understood as expressions of an underlying need or an attempt on the part of the child to test negative self-beliefs, adults in caregiving roles, and the world around them. This shift in thinking is a central component of the ITTM; moving away from working to address symptoms and behaviors, but rather using those same behaviors and symptoms to monitor the effectiveness of treatment and adjust treatment direction in response.

Original Thinking/Response to Involving Caregivers in Their Own Treatment—Then and Now

As a clinician working within a family-based children's mental health treatment center, the idea of working with the primary caregiver to address their own childhood trauma history and, by so doing, increase their "emotional attunement" to the child/youth was not new, but was built on an understanding of the degree of influence the parent and environment have over the overall well-being of the child.

The ITTM offers tools for systematically working with the parent to effect positive change daily, having immediate positive effects on the parent-child relationship and environment. We now know that "serve and return" experiences in infancy and childhood light up neural firing in the brain. The ITTM in effect ensures that parents are more present in relationship with their child, which is both healing and immediately felt and experienced by the child.

Caregivers and ITTM Therapists become agents of change, as they guide parents first through a psycho-educational group experience in Phase A, and then one-on-one therapy with the caregiver in Phase B. Throughout this time, the child experiences an emotionally engaged parent for the first time, a re-engaged parent following trauma, or a greater depth of relationship with them. More and more evidence is mounting related to the key role relationship and full emotional engagement of the caregiver has in the development of the brain around all aspects of cognitive, social, and emotional functioning.

Caregiver assessment at the beginning of Phase B (Trauma Parent) assists the therapist in co-creating with the parent/caregiver, goals of treatment in preparation for working with the child or youth in Phase C. The ITTM provides tools for identifying the primary focus of therapy in this phase. Tools such as the caregiver's rating of their level of *Emotional Attunement* to the child, and *Parenting Pathways* to identify the level of connection that the caregiver can maintain with the child while setting limits, help the caregiver to make ongoing changes in relating to the child, which are documented by means of daily charting homework.

Examination of the caregiver's *Behavioral Loop* assists the parent to identify self-defeating patterns of thoughts/feelings/actions that form behavior patterns as well as provide a mechanism for changing these unwanted patterns through daily charting exercises. As well, the *Parent-Child Behavioral Loop* helps the therapist and parent discuss the level of attunement and self-regulation practiced by the caregiver in difficult moments with the child. Loop charting in conjunction with Parenting Pathways charting forms a basis for implementing and tracking positive change in the parent-child relationship. Reports of positive changes in the behaviors and symptoms of the child are also tracked during this phase as parents/caregivers continue to chart *Parenting Pathways*, *Adult Behavioral Loops*, and *Parent-Child Loops* and rate their level of *Emotional Attunement* with the child while entering individual work with the therapist and caregiver.

The ITTM introduces a mechanism or set of tools which are utilized to deconstruct internal working models (core belief systems about the self), and understand how they were formed because of the brain's inherent drive to reason which are further reinforced by trauma or significant life events. Using advanced CBT diagramming techniques enables the therapist to construct *PAST-PRESENT-FUTURE caregiver diagrams* with the parent/caregiver. These diagrams provide a framework for the parent with the support of the therapist to examine core beliefs or identity conclusions their brain constructed as child, and offers an opening to free themselves from their inherently faulty beliefs, given they were made by putting themselves in a causal relationship with impactful events occurring in childhood. The parent thereby experiences for themselves first the benefits of this resolution in advance of their child, which in turn increases the intrinsic motivation levels of the caregiver and equips caregivers with first-hand proof to feel empowered and competent to break intergenerational cycles of trauma impact with their own child. In subsequent sessions, the same set of diagrams are completed for the child by the caregiver and therapist in preparation for working with the child in the last phase of treatment.

While Phase B and the preparation for Phase C is taking place with the caregiver, the child has already begun to experience positive shifts in the caregiver as the caregiver implements the charting tools introduced in the Trauma Information Sessions (Phase A) which has already shifted the caregiver's understanding, appreciation, and behavior responses with the child. Behaviors are now reframed as their child's mode of communicating what they are unable to verbalize, and become a way for the caregiver to monitor the effects of changes they have implemented at home, which are relayed back to the therapist.

The ITTM is inherently a strengths-based model, as the framework separates and understands traumatic event(s) or circumstances as external to the child, and positions the parent and therapist, and then child or youth, such that they may consider together responses of individual family members to trauma events, and understand that responses of the parent and child were "in the moment" adaptive survival mechanisms or responses.

Advanced diagramming techniques introduced in Phase B with the caregiver are then adapted to develop the treatment for the child where directed sand stories and board work are used to accurately assess and identify the child's first negative self-belief. The board work is geared to the developmental level of understanding of the child, and includes the possibility of incorporating trauma responses of the adult, or the child in the last phase. In this way, the therapist facilitates development of more complete trauma narratives that include and incorporate active responses of the parent/child in the face of traumatic events. Prior to this exercise, parent and child responses were solely understood as events that happened *to* them as passive recipients. Elucidating an individual's responses to trauma is key in terms of developing a greater sense of personal agency and thereby a reactivation of the self, often seemingly lost as a direct result or effect of the trauma. (White, 2005).

The presence of the ITTM as a treatment model assisted ROCK to further evolve clinically in understanding the best course of treatment for children and families. The introduction of the ITTM to ROCK assisted us in determining more clearly with children (especially with children under the age of 6), whether the parent-child attachment relationship was the primary treatment target and best referred to Parent-Child Therapy, or whether working with the parent to prepare for addressing the child or youth's internalized negative beliefs about themselves stemming from the trauma was required to be more central to the work.

In the latter case, one might question the importance of working with the parent or caregiver first. In this situation, it is important to ensure the caregiver/parent is not inadvertently reinforcing—by behavioral responses to the child—the child or youth's internalized negative belief system about themselves in response to exhibited behaviors and symptoms. As such, the ITTM assists in co-development with the caregiver an understanding of the impact of trauma on this relationship and subsequent responses to the child.

The ITTM also provides a lens through which we can understand breaks in a caregiver's ability to provide safety and comfort to the child during moments preceding, during, and following the trauma. Attachment disruptions are themselves more fully understood as traumatic in and of themselves. The trauma itself may have impacted the ability of the child to receive what the caregiver has to offer in the arena of physical and emotional safety and attunement—or the ability of the parent to provide containment to the child in the form of emotional attunement and limits and structure to the child's life, as impacted by parental sense of feeling sorry or guilty that their child had to sustain the trauma and overcompensation for this fact. Naturally, consideration of the nature of the attachment relationship prior to trauma events is an important consideration.

Through the ITTM, *trauma*—a word that initially elicited interpretations of victims—was transformed into a therapist stance of curiosity with parents and children, with a quest of gaining understanding and insight into the *impact* of life events that shape us directionally in development of our sense of self. Turn to examples in nature for evidence of how natural events form beauty and strength . . . trees that grow in a certain direction in response to prevailing winds, rock formations that are sculpted by that same wind, or insults and stress that grow scars and form beautiful shapes in response to trauma.

The ITTM has become a "template" or lens through which I view and understand clinical cases. The idea of "t" trauma as opposed to "T" trauma is now understood as the degree of impact, which stems from many factors but ultimately is a completely individualized experience in response to many predetermined factors, encompassing bio-psycho-social factors, and propels us towards working with the child to ameliorate and relieve the child of negative and limiting self-conclusions that he or she has formulated as a result of external events over which that child had no influence.

The ITTM has assisted us in understanding the child's behaviors and responses to trauma in the context of brain development processes, predetermined biological survival factors, and attachment relationships. Further, any conclusions that child deduced because of trauma are a result of that child's attempt to make sense of what happened, and falsely attributing his or her actions/inactions either directly preceding, during, or immediately following the trauma (in the face of these events) as the cause. The ITTM is a framework built around an understanding of developmental traumatology, an understanding that was not more broadly understood until Bessel Van der Kolk's proposed inclusion of a "Developmental Trauma Disorder" in the *DSM-V*.

Perspective on the Program 16 Years Later as a Clinical Manager

The ITTM has assisted ROCK in better assessing when a referral to Family or Individual Therapy for a child or youth is most appropriate, thereby giving clarity to not only appropriate referrals to the ITTM, but also when it is not appropriate. As well, the ITTM has given us a trauma-informed understanding of all cases who present to the clinic for treatment, and training in the model is key for all staff, especially for those working within Brief Services including the Walk-in Clinic and Brief Therapy programs at ROCK.

Insights and Recommendations

Agency Structures

- Important to have dedicated in-house, ITTM trainers to prevent "model drift."
- Key to have support for the model up the system within an agency.
- Important to have a trauma team or community of practice to review cases, and to provide case consultation within a team that has a thorough understanding of the ITTM model and can address impasses in treatment.
- Ongoing training of new staff (to address the regular turnover of clinical staff within the children's mental health network).
- Clear referral criteria to the program.
- A consultative process to ensure that trauma is not ongoing prior to referral to the Trauma Group.
- Consultation process at the end of the group, as cases wait for pick-up following completion of the group, due to limited resources.

Processes

- Referral guideline for clinicians.
- Completed Referral Checklist.

- Required consultation process with a fully trained ITTM clinician to identify needs with respect to:
  - Safety planning and ongoing trauma,
  - immediate need for psychiatric intervention,
  - referral for psychological assessment,
  - more immediate crisis intervention, and
  - other more supportive counseling for family could be made available; caregiver may need to enroll in their own individual therapy to address unresolved trauma that may be impacting their emotional availability to the child/youth.

Reference

White, M. (2005). Children, trauma & subordinate storyline development. *International Journal of Narrative Therapy and Community Work: Responding to Trauma* Nos. 3&4.

Appendix 4.8

Endorsement for the Intergenerational Trauma Treatment Model (ITTM)

Adrian Jacobs
Clan name: Ganosono of the Turtle Clan, of the Cayuga Nation of the Six Nations Haudenosaunee Confederacy
Keeper of the Circle at Sandy-Saulteaux Spiritual Centre, Beausejour, Manitoba

As community liaison for the Mobile Diabetes Screening Initiative (MDSi), I took the initial 30 hours of clinical training offered by Valerie Copping, PsyD, at her office in Guelph, Ontario in 2010. The idea of treating the caregiver before treating children in crisis made sense to our work dealing with the underlying causes of Type 2 Diabetes (T2D) among Indigenous people in Alberta. Our research was uncovering chronic unrelieved stress as a significant contributor to this chronic disease. Social determinants contributing to the prevalence of T2D among Indigenous people included chronic stressors such as poverty and the life-impacting nature of adverse childhood experiences. We were also discovering the intergenerational nature of trauma affect in the Indian Residential School survivors.

Copping very clearly presented the wisdom of dealing with caregivers to mitigate the intergenerational transmission of trauma affect. Part A of this short-term counseling program deals with the impact of trauma. Part B helps caregivers to attune to the child and not project their trauma response or assumptions onto the child but to help them hear the child's perspective. Part C is where the caregiver with the assistance of the ITTM clinician treats the child and supplies the care not given during the impacting moments of the child's upbringing. The most dramatic results come from the Regressive Re-enactment encounter where a healthy response to the child's trauma experience is supplied to counter the original unhealthy one.

In my work as community liaison with MDSi, my own educational plans, and in my work now as Keeper of the Circle for Sandy-Saulteaux Spiritual Centre (SSSC), the Indigenous ministry training center of The United Church of Canada, I have sought to find ways to incorporate both the clinical training I've received in my own work and to bring this training to other Indigenous leaders. Adaptations of the ITTM to the Indigenous community will be key to addressing in a deep way the underlying causes of many chronic problems. SSSC intends to produce hundreds of problem solvers as we seek the rejuvenation and healing of our people.

Chapter 5

Phase B: The Caregiver Sessions

I have emphasized the importance of evaluating maternal depression, emotional self-expressiveness, and family cohesion and neglect variables, as well as the need to pay close attention to the mediating effects of caregiver mental health issues prior to planning therapeutic programs and strategies for children. Phase B addresses particular, individual, caregiver emotional issues grounded in their own unresolved childhood trauma—as these adult concerns typically are (McCarty & McMahon, 2003; McCormack & Thomson, 2017). It is very important to approach such issues, obviously for the caregiver's sake, but also because caregiver (and family in general) attitudes are the single most important factor negatively impacting or otherwise mediating and moderating the efficacy of children's treatments (Baker-Ericzen et al., 2010, p. 401). In Phase B, caregivers participate in up to eight individualized sessions. The sessions are typically scheduled once weekly. This allows caregivers adequate time and energy for processing, integrating, and applying the material learned and completing homework.

Moving into Phase B

I use the term "caregiver" in both singular and plural forms, but most cases of traumatized children, at least at the outset, involve more than one caregiver. Usually both parents (or foster parents, grandparents, etc.) will refer the child and attend sessions together, often completing Phase A together. Phase B works to optimum effect precisely because it is individualized to suit particular needs. The completion of Phase A leaves the clinician prepared to decide which of the caregivers should continue into the next phases. There are certain criteria to consider in order to arrive at the selection that will most benefit the child:

Which caregiver . . .

- Was most closely related to/involved with the traumatic event, for the best reparative outcome?
- Can commit to attend all sessions as scheduled?
- Spends most time with the child/youth?
- Has the closest relationship with the child—or is closest to the event (as previous)?
- Is the most "appropriate" caregiver in view of the child's age, developmental stage, and gender?

Phase B, Session 1 Assessment Goals

Goals

- To assess and identify where the caregiver is in terms of significant personal trauma treatment issues; barriers to treatment; and areas to be re-addressed prior to proceeding.
- To determine and identify which primary caregiver will continue through Phase B and Phase C.

TABLE 5.1 Potential Barriers to Treatment and Recommendations

Barrier	*Clinician Approach/Treatment Recommendations*
Current drug or alcohol addictions	Refer the family for an alcohol and drug use assessment, and ask the agency concerned to hold a joint session with the clinician and the family to review outcomes and recommendations prior to proceeding with ITTM. If the family does not agree to an assessment, the family can't proceed with the ITTM as there is then no way of ensuring that the ongoing alcohol or drug abuse is not itself a recurrent and ongoing traumatic event.
Current anger concerns in the home (either repressed anger or inappropriate anger outbursts in the home, or concerns about anger—parent's or child's—expressed by the caregiver)	Where family violence is known to have occurred, the Anger Release Program will almost always be implemented with the caregiver first and then the children. After beginning the Controlled Anger Release Program with the caregiver, and after the caregiver has begun to experience the benefits of charting their own anger release program at home, review the steps with the caregiver so that they can implement the anger release program at home with the child. Encourage the caregiver to build or buy, or plan to buy, an anger release bag for the child(ren)—or another method if anger bag is complete and utter impossibility. Set an appointment for the caregiver to bring in the child for an anger release program demonstration prior to this stage being initiated at home. ****See Anger Release Program handout.**
Family violence/power and control issues	Even if partners are not living together, but where abuse (power and control) issues are still occurring, facilitate a referral to a family violence program. Place their file on hold for up to three months; if there is no update or follow-up by that time, close the file. If the (adult) client is in a situation that suggests a subtly controlling relationship, complete the Power and Control Hypothesis Diagrams with the client, both the male and female versions. These diagrams could be completed prior to initiating the core material of Phase B with the PAST/PRESENT/FUTURE Diagrams, or alongside these if the control dynamic becomes evident as you proceed through Phase B. Both diagrams link closely and are important to the successful completion of the Faulty Belief System Diagram. If the client has interrupted the abuse cycle, but has never received any individual support and/or processing regarding the abuse, and they clearly appear low in energy (i.e. little sense of self, meek, depressed, helpless, victim stance), recommend or refer them for short-term adult individual counseling prior to proceeding. The first priority is the completion of family violence counseling. Get an update after approximately nine sessions of such counseling to determine their readiness to proceed. If the client has energy, recommend individual family violence counseling in alternate weeks with ITTM counseling.

(*Continued*)

TABLE 5.1 (Continued)

Barrier	*Clinician Approach/Treatment Recommendations*
Custody access battle; current, or court date set for the future	If at any point during the ITTM implementation, custody or access issues create conflict for the child or family, the ITTM file is placed on hold. Assessment regarding the efficacy of offering alternate counseling services for the family should be explored. The family resumes ITTM counseling when custody and access have been established and agreed upon, and/or the caregivers have successfully negotiated a resolution.
Lack of established access visits or inconsistency of access visits	If the clinician identifies that inconsistent access or lack of access is affecting the child and/or family, the file is placed on hold until the issue is resolved. Children cannot be treated for traumatic events when the access arrangements with their primary caregivers is inconsistent, highly conflicted, erratic, or non-existent. Encourage mediation or legal settlement of an access plan, and establish caregiver commitment to honoring it.
Personal boundary issues (feel they are giving too much or that others are constantly taking advantage of them)	Complete the Membrane Diagram and charting practice with the client for at least three weeks.
Depression/anxiety or suicidal ideation on the part of the caregiver or child (as reported by caregiver) in Phase B, or prior to or during the time when the clinician is seeing the child in treatment.	Refer to the family doctor or emergency department or for psychiatric assessment. The file is sometimes placed on hold, depending on the severity of the situation, until an assessment is complete and available energy is restored to the caregiver or child. Anxiety will likely increase during Phase C treatment with the child. Where the child in Phase C is reported to, or appears to, be suffering from anxiety, a medical/psychiatric assessment is called for if the child seems unable to integrate any of the materials and activities of Phase C. Where the child can manage, and the caregivers can manage, see if the family can cope through to the end of treatment. Re-assess the anxiety level and possible need for assessment at the end of treatment. Encourage the caregiver and child to push past their discomfort during Phase C as much as possible without experiencing continual and severe discomfort (i.e. are they able to carry out their daily duties? Are they eating and sleeping adequately?).
Personal issues that hold back the caregiver from committing their time and energy required for the program	Decide with the client whether to place the ITTM on hold to allow them to pursue or continue individual counseling services elsewhere, or agree to alternate Phase B appointments with individual counseling appointments. Close the file if the client pursues services elsewhere and you do not hear back from them to follow up in 2–3 months. Complete the "Percentage of Available Energy" diagram.
There is a chance that child will not be remaining in the home of the caregiver	The file is held; an assessment is conducted to determine whether other counseling services might be efficacious in the interim.
The caregiver has poor boundaries	Use the Membrane Diagram and chart for at least two weeks with the client prior to proceeding to the rest of Phase B.
Insufficient completion or understanding or application of the Trauma Information Session material.	Review the TIS material if small amounts of information or some of the topics need re-explaining; otherwise suggest that the caregiver attend another round of the TIS. The file is ideally kept open and the client is then directed through Phase B to review the Trauma Session material week by week, thus not having to sit on any Phase B wait list).
The other caregiver's participation in the ITTM seems important to the program's successful completion.	On occasion, you may be seeing one caregiver in Phase B and will recommend that the other caregiver in the home attend a Trauma Information Session Group also. You can put the first caregiver "on hold" until the second one completes the TIS, so that they can proceed together to Phase B.

Materials required for caregiver selection (see Phase B, Task 1)

- Caregiver Assessment Sheet
- Depending on the barriers and/or "gaps" identified: the behavioral loop and/or charting sheet; the Membrane Diagram; the Percentage of Available Energy Diagram; the Power and Control Hypothesis Male/Female Diagram; the Anger Release Program handout.
- Blank Pathways Charting sheets.

As you move through this session with the caregiver, consider the following:

- What is the learning style of the family/caregiver?
- How do they process information?
- What is the appropriate pace for this individual/family?
- What are the specific issues for this client?
- What are the red flags?
- Do the ITTM information sessions need to be repeated?
- If FCS is involved, make sure they are aware of their movement into Phase B. Have a meeting if necessary to set out roles and responsibilities during this phase of treatment.

Ask the caregiver:

- What stood out for you the most from the TIS?
- What has improved at home since the TIS ended or began?
- How do you explain those changes?

Explain that crises will likely occur through the course of treatment, but as a clinician you will not be jumping in to resolve the crisis of the moment. You will be relying on the caregiver's ability to resolve the crisis on their own and/or with their regular supports, personal and professional. Develop a plan with the client detailing what to do if a crisis arises.

It is expected that the child's problematic behaviors may increase at the point of intervention, but our role is to help the family progress through the treatment program to its conclusion, knowing that as the caregiver's hopefulness increases and the program is carried out, the child's behaviors and symptoms will decrease—though not at any predictable rate or degree.

Short of suicidal ideation and/or other very high-risk concerns, we do not stop the treatment program to address the crisis. In other words, treatment progresses despite crisis. Doing so introduces a new approach to successful completion, attainment, and containment of day-to-day, real-life conditions. Often, week-to-week crises determine the sessions' content for the clinician and client, which will often prevent both from achieving sustainable outcomes and lasting change. The ITTM assumes the client will take the necessary next step to address the crisis outside of the ITTM treatment sessions. If the client requires five minutes at the start of the session to identify what their next step is regarding their current crisis, this is provided, but only if it is absolutely required. Otherwise the client is applauded for having come to understand what is going on in their world and what they need to do next, and the ITTM treatment continues through the storm. In this way, clients learn they can progress and achieve change despite the crises and challenges that arise in day to day life, and that these should be expected and can be overcome. School issues are typically addressed after improved relations between caregiver and child have been attained at home. After that, school concerns are addressed and responded to if the school has not already done so.

It could take a clinician as many as five sessions to get the caregiver in the "ready position" for beginning the core material in Phase B. The number of sessions depends on the "barriers to treatment" and the completion, to the program's standards, of the Phase A Trauma Information Sessions. For example, if the homework "review pathways" charting has not been completed or is completed incorrectly, the homework at the end of the session is to chart again for two weeks. Or, if while exploring the barriers to treatment, boundaries or personal energy issues are identified, it is appropriate to send home the Membrane Diagram and its accompanying charting exercise. The clinician should not take the caregiver to the next step until the assessment process is satisfactorily completed. At this point, there may be a necessary re-assignment of homework, depending on the barriers and/or gaps highlighted by the assessment.

Reviewing the Caregiver's Trauma Information Session Responses

Reviewing caregiver responses to the preparatory phase—the Trauma Information Sessions (TIS)—is necessary to discern their degree of impact, hence the extent to which, at this early point, they have already implemented changes. This dual assessment makes the client accountable for their participation in Phase A, while also indicating their readiness to enter Phase B. The clinician asks the caregiver what stood out most for them as they proceeded through the TIS; whether, and what, has improved at home since the TIS began or ended; and how they understand and explain these changes.

This process is meant to be as specific and as tangible as possible. The clinician should have a clear sense of the fundamental details (who, what, where, when, and—sometimes—why).

The clinician then reviews the basic elements of the TIS with the caregiver:

Review of Trauma Information Session Material With Caregiver's

1. pathways,
2. behavioral loops,
3. "ABC's" of anger,
4. 1–10 attunement,
5. support structures,
6. proportion of available energy, and
7. general information on trauma.

This review does not have to proceed in the order of 1–7 as listed here; it should unfold in the manner that makes most sense in terms of what the caregiver appears to have learned. The review's purposes are three-fold: to strengthen any aspect of the TIS that is weak for the caregiver, to reassign homework if there is not enough progress tracked in the charting process, and to assess the caregiver's capacity to commit time and energy to the treatment process. The ideal is to have them connect the new information with positive changes, a small but essential step in encouraging hope and motivation, the cornerstones of caregiver participation.

For the clinician:

- Be sure you see the completed homework from Phase A and note to what degree of inclusion the caregiver can explain it. This will demonstrate their understanding of the purpose and results of the assignment. Also confirm that it shows at least two weeks of up-to-date charting prior to commencing Task 3 (core Phase B material).
- If the caregiver has not completed, or has not understood, the diagrams and related homework, the assignments must be redone before proceeding. If the caregiver clearly has not done any of the homework assigned in Phase A, they are asked to repeat the TIS before moving on to Phase B.
- Review each topic individually by having the caregiver describe/define the topic to you first, prior to having them rate it in terms of impact and implementation.
- Make the process visual by noting the impact and implementation scales on the whiteboard as each topic is discussed and recording the caregiver's answer on the checklist sheet.

Example: Topic—Attunement

Get Information: Tell me what you remember about this topic: what does "attunement" mean?

HANDOUT 5.1 Trauma Impact

Give information/reminders to help them recall

↙ ↘

The Degree of Impact	**The Degree of Implementation**
How did it **affect** you when you first heard about "......."	How are you currently **applying** "......?"
1 2 3 4 5 6 7 8 9 10 ↓	1 2 3 4 5 6 7 8 9 10 →

By reviewing each topic individually, you can determine where the caregiver needs further review and/or review plus additional, or a re-doing of the same, homework. Do not accept general, non-specific responses. The temptation to move on to the next treatment step prior to achieving the required outcome of the current goal will be sure to come back to haunt you as a clinician through the lack of continued successful outcomes by the client.

Phase B Task Outline

Keep in mind the distinct nature and purpose of Phase A and Phase B homework. Phase A homework helps the caregiver understand what drives their behaviors and helps to move them towards making definite positive changes; the homework in Phase B enables the caregiver to maintain this change for the necessary three to four weeks for the brain to solidify the change. Phase B sessions are scheduled every week to increase the benefits of daily homework reinforcement and personal change. Missing weeks is likely going to result in having to go back to the previous session(s) to ensure that the client can reiterate and verbalize their knowledge, and the extent of application and sustainability of the previous week's material. The space between sessions—whether the recommended single week or more—nonetheless ultimately depends on the clinician's judgment regarding the individual client's needs.

Task 1: Caregiver Assessment

There are four steps in Task 1. Ideally each part is completed in the order outlined here. Exceptions can be made at the clinician's discretion; for example, if a client presents at session B1 unable to focus and in tears, with a significant drug problem, etc., the clinician may judge that it is best to begin their assessment with **Part 4: Barriers to Treatment**. If the client does show the required state of preparedness for treatment, the clinician goes on with the review of the Trauma Information Sessions.

Task 2: Determining the Caregiver's Readiness

Here the clinician introduces to the caregiver any number of previously unseen diagrams that might be useful to them, according to the nature of their particular traumatic history that may be a useful tool for them. These additional diagrams build on what the caregiver already understands and help them integrate their understanding and move towards change.

Phase B Diagram Examples

Step 1: Diagrams and Charting

Complete the Following: Membrane Diagram

FIGURE 5.1 Cell Membranes

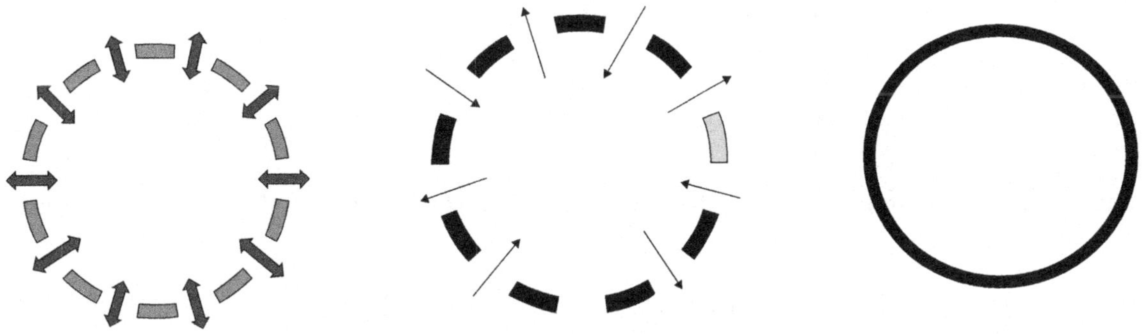

PERMEABLE MEMBRANE No *energy* for the self ➔ Lets everything in and out	SEMI-PERMEABLE MEMBRANE Some *energy* left for the self ➔ Some things in and some things out	NON-PERMEABLE MEMBRANE Lots of *energy* for the self ➔ Nothing in and nothing out

Poor Boundaries

- Non-discriminatory
- Little energy left for self
- Like a sieve
- All in and all out; a wash-out
- No self-care
- Exhausted
- Give, give, give—but never get
- Always the giver; martyr

IDEAL Boundaries

- More discriminating
- More energy left over for self
- Checks in and balances what is given, what is taken in, and what is reserved for self
- More self-care
- Balanced

Overly Self Protective/Focused

- Over discriminating
- All sorts of energy—only for self
- Non-interactive with world
- Hoarding
- Isolated
- Burnt out
- "I don't give anymore"
- Trying to save the self to a fault

Su			
Mo			
Tu			
We			
Th			
Fr			
Sa			

Percentage of Available Energy Diagram—Phase B Readiness

How to Use the Diagram

Mark off sections within the circle identifying: a) what the activity or commitment is and b) what percentage of available time/energy this activity "costs" the caregiver.

Activities include: housework, job, looking after the children, spouse, court, hobbies, school, and so on.

Remember the time commitments for ITTM are: 5% Phase A; 10–15% Phase B; 20% Phase C.

100% Personal Energy Circle

FIGURE 5.2 Power and Control Hypothesis: Women's Version

Intergenerational Trauma Treatment Program

Power and Control Hypothesis Diagram – Woman Abuse – Female Version

Father (Father-figure) Traumatic event
Absent physically and emotionally
Rejecting physically and emotionally
Abandonment – Unavailable e.g. addictions

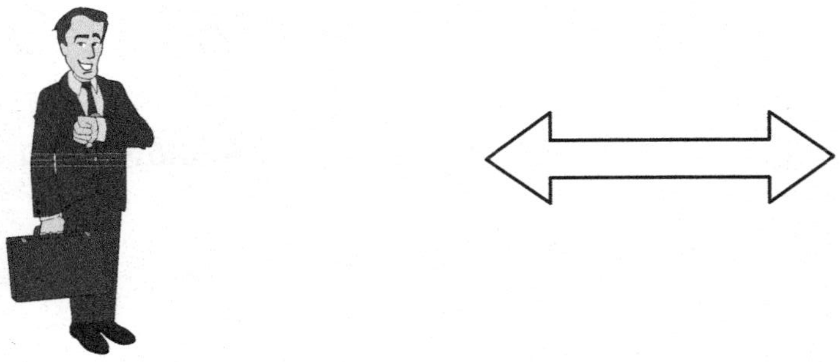

Child – Traumatic Theme & Faulty Belief System

TT: Unworthy → FBS: I am not worthy enough
TT: Incompetent → FBS: I am not good enough
TT: Unimportant → FBS: I don't matter

⇨ **T:** He will arrive/come back/ be there, and then I will be OK and the longing will stop

⇨ **F:** LONGING

⇨ **A:** Behavior: trying to get him to come back/arrive; he will not leave

Partner
Somewhat available
Controlling
Away from her, e.g. addictions

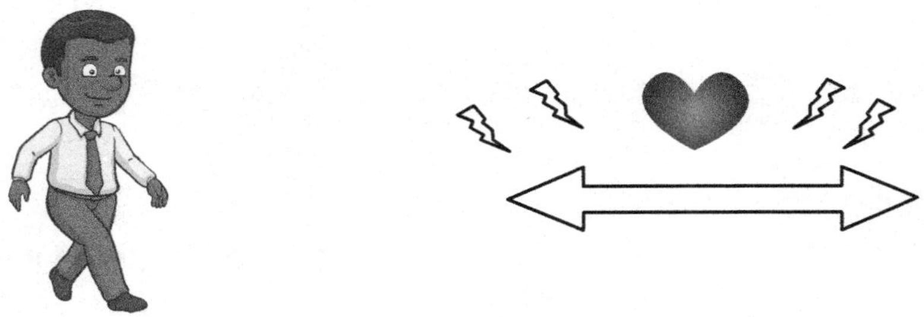

As a Woman
Unresolved TE Impact
Solution to problem never arrived
Unaware of how the FBS and the TE Impact is being played out

If the dream comes true: He arrives fully available in front of her, then she is good enough. Not only has he chosen to be fully there for her, her efforts have paid off → She feels competent after all → I AM GOOD ENOUGH

It is an attempt to resolve the *unresolved Traumatic Theme* and *Traumatic Event Impact* in her life.
She is not fully aware that the *intensity* of the attraction is partially due to the attachment to the trauma-object (identified adult male).

FIGURE 5.3 Power and Control Hypothesis: Men's Version

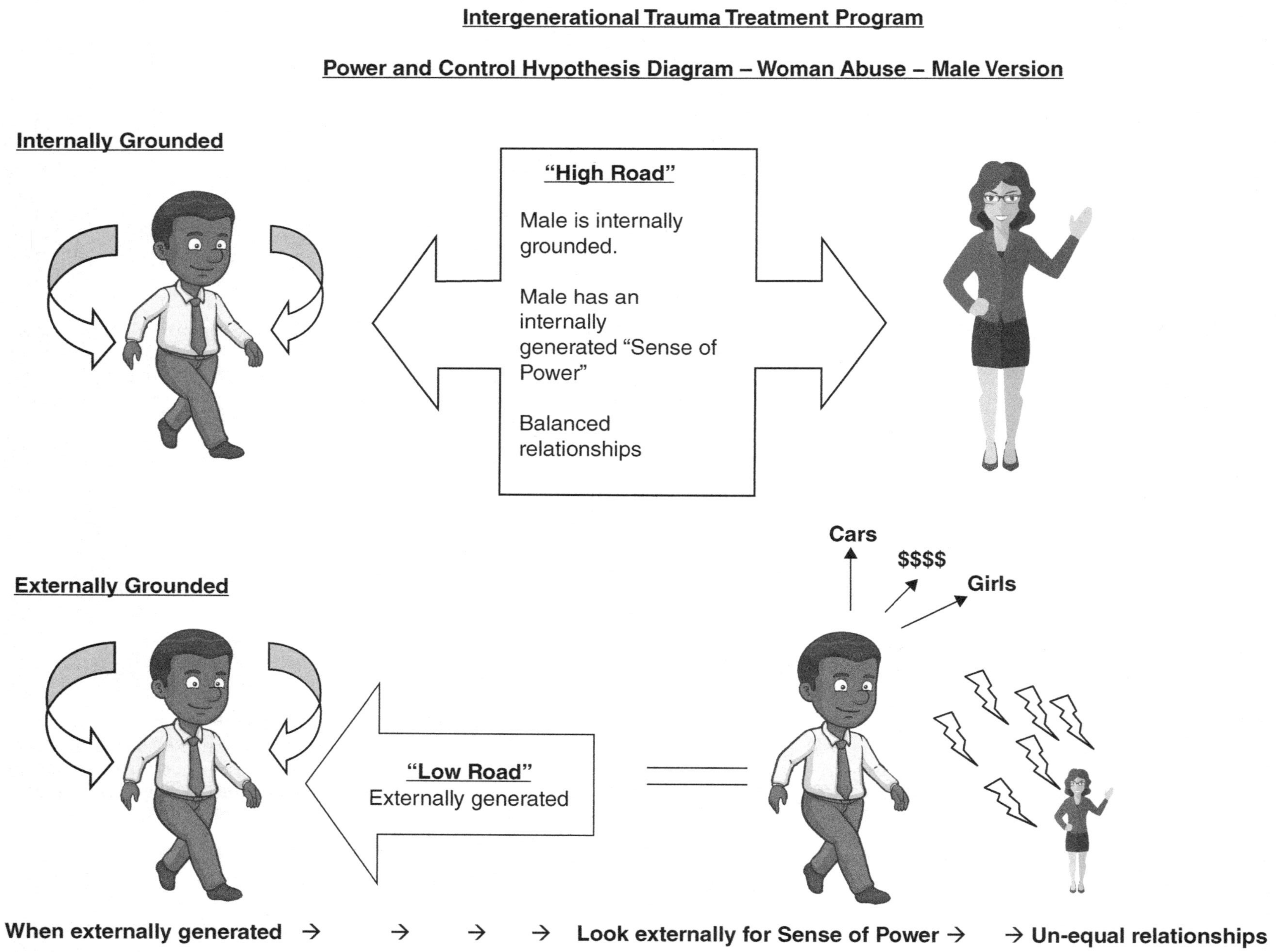

FIGURE 5.4 Thoughts, Feelings, and Actions of Child Witness/Victim of Family Violence—Parent Completion

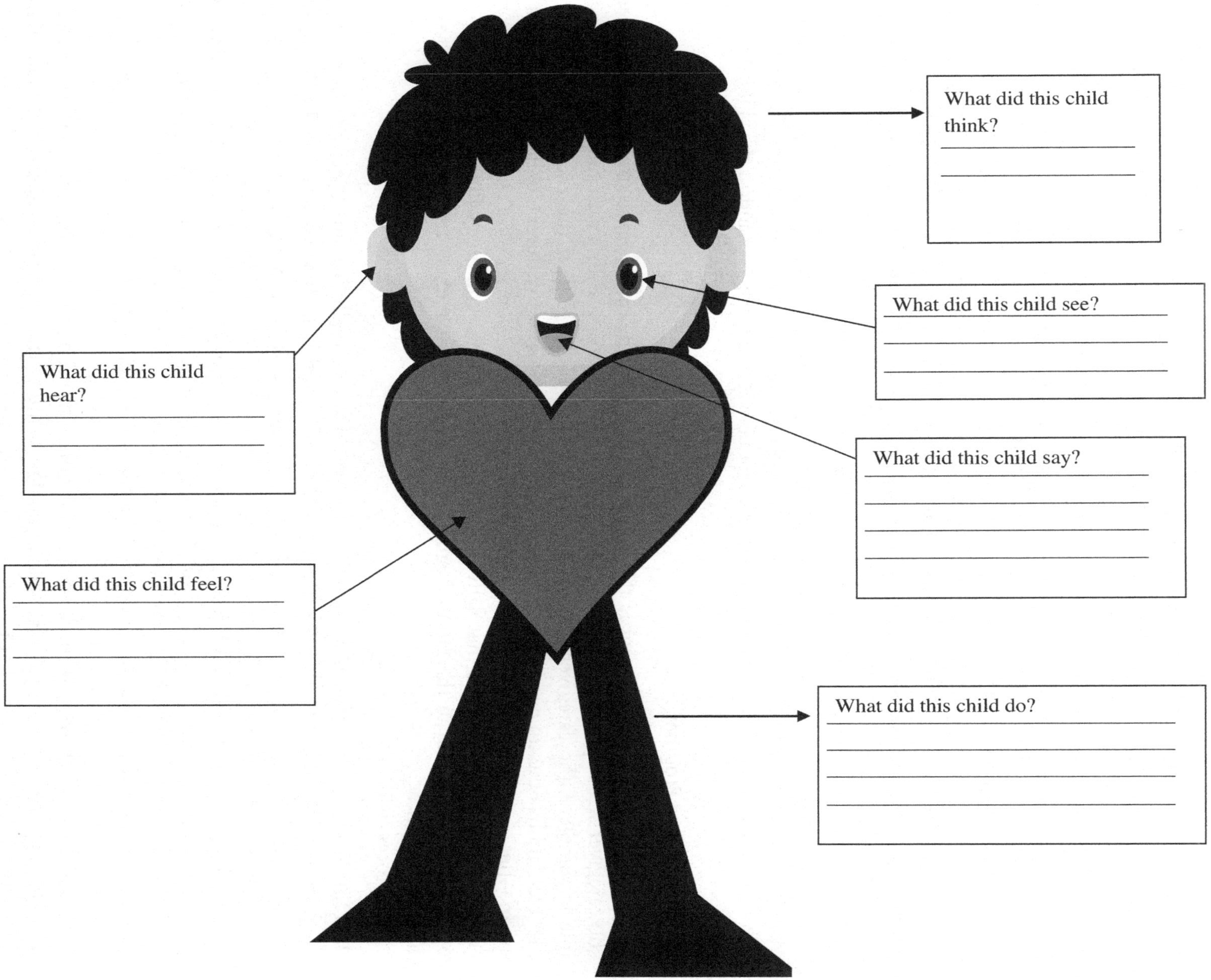

Step 2: Caregiver-Directed "One-on-One" Quality Time With the Child

In this step, the clinician discusses the one-on-one quality time program with the caregiver. For the session immediately preceding the program, the caregiver is asked to bring in the required materials for this work: a calendar, a list of one-to-one activities they have planned to do with their child/teen, their decision about which two periods per week they have set aside to carry out the program, and a demonstration of how they will introduce the program to their child/teen. This program is initiated early in Phase B, with every caregiver who has a child under 14 years; clinicians will adjust the program and activities to meet the needs of 15–18-year-olds. Details about this program and how it is implemented *must be described detail for detail*, as outlined here, with each caregiver, no matter how high-functioning they are, and no matter how familiar you as a clinician become with the program. The clinician takes nothing for granted in the description or in the follow-up of this program's implementation over the next several weeks.

This program paves the way for the "at home" treatment time that will begin towards the end of Phase B and throughout Phase C. It serves to deliberately carve out a space, time, and level of interaction for the caregiver and child: a program that the child sees as being initiated and followed through by the caregiver alone, and not the clinician. Its implementation has been shown to reduce many of the child's unwanted behaviors and symptoms, and to increase their compliance and affection. These improvements then help to weed through and sort out residual trauma-related behaviors and symptoms that we will be seeking to resolve and dissolve in Phase C. Prior to starting this program—prior to the reduction (or not) of symptoms and behaviors in the children—it is difficult to ascertain what exactly needs to be treated in Phase C, because we can't tell if any number of the child's symptoms and behaviors were occurring due to lack of time with the caregiver, or decreased emotional attunement between the caregiver and/or the child/teenager.

The Quality Time Program

The child identified for treatment is the one who will begin the one-on-one time with the caregiver. The caregiver will explain to any other children involved that it is Billy's turn first, and that once his time is complete, the caregiver will follow through with each child. If the caregiver is an at-home caregiver and has the time and the energy to complete the program with each child at home, this is an option—but we recommend that the caregiver's energy be focused on *one child's treatment needs at a time*. The client tells the other child that Sally will complete the process and they will be next. It is important to note that every child in the family begins to experience the benefits of the caregiver's and starting child's treatment.

The process is detailed here:

1. During the quality time program, the caregiver will essentially become a performer and will act as though there is NOTHING in the whole wide world that they would rather be doing at that moment than the activity with the child (which may require, for example, "playing dress-up"). The caregiver will consciously demonstrate and interact with 100% engagement and enjoyment level of the child's play interests. The clinician needs to review this approach and ensure that the caregiver understands its purpose, as well as understanding the program's larger purpose: without this understanding of its benefits, there is unlikely to be compliance or follow-through.
2. The caregiver and clinician working together start a list that reflects the child's character and special interests. From this preliminary list, they highlight at least 10 of the child's most-loved activities, of the kind in which they would be delighted to have the caregiver's dedicated involvement. The list *never* includes activities such as tagging along on adult errands—banking, grocery shopping, bill-paying, or anything else that is done to meet the caregiver's responsibilities. For 5–8-year-olds, the list could include playing with dolls, trucks, or blocks, playing board games or outdoor games, dressing up, going fishing, going to a movie, etc.

3. The caregiver's homework for the week is to refine and complete the list with activities that will create happiness for the child. The clinician reviews that list in the following session.
4. The caregiver is also asked to purchase a calendar that will appeal to the child: that is, a calendar that has large boxes on it. The caregiver is asked to bring that calendar and some sticky stars with them to the following week's session.
5. With the clinician, the caregiver will distinguish a *one-hour, twice-weekly interval* to spend with the child, even if it means taking the child out of school to do so. The caregiver will spend these two hours dedicated solely to the child on the weekend only if there is no other option to carry out the one-on-one time on two regular weekdays. The planned activities are noted on the calendar with the exact time and date in an age-appropriate way that the child can make sense of.
6. Once the calendar, the stars, and the list are ready and the time is identified, the caregiver fills in the calendar with the activities noted on the list to cover a 2.5–3-month period.
7. The clinician reviews with the caregiver how this *very special program and longed-for wish* on the caregiver's part will be introduced to the child.
8. The caregiver holds a special meeting with the child, at a special place and time, such as a favorite restaurant. The caregiver then tells the child that this is something they have wanted to do for a long time but have not had the time to do. The caregiver will say that they just cannot wait any longer and will now make it happen.
9. The caregiver explains what is going to happen twice a week. They will show the list to the child, and tell the child that after three months they will make a new list together—but until then, they will go by this list that represents all the activities they have long been wanting to do with them alone.
10. The caregiver then shows the completed calendar (covering 2.5–3 months) to the child and tells them that it will be placed prominently on the fridge (or another visible location). That way, the child can see and anticipate what is planned and what has occurred, and that there is a next time coming up.
11. The visual aid of the calendar increases the child's understanding that they can count on their caregiver to follow though, and enhances a sense of predictability, order, and control in the child's life. Each time the one-on-one time is completed, the child will be invited to place a star on that calendar space.
12. The caregiver will tell the child that in the event of an unforeseen or unavoidable change the caregiver will *immediately* reschedule their planned activity to another time *that week.*

This program is *never* to be used as a "consequence" or punishment for the child's failure to comply with, or follow through on, a request or responsibility during the week that it occurs. The caregiver during these instances should respond with the "usual" consequences, but this program must be kept as *a distinct and unique contract* between caregiver and child. On rare occasions, as a result of a child's acting out that morning, for example, the caregiver may find it unrealistic to go ahead and act as though they are fully enjoying the child's company during the scheduled hour. I recommend that they announce their need to reschedule their one-on-one time for the next day—without connecting the incident to the postponement. Finally, the caregiver will observe and record the child's behavior after the one-on-one time each day that it occurs. The caregiver will note any behavioral changes, such as the child becoming more compliant, more helpful, more affectionate, more positive overall, and so on. The program's implementation allows for concrete examples of change and the potential for change that will be key to the activities of both caregiver and child in Phase C. There are no reports (over the years) of the program failing when the caregiver implements and sustains it within three weeks of the clinician's introduction of the practices involved. The program begins *only* when the parent feels ready and able. If the clinician senses any potential issues that raise doubts about the caregiver's capacity to adhere strictly to the program, or their likelihood of doing so, individual work with the caregiver is indicated. They must understand the importance of constructing a different reality and lived experience for the child. If there is no positive change in the child, the first area that needs to be reviewed is the caregiver's implementation of the plan detail by detail as originally

FIGURE 5.5 Quality 1/1 Time, Program Activity List

Intergenerational Trauma Treatment Model

1 / 1 Quality Time Chart and Explanation

The purpose of this activity is to prepare "You," the caregiver, for treatment initiatives that will be followed through on at home once your child is being seen in Phase C.

→ Need to spend 1 / 1 time with your child an average of 30 minutes every other day. Pick the days and stick withthem. **Must become a priority. Must follow through.**

→ You and your ITTM Therapist will develop a list of activities.The activities are led by "You" the caregiver, keeping in mind those activities that your child enjoys.

→ The activities are meant to be enjoyable. This is not the time for homework, studying for a test, or any type of negative consequence. Activities must require interaction and do not include watching a movie, playing a video game, or other similar electronic activities.

List of Activities:

____________	____________	____________
____________	____________	____________
____________	____________	____________
____________	____________	____________

FIGURE 5.6 Quality 1/1 Time, Activity Schedule

Intergenerational Trauma Treatment Model

1/1 Quality Time Chart and Explanation

→ Mark the days when the 1/1 time is scheduled to occur. Add a sticker or some sort of marking to indicate that the 1/1 time happened.

Sunday	Monday	Tuesday	Wednesday	Thursday	Friday	Saturday

outlined. The program is caregiver-led, not child-led or determined. The clinician needs to review the program with the caregiver step by step to find the gap in understanding, and/or the reason for the deviation from the required steps; for example, the caregiver may have decided to reduce the scheduled period of one-on-one time from twice a week to once a week. It is important to get at their motivation for this reduction and to explain why the program will not work successfully if such modifications are made.

Step 3: Anger Assessment

The Anger Release Program

In all cases, always, *safety risks must be assessed* before moving on to treatment. The Anger Release Program is a highly contained, self-regulation development program not described in this book. **See the ITTM manual for the program details and instructions for implementation.**

Task 3: Caregiver Core Treatment

This aspect of treatment is the core Phase B material. All prior work readies the client for this core treatment, by first addressing and resolving any barriers that, if left unresolved, are highly likely to resurface and interrupt Phase B's core treatment interventions. Any diagrams designed to address potential barriers at the start of Phase B are charted simultaneously with the continued charting of Phase A diagrams, to ensure the tallying target numbers (whether reduced, increased, or both) are achieved. After two weeks of charting any diagram, the client's energy to do so typically falls off. At this point, a new diagram with charting homework can be assigned for their completion. Charting practices introduced in Phase A are meant to familiarize the client with the tallying process, and to incorporate charting into their daily routine. Clients continue to chart Phase A diagrams in the period between the end of that phase and their first Phase B session if a waiting period between the Phases is required. Even when a waiting period is decided on, clients agree that keeping up with the charting homework helps them feel that treatment is, in fact, also continuing, and that they can benefit from this rather than merely waiting for a restart. When polled, clients indicated that they preferred this active approach while waiting for Phase B over being placed on a wait list for weeks or months before returning to active treatment.

The key steps are outlined here:

1. Begin to complete the caregivers' PAST/PRESENT/FUTURE Diagrams. Define which caregiver or how many caregivers are appropriate and necessary for completion of Phase B diagrams. Most of the time, you will only need to complete the PPF diagrams with one of the caregivers.
2. Decide if one or both caregivers will be present during the PPF completion. Will one of the caregivers benefit from the other's support in the room, or would that caregiver prefer to proceed on their own through the sensitive material? Explain to them that the other caregiver will be invited to re-join further along in Phase B; review that caregiver's progress through the material and the reasons why including them in Phase B is important.
3. Identify the caregiver who was most closely related/involved with the child and/or the traumatic event because their continued involvement constitutes the best opportunity for reparative outcome.
4. Complete the PAST/PRESENT/FUTURE Diagrams with the caregiver who is, first, able to attend appointments each week; and second, spends the most time with the child/youth.

Again, 80% placement and sustainability of the client in relation to each diagram is required before charting on that—and every diagram—is considered complete.

The ITTM recognizes that the client's thoughts, feelings, behaviors, and symptoms, as experienced over many years, are the body's way of alerting the "operating system" that is the brain that something is off/

wrong/not good for the body, mind, and soul: here is the substance of the negative self-belief system. More specifically, the ITTM attests that the first NSBS constructed in early childhood is always false, based on what requisites the brain applies for developing everyone's capacity to reason (by constructing general and self-belief equations) in early childhood. Generating unhelpful thoughts, feelings, and actions is likely the body's best method to alert the individual system to the fact that the NSBS is false. This "falseness" leads to the incongruence within their operating system that prods them to seek help to return it to homeostasis and congruency. Why don't positive self-beliefs also produce bodily symptoms and encourage certain behaviors? Put simply, positive self-beliefs are good food for the mind, body, and soul. Because they are nurturing, they do not "stick" to the brain in the same tenacious manner that negative beliefs do—even if they too are proven to be false. The 4–6-year-old brain has neither developed the capacity to mathematically test the conclusion for falsity or validity, nor has the child gained enough life experience to dispute the concrete premises the brain selects to develop reason and formulate logical equations.

Negative impact such as trauma, complex trauma living conditions, and stress during sensitive periods of brain development are "re-impactments" of the adult's or child's first negative self-deduction formulation. The brain develops self-deductions only after it has secured its capacity to formulate general conclusions (if the sky was blue yesterday, and if the sky is blue today, then that must mean the sky will be blue tomorrow).

Case History: Sarah

To reiterate, the ITTM's Phase B is a step-by-step process that leads the clinician to the accurate assessment, deconstruction, and reconstruction of the client's primary, core-negative, self-belief-system (NSBS). In Sarah's case (introduced in Chapter 3), as well as most others, the primary NSBS has been consciously and/or unconsciously reinforced by the brain's pattern-seeking drive in the face of stressful and traumatic events. Any additional trauma simply reinforces that drive. Distressing symptoms and behaviors can't help but arise and worsen over time because Sarah's primary childhood NSBS has not been assessed, addressed, and resolved. Again, I use this to emphasize that positive outcomes from trauma treatment and other mental health treatments would significantly improve if the primary negative self-beliefs automatically constructed by the brain between the ages of 4 and 6 years old (depending on age of recall) were resolved first. Where children are concerned, the primary negative self-belief of parents will benefit from being deconstructed and reconstructed first, prior to accomplishing the same with children and teens.

The following case example demonstrates (in summary fashion) the ITTM's theory and core treatment process, as applied in Phase B, with a 42-year-old client named Sarah. Sarah is the single mother of two boys (8 and 6). She referred her two children for trauma treatment because they witnessed family violence and the highly contested divorce that transpired between their mother and father. Sarah's parents were also divorced and her mother raised three children alone. Sarah enters Phase B with the apparent core conviction that she can't trust anyone but herself to meet her needs (or her children's). Sarah is depressed about having to refer her children for help in the first place, because it signals to her that she is not good enough at providing her children with what they need. She had promised herself that she would never find herself alone and on her own like her mother did, yet here she is.

Step 1: The PAST TFA Diagram

Extrapolating the Caregiver's PAST Trauma Theme & Negative Self-Belief System

1. After giving it considerable thought, and with discussion guided by the clinician, the adult client identifies three specific instances of when they were most disappointed by, or experienced traumatic impact because of, their primary caregivers/siblings or another significant adult as a young child (4 and older).

2. They then prioritize the three examples from the most to the least impactful *as they perceived them at the time of the experience* (not as they see them in the present).
3. The clinician identifies a potential traumatic theme from this prioritized list.
4. The clinician identifies the potential negative belief system(s) that accompanies this traumatic theme.
5. The client is assigned the charting homework that corresponds with and provides support for the PAST TFA Diagram.

Sarah is given all the time she needs to provide 4–5 examples (between the ages of 4 and 15), which may or may not be examples of trauma as typically defined. A client may take two or more sessions of gently asking the brain to recall and retrieve. If only one example emerges, we go with that one: there is no pressure. There must be an ample, relaxed amount of time for the client to continue to ask the brain to recall the necessary details, lifting layers of memory to get to what is being searched. As I have observed over 25 years of practice, the earliest example will almost always emerge to be an experience at around the age of 5 years. Some of the reasons for this are also discussed in Chapter 2 (The Brain's Drive to Reason; Negative Self-Beliefs). The trained ITTM clinician realizes that, usually within seven sessions, the first disappointment will emerge (one way or another through the Phase B process). Other traumatic or impactful events are then listed (to current age) and included in the final list.

Over the next couple of sessions, alongside the treatment of other targets, Sarah comprises a list of her six most impactful events, again prioritizing from most impactful to least impactful:

1. She was in foster care from the ages of 2–5; when she was about 4, her mother came and went during one of her visits to the foster home without waking her from her nap.
2. She was bullied in elementary school by a competing athlete.
3. She sustained a serious medical emergency at 12 years.
4. She had a near-drowning experience at 6 years and was hospitalized.
5. Her mother told her to leave their home when she was 15, and again at 21.
6. Her living conditions at home were characterized by complex trauma.

How does the ITTM-trained clinician decide which trauma to target in Phase B treatment with the adult caregiver? Sarah referred her children to the ITTM because of traumatic events: family violence and their parents' highly contested divorce. In most cases, the parent's trauma or emotional impact history does not enter the conversation or assessment protocol during the referral process of children or teens. In most cases, if children are referred, clinicians are expected to focus on the event that the adult caregiver/client identifies at intake. The referral could also be initiated by the school or by a child welfare agency, as well as the parent, because of the long-standing and worrying behaviors or symptoms of the child or children. The assessment process may or may not inquire about other historical traumas in the child's life. Usually, the clinician will be required to treat the trauma presented at intake—which may end up including treatment for one or more other issues. How, and under what criteria, clinicians decide what to treat is often left to the discretion of the clinician who receives the file and their area of professional interest or expertise. Sometimes clinicians choose whatever issue is intuited or understood in the literature to be most impactful, for example, placement in foster care at 2 years. Notice that Sarah did not select this event as the most impactful event on her list.

As applied in the ITTM, the first Phase B PAST Diagram with Sarah begins with her own earliest recalled and selected disappointment/impact/trauma which occurred when she was 4 years old—not the clinician's personal assessment of what that might have been. The other events listed may also result in the creation of a PAST Diagram, but clinicians learn how to assess the first diagram and make that decision (about further diagramming) in ITTM training. When asked, Sarah responded with surprise that she ultimately selected her mother's "non-visit" as her most impactful event. She had always believed, given what her own interpretation suggested, and what her friends recalled, that her most traumatic childhood event was the near-death drowning when she was 6 years old and the subsequent hospital stay where she was placed in an induced coma for five days.

For the clinician:

- Draw the PAST Diagram on the whiteboard.
- Record the client's language ("thoughts") on the board in as few words as possible.
- Try to use a single word in the "feelings" category. Provide the client with a "feelings vocabulary" handout to help them select the precise words to describe their feelings.
- Use point form to record "actions." This technique works to contain the client's emotions, a critical safety component for them.

Many clients will be providing the details for the first time, and even if they have told their story before, the telling is emotional and potentially overwhelming. Creating this diagram, and keeping the words on it both precise and accurate, demonstrates to the client that the event and its impact are containable and manageable—more so than when they had been trying to "keep a lid on" their feelings. When a client knows that they can contain their own impact, their hopefulness and confidence about also containing and managing their child's trauma impact is greatly strengthened. The client works on the diagram's categories as much as is possible and the clinician, in discussing with the client and ascertaining any missing thoughts, feelings, and actions, adds these. The client copies the diagram on the board and on the diagram handout they have been given. For homework, they will take the PAST Diagram home and add three more points under each of the T, F, and A columns. The clinician photocopies the original diagram for the client's homework use, and files the original until the next session. The clinician then formulates the potential traumatic theme and their best estimation of the faulty belief system that may have been created during childhood because of traumatic impact.

In summary, as Sarah's story suggests, when complex trauma conditions or acute events occur after the first negative self-deduction has been formulated (at 4–6 years), the impact's intensity in that moment is such that the adult will fall back into the same depth of impact that was the first established in the child's previously unimpacted brain. As such, the individual will often feel the same emotional and cognitive age—and consequently the same sense of powerlessness—of a 4–6-year-old whenever further traumatic events occur, or chronic stressful conditions are present. The brain seems to return at that point to its (literal) lowest common denominator. The individual will blame themselves for feeling in this "childish" way, and will most often interpret this to be a result of their personal inadequacies. Imagine sustaining a traumatic event, or a series of ongoing stressors, that repeatedly reinforce your earliest negative self-belief formulation at the age of 5 years, with no notion that this is what's taking place. The brain's process of developing our capacity to reason and constructing the "I" through self-belief equations occurs automatically and outside of our awareness as children and adults alike.

ITTM theory posits that this automatic process is universal and non-contingent: it occurs in every human, whether there is a history of traumatic events or not. Very few adults who are raising children are aware of the development, impact, or longevity of their own Primary Negative Belief System formations, let alone those of their children. Even if they were, it would remain impossible to prevent the development of our children's first negative self-belief systems.

Now that Sarah's PAST Diagram is complete, the ITTM-certified clinician knows whether to complete additional PAST Diagrams for each trauma that she listed at the start or to decide that the first is sufficient on its own.

What follows is a representation of Sarah's diagram:

FIGURE 5.7 Caregiver's PAST, Thought, Feeling & Action Diagram

PAST

thoughts
(before nap)

- I don't want to take a nap
- Aunty is telling me they are going to wake me up when Mommy comes but I don't believe her
- For some reason, I don't believe her
- I have a very bad cold—that's why Aunty wants me to nap
- If I fall asleep they might not wake me up
- I don't want to miss seeing mommy
- Aunty promises me over and over she will wake me up when Mommy comes
- Very hesitantly, in the end, exhausted from crying, I decide to believe her

thoughts
(after nap)

- Where's Mommy? Mommy came and went?
- I am told Mommy didn't wake me up because I was so sick and needed sleep
- I knew I shouldn't have trusted what Aunty said
- I'm all alone—I can't count on anyone
- I hear someone say when I'm outside, alone and sad, "shouldn't we go to her?" then "no, leave her be" (I remember thinking, "that's not what I need")
- I can't trust anyone to know what I need or that they will give me what I need

feelings
(before nap)

- Scared
- Mad
- Untrusting
- Frustrated
- Worried
- Panicked
- Exhausted
- Powerless—tired and sick with cold

feelings
(after nap)

- Devastated
- In a state of disbelief
- Stunned, shocked
- Lost
- Alone
- Beyond sad
- Silent
- No words

actions
(before nap)

- Fought with all my might
- Refused to settle for nap
- Cried
- Cried …"no, no, no"

actions
(after nap)

- Whimpering, crying softly
- Walked around house alone, in a daze, looking for Mommy
- Went outside farmhouse to the yard alone
- Hoped and waited for someone to come outside to make me feel better

Step 2: Building on the PAST Diagram

For the clinician:

- Ask what stood out (impacted them) most from the last session, and why. How long did the impact last? This question will begin to reveal the client's processing time, and consequently which treatment tasks, goals, and expectations can be most efficiently employed.
- As after each session, check the last session's homework.
- Review the client's feelings about completing the diagramming process on their own on paper. Were these different in nature and intensity than what they experienced when completing the diagram under the clinician's watch and with their assistance?
- Review the just-completed PAST Diagram with the client and place that copy in the client's file, discarding the original one from the previous session.
- Draw a picture of the PRESENT Diagram (at this time representing a very stressful day) on the board (see Figure 5.8).
- Mark the client's trauma theme at the top of the board. The skills for completing the diagrams and for extrapolating the primary and accurate theme with each client occurs in the ITTM training. The theme informs and guides the words you will select from the client's narrative for use in constructing the PRESENT Diagram. Try to use words that are similar or even identical to those chosen for the client's PAST Diagram.

You may notice that the words the client is choosing and the experience they are describing for their PRESENT Diagram (on a very stressful day) strongly resembles their PAST Diagram. This is the goal. *Do not* reveal the similarities to the client yet. The client is likely noticing or intuitively sensing something about the diagrams, but will likely be unable to put their finger on exactly what it is at this point: this experience is a perfect "blind spot" example. When this happens, you know that you're working with the precise material of the past that will enable you to "crack" the root of the client's case. Don't present your observation before the client has worked through what is necessary for them to realize it on their own. The charting accomplishes this. If the client notices that the diagram looks similar, acknowledge their insight and indicate that there will be a closer look at both diagrams, singly and together, in the next session. Do not pull out the PAST Diagram and compare at this point, because it could be very discouraging for the client to see that their "present," which they thought was of their very own design, replicates their past in so many ways. It is best to examine the two diagrams after the third diagram—and present the primary theme after the PRESENT (on a non-stressful day) Diagram—is completed. For the moment, encourage the client to focus on the PRESENT Diagram, as if it is a "stand-alone" depiction of the present-day life of the client.

Conceptualizing the NSBS

At this point in the ITTM program, the clinician attempts to conceptualize the client's primary NSBS but does not yet share this with the client until certain of its "fit." Returning to Sarah's diagrams, her most accurate primary negative self-belief system is her recollection about the foster home visit when she was 4 years old—which she herself has given the number one position on her list of six. At that age, her reasoning of the incident would be something along the lines of:

> if my Auntie promised that she would wake me up from my nap (even though I had a bad cold) when Mommy came for her monthly visit to see me and my sisters and if Auntie—and Mommy—didn't

wake me up when Mommy came, then that must mean I should never again trust people to keep their word about what they say they will do.

Given that Sarah made this first on her list, and considering her surprise when it was pointed out to her, as well as her own diagramming, this is a reasonable and viable formulation of her primary NSBS. Homework should consist of adding three more points to the PRESENT (on a stressful day) diagram in each category of thoughts, feelings, and actions.

Step 3: The Non-Stressful Day Diagram

Once again, the clinician asks the client what stood out most or otherwise most impacted them about the last session, and why this was so, and then reviews the diagram enhancement homework with client. This ensures the "memory work" required on the client's part to understand and internalize changes to their outlook that are in process. Together they will fill in the PRESENT Diagram (on a non-stressful day). The "stressful day" version is posted on the board to assist in the third diagram's construction. The client is asked to imagine what a day is like when they are feeling good about themselves, their lives, their thoughts, their feelings, and their actions. On such a positive day, did their thinking and feeling differ from the PRESENT on a Very Bad Day pattern? They might not have felt that the trauma was all-consuming, for example, but rather that "Bad things happened to me, but I am not feeling dragged down about them today." The homework will consist of adding three points to the PRESENT Diagram(s) for a non-stressful day (see Figure 5.9).

Once the client has completed one PAST Diagram, and both PRESENT Diagrams, but before they have been shown the similarities between the PAST and the "stressful day" PRESENT Diagram, they will be asked to begin to *chart their position* within all three diagrams. If they have not already noticed the similarities of the PAST and the PRESENT (on a stressful day) diagrams, they likely will after one week of charting. The client's charting results after one or two weeks will reveal the clinician's next step. It is imperative, therefore, that the clinician be very clear about how the charting is done and the precise instructions to follow. Misunderstanding on the client's part will require them to begin again, resulting in an unnecessary delay in their treatment. Charting must be completed at specific times (that the clinician will establish) throughout each day, or once at the end of the day. The client also needs to re-read the diagrams, line by line, at least once daily, even when they tire of going over them again and again and feel that they know the details of the diagrams entirely. Re-familiarizing themselves with the diagrams' content in this ritualized manner is critical to shifting their thoughts, feelings, and actions and their movement from the PAST Diagrams into the PRESENT. This is the point at which change really begins.

For the clinician:

- Post the three diagrams on the board and ask the client to study them closely. Are there similarities between the PAST Diagram and the PRESENT Diagram (on a stressful day)? They should be able to see the similarities when the two diagrams are placed side by side.
- Sit and look intently at the diagrams at the client's pace.
- Prompt the client only if they seem "lost for words" or are beginning to display emotion.
- Ask what the client is seeing and feeling and support them in these.
- If the similarities are obvious but the client does not see them, do not push this with the client. The client after one or two weeks of charting will get there.
- Rather than speed up the client's awareness, focus on slowing them down and have them look at these diagrams for as long as it takes them to process the similarities.

- If the client does remark on the "sameness," explain that "sameness" occurs because, when under stress, it is common to revert or regress to previously stressful, most impactful or unresolved trauma states.
- In any case, even if the client does not notice the similarities, the PRESENT (on a very stressful day) Diagram is renamed PAST. Now the client has two PAST Diagrams.
- Ask whether the client ever been aware, even on a minimal level, that they might be reliving past trauma—including their caregiver's—in the present, even though their present lives may look, at least on the surface, different than their past.

It is important to tell clients/caregivers that if our lives in the present clearly replicate or at least resemble our lives in the past, we need to call it for what it is. Doing so permits both clinician and client to get to the roots of the problem. Usually this process provides some relief and allows a measure of self-forgiveness as clients begin to see how their lives have been informed, and continue to be formed, by trauma. At times clients are reluctant to accept this view beyond acknowledging that *it is about the past*, and refuse to "let go" because they are very attached to their own view. Most often these clients will change their position once they realize that they are able to choose and to control which life they are living: either one of their own design that reflects their needs and wants, or a repeat of their own caregiver's life—with very possibly the same intergenerational impact. On occasion the two diagrams reveal obvious differences rather than similarities. The clinician will share this observation with the client, and commend them for the likelihood that they have already resolved the greatest impact of their traumatic experience. As such, it is not imposing in a problematic way on their present day-to-day functioning or interactions with their children. Ultimately, this exercise demonstrates the importance of treating children affected by trauma **as close to the time of the experience as possible**. Doing so will go a long way toward preventing the domination of the present by the negative and unresolved traumatic impact of the past.

This is usually an emotionally and cognitively demanding session for both the caregiver/client and the clinician. The client will initially feel overwhelmed, shocked, or saddened by the likeness of the two diagrams. If this is not their response, however, the clinician needs to encourage dialogue about *what it is* the client sees, and *how it feels* for them to see it, and also about the implications for their daily life and relationships that such similarities exist.

Clinician Steps for Negative Self-Belief System Work

- Present the faulty belief system (FBS) Diagram to the client very gradually, as outlined in the step-by-step process described on the FBS handout.
- Working with the client, revise and "perfect" the diagram where necessary or helpful.
- Send a copy of the FBS Diagram and the corrected FBS home with the client to supplement their charting of the PP/PP/F Diagrams.

The Charting Homework

The charting homework is to be considered completed only once the caregiver is spending no more than 30% of their time and energy, as indicated by the number of "tick marks" in the PAST (both PAST Diagrams) or when the client announces that they are sticking with what they have been thinking, feeling and doing all these years, because it's their life, etc. Always take the client's word and do not try to convince them or "cheer-lead" them into a different position. Rather, explain to the client that we cannot go forward if they are charting more than 30% in their PAST because this signifies that they are not expending much of their available energy for their own PRESENT, and therefore to assist their child to move out of their own PAST into the PRESENT so that their traumatic impact does not dominate their FUTURE. Likewise, we do not want to see a client who is charting themselves to be 80% in the FUTURE: a firm rooting in the PRESENT is the goal, allotting no more than 30% to the PAST or the FUTURE. A client focusing only on charting over three or four sessions will start to move themselves into the desired position on the chart. In doing so, they begin to feel the hopefulness and power uncovered by committed daily charting. The charts that they create for themselves function as a visual "tracking" of personal progress that is very significant in demonstrating to them their own power to overcome the PAST.

We respect the client, no matter where they are in the process: we recognize that each client may need to "overstay" their visit in any one place to build their stamina for the next step towards the FUTURE. If the client agrees to keep charting, they are advised to inform you when they discover that they are not charting any more than 30% in the PAST. This could take four weeks or two months, but at least the client takes a break fully knowing what needs to happen to allow them to proceed. They are not pressured in any way, and are provided with all the "permission" they feel they need to stay in place a while longer. Again, we are looking to assist the client in slowing themselves down and becoming aware and compassionate about their own processing and movement through these issues (and others). They need to understand that, once the percentages are in their ascribed areas of the diagram chart, treatment in Phase B will proceed, and treatment with the child in Phase C is also closer to commencing. Until then, their file can be held; alternatively, you can explain that it is understood that no contact once three months has passed will signal (to both of you) that the file should be closed.

Fourth session homework:

- Charting exercise of the two PAST Diagrams and of the one PRESENT Diagram "on a Good Day." Charting is one line per example each day (on average there should be at least 15–20 ticks in a week).
- Review with the client what stood out from the last session.
- Review homework and the experience/results of charting. What has the client noticed about their diagrams? What have they noticed about the charting? How often are they charting? Ensure that clients are charting accurately. Adjust or reassign goals for charting total numbers in PAST/PRESENT charting blocks at the bottom of the diagrams. Reassign charting homework goal numbers. Discuss charting for about 15 minutes.

Step 4: Creating the PRESENT Diagram "On a Very, Very Bad Day" and the PRESENT Diagram "on a Very, Very Good Day"

What follows is a systematic explanation of how the critical TFA work of Phase B is carried out. It is not intended to be used on its own without ITTM training, but simply to introduce the process by outlining its key steps. Further details can be found in the **ITTM Manual**.

The importance of charting to the ITTM's efficacy cannot be overstated. Charting works to shift the client from the PAST to a more PRESENT focus and an acceptance of the FUTURE's potential. The tallies are totaled each week and new target numbers are then assigned for each **Thoughts, Feelings, and Actions** section of each diagram.

1. Construct a PRESENT-Stressed TFA Diagram.
2. Construct a PRESENT-Not Stressed TFA Diagram.
3. Confirm or adjust the charted FBS tallies.
4. Assign PRESENT-Stressed and PRESENT-Not-Stressed TFA homework.

FIGURE 5.8 Caregiver's PRESENT on a Very Bad Day "Thought, Feeling, and Action" Diagram

PRESENT (On a very stressful day)

thoughts

- I'm always going to be alone
- No one really wants to know me, they only want to be with me because I look like who they imagined themselves to be with
- Count on NOTHING
- No matter how resourceful I am I always end up alone

feelings

- Anxious
- Emotionally tired of feeling so alone—it's isolating
- Feeling like I'm very different from most people
- Sorry for myself
- Sad
- Scared
- Alone

actions

- Isolate self
- Don't ask for help
- Don't share feelings with friends
- Get busy relying on myself
- Keep everything inside
- Live a private reality

thoughts

- I've always loved and cared about others more deeply than they have cared about me
- That's just the way it is
- I can't risk asking people for help for anything about my needs because they may say "no" and that would hurt too much, it's happened before
- Maybe in my next life it will be different

feelings

- Resigned to the "unhappy" feeling
- Helpless
- Tired
- Lonely
- Uncared about
- Defeated

actions

- Create my own joy through meeting the needs of others
- Cry
- Wait and keep going
- Smoke
- Wait for the pain phase to pass
- Force myself to keep eating
- Hope for a miracle

FIGURE 5.9 Caregiver's PRESENT on a Very Good Day "Thought, Feeling, and Action" Diagram

PRESENT

(On a very good (non-stressful) day

thoughts

- I am a good and sweet person
- The world around me doesn't have to define me—only if I let it
- Maybe one day I will meet someone who really cares about me for me, not for them
- I am the best person to create and give myself what I need—the perfect ingredients

thoughts

- I have life-long friends who love me
- People care about me even if it is in ways that could be better for me
- You don't always get what you want but hopefully you get the minimum of what you need
- I have accomplished a lot—all by myself
- I've come a long way

feelings

- Optimistic
- Confident
- Love
- Peaceful
- Hopeful

feelings

- Accomplished
- Nice
- Kind
- Fair
- Mature

actions

- Make sure people are good people with values and morals before I trust them
- Keep being kind
- Keep trying to help people where I can
- Do fun things with friends
- Exercise

actions

- Buy some gifts for friends
- Go out for dinner
- Start running again
- Plan a trip
- Stop smoking
- Help others
- Maintain hope because you never know what's around the comer

Step 4 builds on the homework charting outcomes from session to session. To reiterate, this part is considered complete *only* when the caregiver is spending no more than 30% of their time and energy in the PAST (both PAST Diagrams) or FUTURE. The goal is to see a client charting themselves as 80% in the PRESENT.

Comparing and contrasting PAST and PRESENT Diagrams:

- If clinician and client agree that they are more similar than different, re-title the PRESENT-Stressed Diagram as the PAST. Because it now strongly resembles the PAST, it needs to be recognized as the PAST.
- The PRESENT-Stressed TFA Diagram becomes a second PAST TFA Diagram.

Step 5: Creating the FUTURE (Short Term) TFA Diagram

Perhaps not surprisingly, the FUTURE Diagram can be the most challenging and frustrating diagram for clients to complete because they may not be used to imagining themselves in a different—happier—place then they are in the PRESENT. Many can't or haven't dared to imagine anything other than the negative impact of the PAST, even while unaware of how this has been informing their thoughts, feelings, and actions of the PAST and PRESENT alike. Consequently, they have great difficulty imagining, much less believing, in a FUTURE unclouded by trauma impact.

1. Construct the FUTURE Diagram with the client. Decide on two-year goals regarding the thoughts/feelings/actions: the objective is for the client to consider when the traumatic TFA could be completely resolved, at least in their own view. Ask the client to imagine what they might be thinking if the trauma theme were inverted to the positive; for example, if the trauma theme has moved from "I am totally responsible for what my parents did to me" to "I am not responsible for what my parents chose to do to me."
2. Complete the FUTURE Diagram from the perspective of the resolved trauma theme. The FUTURE Diagram reflects the client's goals for themselves and their families (not, at this point, for their referred individual child or children).
3. The details under each Thoughts, Feelings, and Actions classification in the FUTURE Diagram need to be precise and concrete. Especially in the Action section, the client should record the five W's covered for each action listed. Thoughts also need to be definite and measurable: "I am happy" is too vague and general to be useful, so the client should think in terms of "what exactly will I be doing/experiencing that would lead to happy thoughts?"
4. Now ask the client to begin charting all four diagrams, with the goal to be situated primarily in the PRESENT position.
5. By this point, the client should be positioning themselves most of the time in the PRESENT, some of the time in the FUTURE, and the smallest percentage of the time in the PAST. Their charts should look very different than their earlier PAST and PRESENT charts. You will also notice that the client's "marks" in the FUTURE Diagram are beginning to increase: keep the client charting until they increase significantly.
6. When the client is increasingly "checking" in the FUTURE column, it is safe to bring to their attention that much of the FUTURE as originally described is now occurring in the PRESENT. It is time to change the heading at the top of the FUTURE Diagram to PRESENT, making this

the second PRESENT Diagram. The client's future has now become an active component of their PRESENT.

7. We now have two PAST Diagrams, and two PRESENT Diagrams. It's time to design a 2–5-year long-range FUTURE Diagram.
8. The client needs to continue charting all five diagrams for another 3–4 weeks—if necessary, even during the initial sessions of Phase C with their child. In any event, you can and will always be checking in with the caregiver about what is going to occur in the next session with the child, so you can review the client's homework assignments as needed even as you begin to see the child. If the client has not charted the five diagrams long enough (at least three more weeks), they will backslide in their placement on the diagrams, which simply capture visibly what is happening in their life. Clients should continue charting until they are very firmly rooted in the PRESENT.
9. Formulate the Primary Negative Belief System with the caregiver.
10. Introduce the "Under stress, I regress" idea.
11. Explain how the brain establishes its capacity to reason and make sense of the world and the self to the point where the client can repeat and explain the process back to you.
12. Apply the brain's Requisite Rules of Reason to the client's formulation.
13. Demonstrate and illustrate the Adult's Corrected Self-Belief System.
14. Create the (short term) FUTURE TFA Diagram.
15. Assign FUTURE TFA Diagram charting homework.

Charting Homework Trajectory

After 3–4 weeks of continuous charting the client should be able to:

- Gain insight into what is happening for them as the diagram reveals this.
- Take steps in their own life to confront issues of the PAST within themselves or with other members of their family or support structure.
- Move from a PAST to a PRESENT position in their charting.
- Make use of your insights about what might be undermining their strength in shifting or addressing these issues.

If most of these objectives are not yet achieved, you will need to consider a re-referral for individual counseling or victims of violence counseling with an outside agency, or you might want to encourage a break from counseling until they feel ready to proceed in Phase B treatment. This might be as simple as noticing (on their own) a shift in their commitment to charting or a more complex realization that they must address their own traumatic impact in order to understand and contain the details and impact of their child's trauma. Agree to a length of time for the break, pause, contemplation, or review period. Explain that it is very important for them to take the time they need right now prior to proceeding with treatment with their child.

FIGURE 5.10 Caregiver's FUTURE, Thought, Feeling and Action Diagram

FUTURE

thoughts

- I am not alone
- I am not lonely
- I've met someone who really knows and sees and loves me for who I am
- I ask people for help now
- Even though I understand the limitations of my mother, my mother admits that it was wrong to completely abandon me three times and put her needs over mine
- My mother feels pride in me and I am happy for her for that

thoughts

- I am O.K. on my own
- History of past—leads to present if left unresolved
- I will practice being able to trust
- I understand now why I haven't been able to trust anyone
- I am not alone—I can love myself—and I will not feel lonely
- I am the only one who can truly and always give myself what I need or want
- That is a really good and important thing to know and be able to accomplish

feelings

- Happy
- More confident
- Higher self-esteem
- Proud of stopping vicious cycle with myself that led nowhere but down
- Less anger
- Less sadness

feelings

- Proud
- Nothing is missing
- Full
- More trusting

actions

- Practicing asking others for help
- Letting other people in
- Practice not isolating myself when I feel down
- Making goals and achieving them

actions

- Get help for myself when needed
- Try not to be afraid they will say no
- More time and energy for fun with self and friends
- Active and healthy
- Cooking and entertaining friends
- Loving my home and my life

Step 6: Creating the FUTURE (Long Term) TFA Diagram

1. The short-term FUTURE Diagram becomes the second PRESENT Diagram as soon as the client has charted a total of 20 tally marks or more in the FUTURE column. Because the FUTURE has not arrived yet, the short-term FUTURE Diagram becomes the second PRESENT Diagram.
2. With the client, put together the long-term (2–5 year) FUTURE Diagram.
3. Have the client continue the tallying homework.

Conclusion

This chapter has summarized in detail how the ITTM is implemented with adult clients/caregivers to focus them on their own unresolved—and often unacknowledged or even unrecognized—childhood trauma impact. The client is brought into direct partnership with the clinician, whose role in Phase B is principally to direct, assist, and support the client in diagramming their own lives—PAST, PRESENT, and FUTURE—and accompanying these life-pictures with careful tallying, or charting, of their "position" in each of the three categories at various points in as they go about their daily routines. The outcome is intended to be a new emotional clarity in themselves, and consequently a reinforced commitment to continue to Phase C, which brings the child—the *original* client—into the picture. The next chapter discusses this process as we take ITTM treatment to its goal: to bring caregiver(s) and their child/children to a positive condition of trauma resolution.

References

Baker-Ericzen, M. J., Jenkins, M. M., & Brookman-Frazee, L. (2010). Clinician and parent perspectives on parent and family contextual factors that impact community mental health services for children with behavior problems. *Child & Youth Care Forum* 39:6, pp. 397–419.

McCarty, C. A. & McMahon, R. J. (2003). Mediators of the relation between maternal depressive symptoms and child internalizing and disruptive behavior disorders. *Journal of Family Psychology* 17:4, pp. 545–556.

McCormack, L. & Thomson, S. (2017). Complex trauma in childhood, a psychiatric diagnosis in adulthood: Making meaning of a double-edged phenomenon. *Psychological Trauma: Theory, Research, Practice, and Policy* 9:2, pp. 156–165.

Chapter 6

Phase C: Bringing the Child Back In

Although Phase C, the ITTM's culminating stage, shifts the focus from the caregiver, who progressed through individualized sessions alone in Phase B, to the child who is the true center of the treatment process, the caregiver remains very much involved. Consequently, the initial step is a brief informative session that orients the caregiver to their active participation in the child's treatment. This requires the caregiver's input in three guided exercises—including individual homework—that focuses them explicitly on the child's trauma *as they see it.*

Step 1: Caregiver Orientation to Phase C

To begin, the caregiver will be asked to:

Phase C—Caregiver Check-In

- Recall the child's most impactful memory, noting their sense of disappointment/disillusionment; this will be drawn out, literally, with as much detail as possible.
- Complete the child's PAST, PRESENT, and FUTURE TFA Diagram.
- Examine the child's PAST, PRESENT, and FUTURE Diagram with the clinician's interpretive/comparative assistance.

As the caregiver recounts their child's trauma, and works on their child's diagrams and charting, the clinician pays close attention to the caregiver's perception of the child, noting whether this perception is shaped—perhaps distorted—by a number of factors: their personal trauma history; the caregiver's empathy level; and the caregiver's ability to provide containment for the child's traumatic experience(s) and symptoms. Distortions, failure of empathy, disinterest in learning containment practices, and so on, *must be* addressed before moving on to the child's treatment in Phase C.

The caregiver will then hypothetically identify their child's three most impactful traumatic events. By definition, this will be the caregiver's "best guess," where experience has shown that this best guess is usually accurate. At this point, it is crucial to distinguish between the **most traumatic event** and the **most traumatic impact** because of that event. While the caregiver relates the most impactful events, taking time to give *all the most specific details* recalled concerning the child's most traumatic event, their perspective is recorded detail for detail. For example, the exchange between caregiver/client and clinician might follow these lines:

Caregiver's recollection:

The father (who was dying of cancer) was visited by his 8-year-old daughter during his final days in the hospital. The daughter noticed that her father was dressed in a light-green gown, and looked very different than the last time she had seen him, before his admission, a month previous. "I remember Jane saying that Daddy didn't look like Daddy any more. Daddy was eating green jelly and drinking ginger ale through a straw. There was a bird chirping outside and it was raining. Jane could see that Dad had three tubes hooked up to his hand and arm."

Clinician's response:

Which hand? What colors were the tubes? What time of day was it? What did Dad say when he saw Jane? Could Dad speak? [and all details that the caregiver can remember from her observations of the situation]. Then what happened? . . . and then what happened? What did Jane say? And how was Jane in the first few minutes/hours after she left that hospital room? Did she leave with you or did someone else take her home? What happened then? Did you have a chance to talk to her shortly after that visit to the hospital?

It is essential to collect as much information as possible from the caregiver at this point: the greatest negative impact is often experienced in the pre- and post-minutes/hours of the traumatic event. To permit the clinician to compare details and recognize extra, different, or missing details and emphases, the caregiver's story is needed before the child recounts their own version. The points of difference or intersection are as important, or more so, as the actual details recalled. Either account could have, and usually does, overlook or simply skip vital details, intentionally or not. The greatest impact on the child is frequently uncovered in the gaps and silences, present in both stories, making close comparison a critical part of the clinician's role.

For homework, the caregiver is assigned completion of the child's PAST/PRESENT/FUTURE Diagrams. When the caregiver returns with the assignment, the clinician checks for completeness and appropriate compassion/empathy/understanding in the caregiver's perspective in their mapping of the child's experience(s). Some direction on the clinician's part—questions, suggestions, clarifications—will allow the caregiver to fill in details, remove details, normalize. At this point, the clinician will position the child's own diagrams beneath those of the caregiver and draw their attention to the similarities (to reinforce and further grow empathy), or will highlight the differences if emphasizing the fact that, for example, the caregiver's S/A (sexual abuse) and the child's S/A are significantly different, strongly suggesting that the child is not necessarily having the same, perhaps anywhere near the same, experiences that the caregiver is imagining or worrying about or even projecting onto them.

If the diagrammatic evidence shows this to be the situation, the next step is to give the caregiver a few more weeks to chart while paying attention *on their own* to the differences or similarities. By having them chart how often they can see the similarities or differences in a typical day, each day of each week, they will substantially increase their awareness and understanding of their own and their child's experience of trauma, and especially its impact. When the caregiver's diagrams indicate an already high level of attunement/awareness, there is no need for further charting on their part. The clinician should applaud the caregiver's ability to see and experience the child's impact and event as unique and individual (especially if the event detailed from both perspectives was similar). The caregiver will move on to the first sessions with the child in Phase C once the clinician has explained what these will consist of, and what their own important role will be.

Step 2: Caregiver and Child Joint Sessions

Once the clinician is satisfied that the caregiver has increased their awareness and empathy as much as is attainable in the first step on their own, the caregiver will move on to shared sessions with the child, usually involving up to seven assessment and treatment sessions. Having acknowledged and resolved their own issues surrounding trauma, the caregiver is now adequately prepared to act as "co-therapist" in the child's treatment.

Therapy with the child is intended to resolve impact related to:

Phase C—Trauma Treatment Goals

- The attachment relationship to the caregiver.
- The injurious effects of the child's primary NSBS.
- The loss of significant relationship(s) in the child's life.
- Shame or guilt for their history of problematic behaviors.
- The traumatic event itself.

Phase C consists of four assessment sessions and four treatment sessions with child and caregiver(s) both present. In the assessment sessions, the clinician utilizes sand tray assessment techniques to gather information about the child *from the child directly* (Thompson, 1990). A treatment diagram for the child is then formulated from the themes and details originating in the child's Sand Tray Stories. The diagram is intended to capture the child's sense-making of the event and its impact from their own "felt" perspective. The result illustrates the thoughts, feelings, and actions of the child as they have attempted to cope with the traumatic event(s). The diagram is placed within the context of past, present, and future and then serves as a tracking tool to monitor and guide changes in the child's day-to-day thoughts, feelings, and reactions in response to the impact the traumatic event(s) have created.

In each of the assessment sessions, the clinician tries to determine the child's predominant presenting affective and cognitive issues. If their presenting issue differs from the traumatic event known to have occurred, the predominant issue now exposed must be addressed prior to exploring the traumatic event for which the child was originally referred. The clinician identifies the coping strategies used by the child for organizing the predominant issue. Their physical and emotional safety—as they perceive it—is also assessed now. The clinician further identifies any symptoms the child has or may be currently exhibiting and determines whether a psychiatric consultation or assessment is required.

The clinician then explores the current attachment relationship of the child to the caregiver using the sand tray therapy technique, and outlines interventions to strengthen or re-create the attachment relationship as necessary. Finally, the clinician explores the child's belief system regarding the people in their life. The clinician checks for distortions within the child's viewpoint in order to determine whether the child's chronological age appears congruent with their emotional age. This allows for the preparation of a list of treatment issues from the diagram and other themes that have been presented, as noted in the sample chart in the next section.

Phase C: Processing the Sand Tray Stories

Purpose of the Directed Sand Tray Stories

The Sand Tray Stories help the therapist generate the list of treatment issues that will need to be addressed, the relative importance of each issue to the young client, and what approaches/messages will likely be most efficacious, given the child's interpretative tendencies (how does the child interpret the world around them?).

As clinician and caregiver complete Phase B, they have together started to predict some of this, along with a sense of what the child's expected impactful event might be. This information, along with the information generated through the early Sand Tray Stories, can be tabulated as follows:

TABLE 6.1A Sand Tray Tracking Sheet

Issues (treatment needs)	*Frequency of endorsement as noted in sand tray/ clinical meetings*	*Overall rank of issue*
Tendencies (How the child seems to interpret events and govern their response to them)	*Frequency of endorsement as noted in sand tray/clinical meetings*	*Overall weight of tendency*

Case example: Eight-year-old Jack's father was incarcerated for violence, which he witnessed, against his mother. She predicts that the final episode of violence, and/or the police removing the father from the home, will be the most impactful events. The early Sand Tray Story reveals that he misses his Dad, and wishes he could see him more often, and that his story emphasizes a special time with Dad. He breaks down and cries when asked a question about Dad's place in a family story. This information *might* be tabulated like this:

TABLE 6.1B Sand Tray Tracking Sheet

Issues (treatment needs)	*Frequency of endorsement*	*Overall rank of issue*
Worry about Mom and her ability to keep herself safe	*xxx*	
Worry about Dad being cared for	*xxx*	
Grieving loss of contact with Dad	*xx*	
Loyalty issues	*xxxx*	
Witness of Dad's arrest	*x*	
Witness of violence against Mom	*x*	
Tendencies (How the child seems to interpret/govern response to events)	*Frequency of endorsement*	*Overall weight of tendency*
Romanticizes Dad	*x*	
Gives himself a lot of responsibility	*x*	

After a number of sand tray sessions, the treatment list might well have been generated, indicating which items are most important to the child, as well as the ways in which he has "framed" the events and consequently some understanding of his tendency to interpret his world in certain ways. This amounts to a substantial amount of information about the child that will permit the design and implementation of the types of interventions that will be most meaningful for him. The clinician will also be able to work in a more focused way to uncover the child's faulty belief system and consequently to devise a treatment strategy that can dismantle it and rebuild it in a healthier manner.

The remaining four sessions further explore issues while establishing a contained affective, cognitive, and behavioral experience for the child. Just as the caregiver received support to make positive changes in their own life, the caregiver is now positioned as an emotionally attuned and supportive, competent, most-informed director for the child in treatment. Once the caregiver is satisfied with the treatment gains achieved by the child as originally set out in the treatment plan, and once improvements in the child's symptoms and behaviors within the home are evident and sustainable, the Behavior Choice Program (BCP) may be introduced most effectively into the caregiver's regular practices to address any remaining problematic behaviors with the child.

The major distinctions between the BCP and other behavioral programs are:

Major Distinctions of ITTM's Behavior Choice Program (BCP)

- The caregiver modifies their own behavior first.
- The caregiver and child share an understanding of the emotional forces driving the child's behaviors.
- The caregiver and child witness the capacity for and experience of behavior change prior to beginning the BCP.
- The "choice" of behaviors rests solely *on the child.*

The BCP is generally carried out in the home for 3–6 months following the closing of the file at the clinic to allow the child to practice self-responsibility and impulse control, and to enjoy the rewards of positive choice under the informed guidance of the caregiver.

TABLE 6.2 The ITTM Trauma Treatment Checklist

Life Themes and Treatment Issues			
Has the child:	*Yes*	*No*	*Maybe*
1. Directly experienced one or more of the following? a) Physical abuse b) Sexual abuse c) Verbal abuse d) Emotional abuse			
2. Witnessed family violence and/or abusive behavior involving his/her caregivers?			
3. Lost a mother, father, or friend to death (unexpected or expected)?			
4. Experienced an unexpected separation from their primary caregiver for longer than three days?			

(Continued)

TABLE 6.2 (Continued)

5. Experienced an adoption process?			
6. Experienced a real or perceived threat to the life or safety of their primary caregiver?			
7. Experienced one or more out-of-home (or foster home) placements?			
8. Experienced abandonment by a primary caregiver?			
9. Experienced neglect by a primary caregiver?			
10. Experienced a frightening hospital experience?			
11. Experienced an unexpected move?			
12. Experienced inconsistent access visits by a primary caregiver where the visits were either frequently canceled or not acted upon?			
13. Been discovered to have been touched inappropriately or been found touching another child inappropriately (even if a similar age)?			
14. Experienced another traumatic event not listed?			

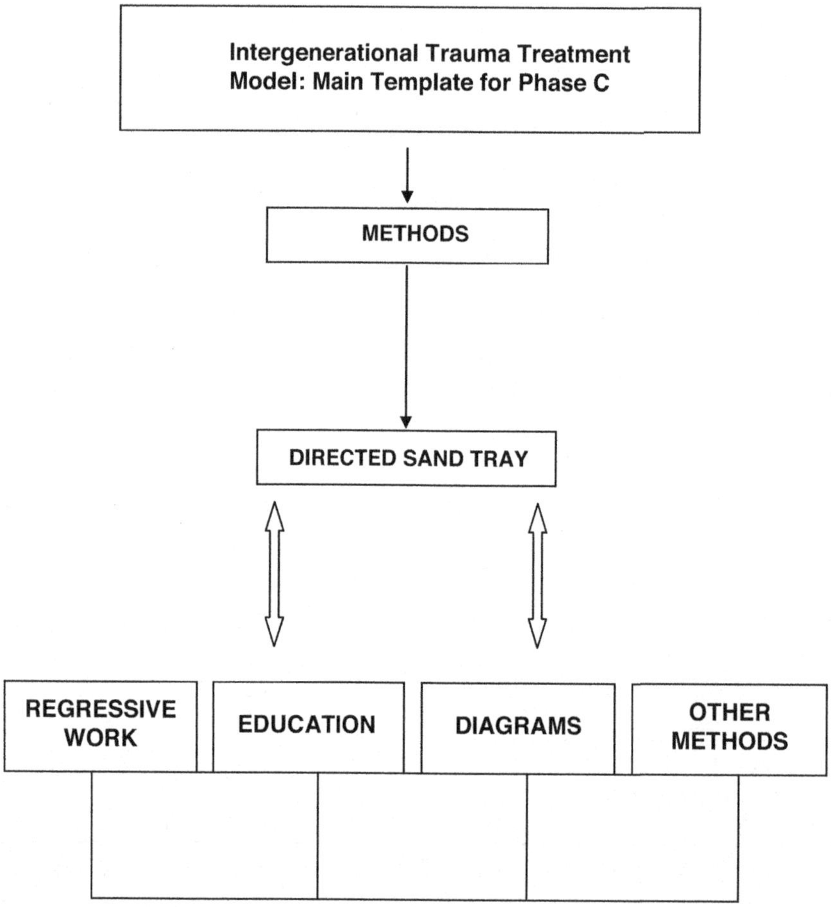

Option 1—Directed Sand Tray Story-Making

- A hypothetical treatment plan has been formed with the caregiver.
- The child has a strong enough sense of self and a solid enough foundation with the caregiver to enter the trauma's details.

Approach

- By means of miniatures and a sand tray, the child is invited to choose 10 miniatures, one of which represents them; the child chooses the age represented by the miniature.
- The clinician directs the child, matching the child's intensity of emotions, as the child makes a story or stories with the miniatures and the sand tray.
- The clinician writes it down carefully and interrupts on purpose to extrapolate and share relevant information.
- The clinician then reads the story back to the child (and caregiver) and photographs the sand tray for the child to take home.

Important: The child is not playing in the sand but may move miniatures through the sand as they tell the story. The story must follow a narrative arc with a beginning—"Once upon a time"—a middle that lays out the details, and a close—"The End."

Faulty Belief System Diagram—Reconstructed (On Board) and Any Action Required to Be Taken

(on the part/behalf of the child)

Story Themes

- General story.
- Family story.
- Family story (if two families/appropriate).
- Story of me and Mom.
- Story of me and my other Mom/Dad (if two families/appropriate).
- Story of the day the bad thing happened.
- Story of the day the bad thing happened (resolved).

Close

Option 2—Regressive Re-enactment (R-E)

***refer to ITTM training and training manual**
****a very high degree of containment is required for R-E with caregiver & child**

- Not every child who has suddenly lost or who has experienced unavailability of a caregiver will require regressive work.
- Treatment intervention time is tripled when the caregiver and child practice the story at home each week, one or two more times in addition to the story acted out in the clinic.
- As the child bores of acting out the story at home, the clinician then knows to advance to the creation of the next chronological age story with the child. The newborn story is always completed on its own, then other ages can be done separately or grouped together in years of two if the child is willing. Child leads this option until they have reached their current age.
- Value of regressive work for clinic forms of caregiver-related trauma where the child is living with that caregiver or foster parents.

***The Regressive Re-enactment time at home replaces the 1/1 quality time spent at home with the caregiver established in Phase B.**

Action (Following the Completion of R-E)

- A child-accessible version of the PAST/PRESENT/FUTURE Diagram is created to highlight the injustice of their past experiences, how the present is different, and how/why there is hope for a better future.
- Other diagrams are created on the board to emphasize that the traumatic event was not caused by or because of them, but most often because of the situation/circumstances/limitations of the adults.
- Discuss the time it takes for children to adopt New Brain T, F, As and how long it takes to find that the new brain thinking is sticking. This is a *process*, not an automatic development occurring just because the impact has been explained to the child.
- Move back to completing the Directed Sand Tray Stories if the T.E. has not specifically been addressed.

****Charting follow-up and homework for caregiver and child.**

Outcomes

- Emotional attachment between the caregiver and child has increased.
- The child has a sense of self, increased self-esteem.
- Behavior has improved-symptoms have reduced.
- Creation of the Faulty Belief Statement-identified dilemma of the past for the child and demonstrated how that dilemma and their related behavior were caused by the trauma impact and the child's attempt to make sense of the traumatic event—what should have happened, safety issues, etc.

***IF the traumatic event has been addressed and resolved through this process, is there any ACTION by the child required?**

Close

Option 3—Education

(used primarily with teens—1–3 sessions—prior to asking if they would like to participate in treatment)

Methods

- The clinician identifies the need to provide introductory education to the teen on the teen's T.E. prior to gaining the teen's commitment to treatment.
- Uses the existing ITTM diagrams, education information, resources, handouts, movies, stories, IF cards, etc. to the teen's specific T.E.

Actions

The clinician does almost all the talking in these sessions. This is NOT a time to gather information or quiz the teen/child, no matter how tempting. You are the teacher here. Following educational sessions, and only once the clinician feels they have formed a relationship with the teen/child, the teen is asked to come back to the next session. At this point, they will report as to whether they are willing to continue treatment. If they agree, the clinician moves back to Options 1, 2, 3, 4, or 5, or a combination.

Homework

- Teen version of the Membrane Diagram: Pathways Diagram to affirm communication difficulties that have occurred with the caregiver.
- Child Witnesses of Domestic Violence Diagram: treated vs. untreated outcomes; risks/roles.
- Power and Control Hypothesis/Female Version Diagram: treated vs. untreated outcomes (risks) roles.
- Power and Control Hypothesis/Male Version Diagram: treated vs. untreated outcomes (risks).
- Effects of alcohol on teens: treatment vs. no treatment outcomes (short and long-term risks).
- Effects of witnessing other traumatic events: treated vs. untreated implications/risks.
- Short and long-term effects of sexual abuse. Treated vs. untreated: risks-short and long-term implication.
- High road/low road diagram: teenagers' life choices—"practice makes perfect" whether positive or negative.
- "Inside the Teenage Brain" documentary—to normalize and affirm feeling of isolation/difference/breakdown of communication.
- "Secrets of the Silver Horse" cluster dolls explore various aspects of teenager's self/soul.

Do Not Close

(go back to options to resolve and/or dissolve T.E. impact and F.B.S.)

Option 4—Diagrams

(will likely only begin here when you have older children [14+] who refuse to go to the sand tray but who are already *very keen* on treatment—this is quite rare)

Methods

- Used when child is really drawn to the whiteboard when they first walk in.
- Use of whiteboard will likely be the first treatment modality until you can perhaps encourage the child to some other options (if needed).

Diagrams

- Play a round of "Jeopardy" with the caregiver, child, and clinician to compile a comprehensive list of treatment issues to address at the clinic.
- Caregiver and clinician leave the room—the child orders the issues from most to least desirable as they see it.
- Make a list of positive/negatives about prior caregivers.
- ABCs of Anger/Anger Buckets—child fills bucket to depict current and desired level of anger in bucket. Pathways discussion with caregiver (past and present context)—Stress and Chaos map of caregiver and child differences-capacities, etc.
- Babies being arbitrarily placed in Good/Happy house vs. not Good/Happy house—did the child choose?—no! Baby potential diagram. Women vs. Mothers diagram. Men vs. Fathers diagram. Meter diagram for Trust vs. Mistrust. Thought, feeling, and action diagrams. Support structure diagrams.
- Traumatic event drawing in the context of the past, present, and future—including pre- and post-conditions.
- PAST/PRESENT/FUTURE Diagrams. Negative self-belief system (NSBS) Diagram for the child based on their individual T.E, impact and theme. Resolved NSBS Diagram. Original/child. **See example at end of chapter.

Actions

- Cognitive behavioral diagramming to identify and resolve NSBS.
- Charts and charting for all diagram(s) listed previously and all others designed.
- Anger release program; therapeutic letters; other actions required.
- Behavior Choice Program.
- Back to other options.

Close

- Corrected negative self-belief system (NSBS).
- Resolution of traumatic effect.
- Attunement between caregiver and child has increased.
- Child has a sense of self-esteem, increased self-esteem.
- Behavior has improved, symptoms have reduced.

Option 5—Other Methods

Methods

- Forming treatment plan-identifying most impactful event for the child (past or present). If traumatic event being revealed in the present life of the child, they must still go back and reveal and resolve traumatic event for which they were first referred
- Through stories, diagrams, and questions.
- Symbolic means to help a child/teen understand that the bad thing that occurred is not about them, to help make sense of the event.

Other Options

- Therapeutic letters.
- Boundary Diagram with child when there is enmeshment with the caregiver, or too much distance.
- PAST/PRESENT/FUTURE Diagram with teenagers with charting homework.
- Creating funeral and/or other rituals for resolving the unresolved or complicated grief/traumatic impact.
- Symbolic forms of activity.
- Rebuild communication between teen and caregiver.
- Positive and negative aspects list of caregiver who caused trauma.
- Child writes a list of questions they would like answered; leave the room while they write them down.
- Dolls.
- Special educational information-materials/movies.

Actions

- Cognitive behavioral diagramming; charting follow-up homework; letter writing, when there is caregiver abandonment, rejection or sudden loss.

Close

- Corrected faulty belief statement.
- Resolution of traumatic event.
- Attunement between caregiver and child has increased.
- Child has a sense of self/self-esteem.
- Behavior has improved.

Phase C

Enter Phase C with:

- A diagram of the child's past, present, and future per the traumatic theme(s).
- A trauma theme.
- A likely dilemma (which speaks greatly to the child's behaviors).
- A belief system for the child: "if this then that must mean I . . ."
- An estimation, or informed "guess," by the caregiver and the clinician, working together, about the event that has created the most impact per the caregiver and yourself.

Example: Betty's Case History

The clinician aims to understand how the child views their world, the people in their life, and their attachment figures. This understanding will help to uncover the child's most pressing issue in their own perspective, and to compare this to what the caregiver sees as the core of the matter.

The Case Presented

Six-year-old Betty has experienced physical and verbal abuse by her parents, as well as their abandonment/rejection and relocation at some distance from their two children, Betty and her brother. They have no contact with the parents, who remain together, and whom Betty has not seen for three years; she lives with her brother and their foster parent. The priority issues that Betty presented are anxiety, lack of containment, and lack of self-regulation. At the time of referral, the foster parent had noted an increase in symptoms at home over the previous three weeks.

The Initial Assessment

Regressive Re-enactment is a strong likelihood. Sand trays should be used to back to process traumatic events and to work on re-attributions if, necessary. Do we need one or more before deciding the treatment plan? Do we have all the information we need?

Session 1

- Meet with the caregiver first: get an emotional check-in (update).
- Prepare them for what is to happen.
- Explain why we use sand stories.
- Explain that the child should lead.
- Explain why the caregiver should not engage at this point.
- Emphasize that the caregiver should be supportive.
- Emphasize that the goal is to reinforce rapport between the child and caregiver first.
- Explain to the caregiver that the purpose is to move together (caregiver, child, and clinician) towards the traumatic event, no matter how many stories it will take to make the child comfortable to approach it. When we get to the traumatic event, the caregiver will assist in uncovering the critical details.

The first evaluative sand story:

- Have the child look, observe, and/or pick up each miniature in the collection. Watch their speed of observation and have them start over again by demonstrating the ideal speed. Ask the child where in their body they "feel" feelings. Have the child return to the collection and ask the child/youth to pick the 10 miniatures that gave them the strongest feeling. Ask them to place their chosen items in the sandbox.
- Ask the child to "pick something or somebody to be you."
- Tell the child that you would like them to make a story, with a beginning, a middle, and an end, using these things.
- Give them 10–15 minutes to see if they can figure out how to do this without further prompting or direction. Once they say they have a story in mind and attempt to "show" it with their chosen pieces, say, "You've done so well. I'll let you pick five more things."
- Ask if there are any miniatures they would like to change, now that they have an idea for their story. To make changes they must replace the original choice with one of the second round of choices. Some children may spend most of the session changing and replacing all the items. The child's selection process will provide information on how the child currently is able to make decisions or not; with clarity and

conviction or do they demonstrate difficulty in making or sticking with any one decision. The process observed will often mirror the child's general decision-making processes in their day-to-day world.
- Final question: "Do you need any more people?"
- Have two sandboxes and give them the option to use one or both.
- Explain that three things always happen in a story. There's always a beginning, a middle, and an . . . (end). Let them finish your sentences; this helps to evidence their ability to succeed and further engages them in the process.
- Encourage them to use as many words as they can: "I'd like it to be a long story and I'm going to be writing it down as you tell it. I'm a very slow writer, so I need you to tell it slowly." Tell them they have free rein to tell their story, but no Christmas or birthday stories or stories they have seen on television or other media.
- Pause frequently. If the child is going quickly, stop them and say that you want them to retell the story to make sure you have it right.
- Encourage containment by asking the child to put the toys back and shake off the sand.
- Close the session by "checking in" with the child: "What did you think of that?" "Would you like to come back?" "You did such a good job with your story. Next time I'm going to ask you to do the same (or get you to do something a bit different)."

Ask the caregiver after this session what* they *observed:

- What did *you* take from this?
- How did *you* make sense of it?
- Get their view first; then offer your own view by expressing ideas in a general fashion—permitting many viable interpretations on their part—rather than presenting them with "solid" views. They need to feel that they are an important part of a partnership, and not simply there to watch and be "told." Be clear that you are working together and that they cannot take it upon themselves to uncover things no matter how tempted. There is an appropriate pace and process that they must agree to respect.
- Advise the caregiver *not* to discuss or ask why the child, for example, did not choose to include their brother Bobby as a member of their family, or what the story meant. The parent congratulates the child on their story.

To summarize, in Phase C we return to the caregiver's PAST/PRESENT/FUTURE Diagram of the child who was the principal assignment of Phase B. We use the diagram to hypothesize about the child's dilemma, main traumatic themes, belief system, and their most impactful traumatic event. We assess and address this with the child (in the caregiver's presence as observer) through techniques that can include Sand Tray Storying. During the telling of the Sand Tray Story, the therapist guides the child through a deliberate, slowed-down retelling of the story; doing so provides the child with the opportunity to contain their emotions and directly experience the feeling of self-regulation. The first story in this case is necessarily titled: "A very good day with Mom/Dad/family." Given that the goal of treatment for this child is reduced guilt and anxiety for having to testify against the parents in court, the clinician must first address as many as possible of the positive experiences and memories of the child's love for their parents, or the child will experience even more guilt and anxiety for telling the story about "the day(s) the very bad things happened." It is important to bring any such positive memories into the real-life context of the treatment at least once (and possibly along the way). The child will tend to resist or dismiss the behaviors of the parent(s), thereby hanging on to their own guilt about "betrayal." The best way to address this and move forward into the specific details is by honoring the positives and child's love and caring for the parents.

During the Phase C assessment stage, the clinician considers important questions as to whether the child is naming the traumatic event, or, if they are not naming it, whether the details recounted about the trauma impact are in order and complete. If the details are scant or scattered, often both, this may require returning to the Sand Tray Stories. A checklist of what the items selected and/or exchanged, potential challenges for the child, what the primary theme and message was of the story, what the trauma theme or negative belief system is and whether the story was a "wish" or "fear" story is completed by the clinician after each sand tray session is over.

With teens, completing the checklist before they leave and giving them a copy to take home permits them to leave the session at least with a fuller and more "real" understanding of their own behaviors. Therapeutic letter writing (see Options section) can be used at the end of Phase C as a very effective method for ensuring the child/teen engages in some form of action-taking to regain a sense of personal power *over* the event. There is also good reason for keeping the child apprised of where you will be going next. For example, "Next week in the story we are going back into the middle of the story to list all the details of what happened and because you were there, you'll be able to help fill in the details, whether you tell the story or whether we tell the story."

Session 2

In the second session, draw a diagram about moving through the middle of the trauma blob and why the child needs to go through the good and not so good memories; provide age-appropriate information to the child and teen on all the reasons why—short- and long-term implications—and that not going into the good increases anxiety and will create problems down the road. The clinician does not need to hold back what reasons are given to the child, or be concerned about whether the child will understand. My experience is that, most of the time, children as young as 4 and 5 can and do understand. The clinician must expend every effort to inform and contextualize the situation's impact for the child/teen. This can be further "teased out" with regressive work.

Clinician Factor Considerations

It is important to ask these questions about the process once it has been carried out for the first time, so that an effective plan can be drawn up:

- What other stories do I absolutely need?
- Do I have all the trauma details I need on specific events?
- Has the belief system of the child identified by the caregiver in Phase B been confirmed or denied?
- At what age would regressive work likely begin with this child?
- Are the caregivers in a position of readiness to go forward?
- Does the child have a strong enough foundation to enter the traumatic details now, or do we need to create that foundation first, i.e. Regressive Re-enactment?
- Does the order of the stories matter with this child, and if so, which one do I prefer to go into?

The clinician's answers to these questions will serve as a "roadmap" to all that follows in Phase C and need to be kept for reference.

Sand Tray Stories

Where the child can go into traumatic issues through sand stories instead of regression, this approach should be used first. The Sand Tray Stories will rework the details of the chaos story with the intent of having the child consider and understand what *should have happened* to ensure their own safety and well-being; or the child tells the story from their own point of view as to *how it should have been*. The clinician attempts in this way to correct cognitive distortions by telling the story and then having the child tell it back to them. The clinician will note when the story appears to be too intense for the child, asking the child to confirm their feelings at that time. An example of the clinician's worksheet follows.

The story-telling process:

1. Tell the story that depicts the child's emotions: use their items or pick different ones to retell their likely range of emotions at the time—fear, anxiety, desperation—and have the child add to it.
2. Tell the story of how the child managed to get through the experience—guess at the role they took on, invite them to correct you if you get it wrong, or have the child tell the story and you intervene to bring out the details.
3. Tell the story of the good day, when someone looked after the kids.
4. Welcome the good and the bad in the stories.
5. "There are days when I miss my Mom and Dad story"—the clinician can tell this story, or at least start it, or have the child tell the whole story.
6. An unmet wish/dream story that the clinician can start or tell, or have the child tell it.
7. The clinician or child tells the imagine story, thinking about what will happen in the future involving the child and their biological family. As the clinician gets closer to the traumatic event, you get more and more specific: you are intentionally searching for more information.

Examples of story subjects:

- The day the parents showed they really didn't care about me (they moved away).
- The day or days my mother tried to choke or otherwise hurt me (and how the child coped with now knowing their parents could deliberately hurt them).
- A day that you wished for time with your Mommy.
- The day I felt so bad for not wanting to see my parents again (guilt/loyalty theme).
- The day I came to live with ________________.
- The hard day when the child worried that someone in their family might be hurt (perceived threat).
- A story about a child who loved their life and worried it would change (displacement/survival).
- A story about a child who had two Mommies.

Once the traumatic details are laid out, the clinician will want to turn over the power to the child to organize and create their own roadmap.

Traumatic Events Not Directly Involving Caregiver Abandonment, Abuse, or Neglect

Traumatic events under this category are numerous and varied. They may include the loss of a sibling, legal battles that have directly or indirectly involved the child where the child is aware of contention, physical abuse (unrelated to the caregiver, except for the child's experience of a caregiver's failure to protect), an accident involving the child or caregiver where permanent loss did not occur, victimization of the child through bullying or other unforeseeable victimizing events, sibling abuse, animal abuse, self-harm, having witnessed or been exposed to inappropriate behavior by caregivers or other adults, cult activities, fear for a caregiver's health (based on actual traumatic health episodes but non-life-threatening), loss of access to one caregiver (but where the child still resides with primary caregiver), unresolved grief, adoption where the child has never known their biological parents, or the perceived risk of a caregiver reentering abusive relationship(s), when the child has witnessed or directly experienced abuse in the past.

Session 1

General sand story with favorite items and general family sand story (family members unspecified). Here the clinician works on building an intense and trusting relationship with the child—quickly. Push to join and align yourself with the child in every way you can.

Session 2

Specific sand story of a child at a certain age when "a bad thing happened involving . . ." The story can be either child- or clinician- or caregiver-generated. It is very important here not to extend or delay time in getting down specifically to the traumatic issue about which the family has sought assistance. The clinician will have enough "relationship" with the child by this time (in almost all circumstances) to move ahead to the traumatic events.

What is being addressed is the loss of *what would have been* if the event(s) had not occurred, as well as the injustice of what did occur. The clinician also seeks to obtain a full and accurate view of the effects of the trauma on the child's past, present, and future thoughts, feelings, and actions, e.g. "I feel like I will never be the same as I was before it happened."

Take the child's lead. The child-identified traumatic event may start off being something quite different than what anyone would have guessed. If this is the case, follow it through with the child but see if incorporating other trauma themes into the current sand stories is possible. If not, the clinician will need to cover, in at least one sand story, the details of the most severe traumatic event, as they know it, to ensure that the child is not simply avoiding it.

A session on the traumatic event(s) will touch on some or all of the following, and related, questions on the clinician's part:

- What happened on that tragic, horrible day? The child tells the clinician, or the clinician narrates the story after the child has filled in some of the details, repeating it slowly, while adding other details obtained from the caregiver, agency file, or other referral sources.
- If the child has not moved the items in the sandbox during the telling, the clinician may move them around in the box while repeating the child's story (with a few details added): "So, let's see if I understand what you are saying correctly . . . there was Joey . . . he was 2 years old . . . he had a

brother . . ." One technique is to say a small detail incorrectly just to engage the child and to check if the child is as involved in the details as the clinician appears to be. The child will likely provide a correction. This technique incorporates a bit of a challenge to the child, in an engaging way, to work with the clinician in taking charge of their own story, for which only they know the true details.

- If the clinician is primarily telling the story (because the child either can't or does not feel comfortable risking it), another possible approach is: "It was 5 o'clock on a Monday. Joey knew it was Monday because it was a school day. . . . He woke up, and he was feeling (Joey puts in his feeling) . . . happy. OK. Joey woke up that day and he was feeling happy. He put on his ____ and he had ____ for breakfast. . . . Then he was at school in math class and the principal came to the classroom and asked to speak to ____." This is as if the clinician, with the child's active input, is writing a letter describing the situation to an outsider, although you are (or Joey is, if willing) re-enacting the story in the sandbox, and doing the collecting for any additional items (details) needed.

This version is the most in-depth story the child will ever have heard on the matter.

Details are paramount, including those regarding ordinary surroundings and people. For example, if the trauma is rooted in a hospital visit to a terminally ill caregiver, note the color of the hospital walls, where the tubes were placed in the patient, what sounds the machines were making, what was on the windows, in the rest of the room, who was present, what was said by each person there, the uniforms of the medical staff, what the mother said to the child—everything that happened before, during, and after the event. If the child says, "I don't know" or "I can't remember," the clinician responds with reassurance and affirmation: "That is OK. Give yourself some time to see if you can remember, because I know you have a great memory," and "You are not supposed to know the answers right away. I know you haven't been asked the questions in this much detail before."

The clinician does not attempt to "get into" the child's feelings during the detail gathering with the child. Trying to work through feelings at this point may divert or impede the story, and the child may have a very difficult time getting back to recalling the event or incident details that are critical to this phase of treatment. By keeping to a step-by-step recall of specific details, the clinician contains the intense, frightening, and/or possibly overwhelming effects for the child. The clinician is also demonstrating, by not addressing the child's feelings of that time, that this is a matter-of-fact recounting of the order of specific events, on that specific day or at that moment, that have no two ways about them: the events came, in a certain order, one after the other, and then it was over.

Obviously, while traumatic events are taking place, children will experience powerful feelings. But the events are beyond their control and are happening rapidly, so the primary emotion is fear. The child cannot simply stop the incident as it unfolds to wonder at their own feelings about it: they cannot be spectators to their own trauma, clearly, and are in no position, due to age and circumstances, to wonder what they can or will do next. They are most often in a reactive shocked mode of being forced to endure what transpires. The clinician must isolate the event as such: it has a beginning, a middle, and an end. Before this session begins, it is important to have reviewed all the details with the caregiver in order to mitigate the likelihood that the caregiver will lose emotional control as the clinician gently but intently uncovers the details with the child. If the caregiver does break down, the clinician should acknowledge to the child that expressing feelings is perfectly fine, and that Mom or Dad or whomever will get a drink of water and then you can all carry on with the rest of the story, and confirm to the child that they are "doing such a good job."

Session 3

When the story in the sand is completed, the clinician takes it to the board and tries to diagram its key details. These details are placed around the periphery of the stick figure representing the child. This process enables the clinician to get to the thoughts, feelings, and actions of the child during and around the event. At this point, the child will have a chance to process the event at all levels, and then to provide information about their process, which the clinician will check for distortions and themes that likely helped to shape the child's current belief systems. The child, however, can go to that feeling level from a manageable and containable distance. The child will also mirror and follow the clinician's lead on containment, which provides additional protection to them. This is very important, especially when the child's experience generated high fear levels, and can be assumed about all trauma in childhood. This becomes the PAST Diagram. Once the child has provided the details of the event and, most important, *their understanding* of what or why the event occurred, the clinician can proceed to explain other feasible interpretations about what happened for the child without worrying about the public exposure of family involvement, for example, the "family name" or social standing. *The child's mental health is the only priority.*

The following dialogue is an example of cognitive restructuring and belief system reframing. Six-year-old Tommy and the clinician discuss what happened and what he sees as the meaning of what happened:

Tommy: "Mommy gave me away, but kept my sister."
Clinician: "Why do you think she did that?"
Tommy: "She said I was too much trouble."

Children will often say "I don't know," whether they genuinely have no real idea or they simply do not want to vocalize it. This is problematic because it affects how the child will make sense of their own value, place in the world, sense of power, faith in others, and so on.

How do we frame a less painful and emotional explanation to Tommy about why his mother chose his sibling? The emotional pain cannot be denied, nor should the child's interpretation be dismissed. A more beneficial approach is for the clinician to work out, based on the actual details of the trauma and the child's own faulty understanding of it, an equation that is both more logical and more believable. At this point, the clinician must work hard with the child to ensure that they are prepared to accept, willingly and wholeheartedly, an alternative, self-liberating understanding of what happened to them and why. The clinician may need to wait until the next session to come back with a recast explanation and therefore a logical interpretation that will convince the child.

My own experience in taking traumatized children through the ITTM process reveals this to be the crux of the treatment issue with many children. *This is a critical point of intervention.* Reconstructed meticulously from the known trauma evidence, the clinician's proposed alternative can lead to long-term resolution for them. The child/victim takes active part in liberating themselves from ongoing, damaging, and disempowering feelings of guilt, worry, grief, self-reproach, self-blame, self-critique, and harshness, and consequently the overall distrust of others which can develop into outright animosity. The clinician must make sure to record all ideas that arise as the new interpretation is being arrived at. Likewise, the rationale and the working "reconstruction" must be set down carefully. Children, at very early ages, are sensitive to any hesitation, confusion, or self-correction on the part of adults. Traumatized children are particularly wary and inclined to distrust on the basis of such "clues." The clinician's coherent explanation of the new interpretation, reflecting their own conviction and confidence in its viability, will go far to convince the child to accept this reframed trauma story despite attachment to their own version.

With reference to Tommy's interpretation of his mother's abandonment, the clinician could take up the dialogue by saying, "It sounds to me like your Mom thought one child was going to be less trouble than two." Then they will explain the rationale for that interpretation, building up a solid foundation to support the argument presented to the child. Until the new interpretation makes significantly more sense than the child's argument and its various support pieces, which the clinician will have recorded prior to suggesting the alternative, the child will resist. In diagrams, the clinician should demonstrate that their own interpretation has more valid "pieces" scaffolding the real explanation than the child's. In short, the child must "see" that the clinician's argument is tight while theirs is not. This, of course, is worth the clinician's persistence because the child's loss (of the argument) is an enormous gain for them, as the clinician will emphasize. They are joining forces with the clinician to free themselves from pain as they discover a better, more fitting, solid, evidence-based explanation for what happened and why.

Returning to Tommy's situation:

Clinician: "What sort of *even bigger* troubles do you think a mother would have by giving up one of her two children? How do we know if your mother is even looking after the one she kept with her? What is *too much trouble* for mothers?"

Tommy: "I don't know."

Clinician: (building support for their argument) "Adults have troubles . . . often bigger troubles because they are older and have had more years to make troubles for themselves. Let us list some things that make adults *too much* trouble.

More support pieces are then systematically put in place:

Clinician: "Children are little. You were 3 when your mother decided to try cutting her troubles in half by going from two children to one. You only had three years' worth of troubles. Your mother has 35 years of troubles. Who has the most troubles? Who has the biggest troubles? (Draw the size of troubles for a 35-year-old, compared to the size of troubles for a 3-year-old). "Whose job is it to take care of the little troubles of kids? *Parents*."

Here is a support for the argument that the child will not be able to ignore:

Clinician: "Why would your foster mother Suzie have eight children to care for, and another three of her own, and have no trouble looking after and loving all of them, and another mother has two children and can't even look after one?"

The discussion can be brought around to general statements applying to adult responsibilities:

Clinician: "What qualities do adults need to be able to love others well, especially children?" "So, let us talk about what *really was the biggest problem* for your mother."
These are listed on the board beside the list of typical 3-year-old-troubles.

Final question: "Who is the biggest trouble?"

At this point, the session should be completed by going over and reinforcing what has been discussed: "Tell me what we have talked about today." The subsequent session should begin the same way, by having the child recount everything that they can remember from the previous critical session. At this point, the caregiver will also report on their own observations about the child's feelings and behaviors during the interim. There should be significant differences—even subtle but important ones such as a new "lightness" in the child's attitude and demeanor—since the previous session.

Session 4

The clinician returns to the sandbox, and tells a story of what *should have happened* that day (or in that time), and what any child *would have and should have* experienced on a "normal" day: *not that trauma, not that crisis*. The clinician makes it clear that the child had no reason to experience that trauma on that day; rather, the child had every right to experience what other children experience on any "normal" day.

It must be emphasized that both approaches and/or outcomes of getting to the traumatic story details are positive. The clinician will either get the details to the traumatic event as they or the child know them (and some not previously known), or will get the details of another story. All details will lead the clinician to the board where diagramming and organizing the traumatic events will occur. From the details, it is possible to deduct the themes and the child's likely belief systems along with the dilemmas that arise for them because of those beliefs. These are the true effects of impact that need to be explained, organized, and often re-organized for the child, and placed into a new perspective. In short, this is the place where differences and similarities between diagrams can be seen. If the child was not initially, but is now, beginning to demonstrate signs of regression at home, or in the sand stories, this is the time to move to regressive work. This step should not be assumed without first preparing the caregiver and getting acceptance for your view and recommendations, and discussion of not only short-term drawbacks—perhaps affecting school and family relations—but also the long-term benefits for the child and family.

Session 5

This leads the clinician and the child back to the sandbox or to the board to work towards designing the PRESENT Diagram with the child. This diagram will address:

- What and who is in the child's life now?
- What is the same and what has changed since the event?

Acknowledging that life is different now, the clinician should ask the child to think about what another child of their age who has experienced the same thing what they could personally tell them about how to get through it as they have. What would they need from the adults in their life to get through it well? What would they tell the other child about how to make sense of what has happened, and about what should have been. When should the other child be allowed to cry? Who is that child allowed to miss, or to have questions about? What would that child tell their friends? Cover all the angles with the child. Identify belief systems, dilemmas, or thought processes that need to be incorporated into the child's future. Let the child direct their own treatment and needs for assistance from adults.

Sessions 5 and 6: The Future Diagram

Explain the grief process for children and how it differs from that of adults. Ask the child how long they feel they have been grieving. Do others know when they are sad or mad? How do the adults know? What are their own dreams and plans for their future?

Sessions 6 and 7: The Behavior Choice Program

Other interventions can be used along the way or following the trauma treatment process as discussed, but only once the steps outlined above have been completed. At this point, the clinician (alone or with the child—unclear) should brainstorm logical, plausible, believable alternatives for adjusting the child's sense-making of self and others.

Treatment for a child abandoned by their caregiver:

Always explore common themes in the behavioral difficulties the caregiver is experiencing from the child:

> **Example:** M.C. was abandoned and neglected by her biological Mom. She was shipped between various foster homes of which one foster mother, gave up—unable to handle the behavior—but kept M.C.'s sister. **A second rejection.** The current behavioral problems presented when M.C. was with a female figure whom she did not particularly like nor trust. The theme is female figures of authority. Because her mother abandoned her all the negative feelings she has with respect to her mother need to be vented towards someone. She does not want to do this with her current mother figure because it may jeopardize this relationship. She wants this closeness. With others, she feels more able to risk or to test these relationships, to prove if they are going to stick around for her.

The clinician makes a chart divided into two types of people:

- Those M.C. trusted.
- Those M.C. could not yet trust or cannot trust.

Discuss how trust is developed, what it means, what qualities it defines (i.e. takes time).

Template for Regressive Work

Primary Caregiver-Related Trauma

Child

TABLE 6.3 Regressive Work Template

Acute	*Chronic*
Sudden and complete loss of caregiver.	Inconsistent access of caregiver.
Accident involving caregivers.	Witnessed violence.
Sudden move from a caregiver (unexpected).	Neglect or abuse by primary caregiver.
Adoption.	Chronic illness of a primary caregiver.
Sudden life/death risk to caregiver.	Unavailability of a primary caregiver.

* Not every child who has suddenly lost or who has experienced unavailability of a caregiver will require regressive work. We consider regressive work when there are *acute forms of caregiver-related trauma*.

- The child has experienced sudden loss, or experienced unavailability by the caregiver who is now lost *and* where the child is regressing;

Or where

- It is known that the child and remaining or current caregiver have too much emotional distance between them that is obviously (however subtly) contributing to the child's behavioral difficulties;

Or where

- The child experienced unmet needs for nurturing by the primary caregiver prior to the loss where the caregiver is now lost, and
- We also consider the value of regressive work for chronic forms of caregiver-related trauma where the child is living with that caregiver or with a foster parent;

Or where

- The child and/or caregiver are experiencing blocks and conflict in the present often related to unresolved trauma of the past via behavioral difficulties.

And where the child has also experienced

- neglect,
- abandonment,
- a short-term but acute period of unmet needs by current caregiver,
- the chronic illness of a caregiver,
- the unavailability of a caregiver,
- witnessing violence, or
- a perceived threat . . . the threat of death or abandonment (unintentional); or
- they are state wards with access, or
- they are state wards without access.

To practice the ITTM which includes the Regressive Re-enactment Segment, practitioners must complete the ITTM training program. Because of the intensity and degree of specialization required to implement the Regressive Re-enactment portion of the program, it will not be described here in greater detail.

Carrying Out a Sand Story With a Child Where Sexual Abuse Has Occurred and the Perpetrator Is Not in the Child's Life

1. Specific sand story to include child's current caregiver (to ensure child has sense of strong supportive relationship and trust with that caregiver, for the sake of revealing that will be forthcoming).
2. Show the movie "Good Things Can Still Happen" if sexual abuse has been verified or suspected, and discuss aspects of movie at end of movie. See how able the child is to discuss the abuse or relate to the movie or not. This will provide insight for you for what the next session is likely to consist of (i.e. who will likely be telling the story).

The next session will require an hour and a half.

1. Sand story about the abuse. The caregiver needs to know in advance that today is the day you will be going for the details of the story, where you will likely access the caregiver for details along the way. This is for demonstrating to the child that the caregiver can not only withstand the details, but also provide more details

in a "matter-of-fact" fashion. If you sense the child cannot verbalize or reveal secret, have them develop a story about Bobby, who is 5 years old, on a day that a bad thing happened, or the day Uncle Sam did that bad thing, or touched Bobby in a "not OK" way. If the child creates a very general story about the trauma but chooses to leave out the worst parts, then the clinician should do a story back to the child as the story was told, but now including all the parts the clinician knows were true for the child. The clinician needs to leave room for the child to add additional details. Also, the clinician needs to ask feeling questions throughout the story like, "I wonder how Joey felt when . . ." If this fails to generate further feelings, then the clinician verbalizes and owns the feeling for the child as the clinician is telling the story "I was so mad" . . . "it made me feel so bad when he did that thing to me, I thought, 'Why is he doing those bad things?' I wondered . . . 'where is my Mom or Dad?'"

Go to the board to take a picture of the past. In a "matter-of-fact" way, record details around the periphery of the PAST Diagram. Include then the thoughts, feelings, and actions of the child.

As you are adding words to the diagram which make up the details of the event around the periphery, pause and provide educational information to the child: e.g. why do perpetrators go to jail? . . . why should they? . . . why did they? . . . why did they not? . . . what are the laws about protecting children . . . about specifically that child's experience of abuse . . . sexual laws . . . it is criminal to violate a child's innocence by taking them to a sexual place prior to the child coming to that place by themselves. Most people masturbate . . . why? What is the difference between masturbation and sexual abuse? Is masturbation OK? . . . is making oneself feel pleasure OK? What are the rules for self-pleasure? . . . when is giving oneself pleasure not OK? (e.g. 16 times a day is too much) . . . what happens in adolescence? How does sexuality change then? . . . hormones, . . . desire, . . . etc.? . . . where does power fit in here with sexual and other forms of abuse? . . . what does it say about the other person's need for power and control? Here you are trying to normalize the child's experience, and likely outcomes of increased self-touching, worries, mixed feelings about pleasure creating etc. Also, you want to normalize the conflict that arises for victims of sexual abuse. . . . You know inside that something feels very wrong about what is happening, yet your body may also be telling you and giving you feelings of being touched that you have never experienced before.

2. Create a PRESENT picture, demonstrating how the PAST is different from the PRESENT, particularly where the perpetrator is involved. Emphasize the safety guidelines that are now in place for the child . . . and the adults that are ensuring the safety prerequisites are being upheld. The child in the present also knows a whole lot more about abuse and the effects of abuse then they knew before. . . . Is this positive in a bittersweet way? Other interesting observations and points by caregiver and clinician.
3. Create a FUTURE picture.
4. Behavior Choice Program for remaining behaviors.

TABLE 6.4 Summary Chart of Treatment Options (First Section)

1-Standards Traumatic Event Treatment	2-Regressive Work	3-Education	4-Other Interventions
	**Even when one of the conditions listed below is/was present in the life of the child, it does not always mean regressive work will necessarily be required or that it should be chosen treatment. **See exceptions.		**When steps 1, 2, or 3 cannot be completed with a particular child right from the start, other interventions should only be used as a stepping stone to lead clinician and child back to steps 1, 2, or 3.

(Continued)

TABLE 6.4 (Continued)

		1: Diagram of children witnessing family violence 2: Diagram of babies not having a choice of which house they get placed with or with what caregiver.	***Board Work*: list of therapeutic issues—caregiver, child and clinician form list of issues to address (child orders list)
Sand Stories:	**CONDITION 1:** *When the events listed are revealed in Phase B by caregiver or when the events or impact of the events (listed below) are revealed by the child through repetitive themes during the process of completing the Standard Traumatic Event Treatment.*	Provide and inform child/teen of educational information—what we know about child's trauma—treated vs. untreated *Movie: "Good Things Can Still Happen"	*PPF Diagrams (with teenagers) *Boundary Diagrams with children/teens *List of positives and not-so-positives about lost/unavailable caregiver *Therapeutic letter writing
1-General	Abandonment/rejection by biological or another primary caregiver	Diagrams	Stories ("Secrets of the Silver Horse" cluster dolls)
2-My family	Neglect		
3-Me and Mom	- Unmet emotional needs - Child has little sense of a grounded or internalized sense of self/fragmented—not enough emotional strength or sustenance to even create the content for the Standard Sand Tray Story Process		Re-building communication/trust between caregiver and teenager, prior to being able to continue with TE treatment
4-Me and Dad 4-Me and the hard day (TE) 6-Others *Me and my other Mom.	**CONDITION 2:** ***Child demonstrating 2–3 of the following at home, in session, or elsewhere.*** 1-Regressive tendencies 2-TE re-enactment through behaviors—setting up repetition compulsion of Traumatic Event or Traumatic Object through the natural reaction of caregiver's responses (however negative) 3-Behaviors		Therapeutic letters
Board Diagrams - Child witness of DV - TFA Diagram - Good house and bad house - Positives and negatives list about caregivers - Others	4-Symptoms—anxiety 5-TE continual (stuck) re-enactment in Sand Tray Stories 6- Hyperactivity/hypervigilant		

Assess and plan to carry out some form of action to be taken by the child, guided by the clinician and caregiver, that will empower the child. This is always required in cases where the traumatic event is/was related to a primary caregiver.

Phase C Treatment Options

Questions to consider:

- In what order to implement Options 1–4?
- Do the presenting child's behaviors/symptoms (Option 2) need to be addressed through regressive work? Or . . .
- Is there another method?

Board Work (Completed by Child)

GOAL: Successful Individual Trauma Impact Resolution

The child can now describe the difference between the way they used to make sense of their impact to the traumatic event to their new sense-making of the traumatic event. The child should be able to rewrite, retell, or redraw the new diagram which will then be an indication of their reconstructed belief system about the event and what the impact of the event is. When the child can draw the "new sense-making diagram" on the board on their own with very little prompting from the clinician, then treatment will be able to be classified as complete.

If the child must be prompted any more than 5% of the time, the child is not ready for treatment to conclude. We have discovered that the child's ability to retell the trauma and the sense-making of the trauma is a reliable indicator of the child's integration and application of the new and the logical way to understand the trauma. The child's integration and application and ability to describe the new schemata on the board in the form of a diagram results in a notably more peaceful effective experience for the child, as well as in a significant and notable reduction in behaviors and in symptoms of the child.

The clinician has formulated the diagram and the new logical perspective for the child's revamped understanding of the traumatic event based on a clear and indisputable argument (specifically designed to reflect this child's traumatic history). Ultimately, the child/teen can now also describe what the risks to themselves, and what the triggers may naturally be for themselves in the present and in the future.

Choosing the Order of the Options

Always set about starting Phase C with Option 1 with children and teens. You need to set up the commencement of the first session of Phase C with this intention and with the introduction to the child/teen right off the bat. Without this approach, you may never get back or into the sand trays at all.

**See special tactics for introducing Option 1 to teens, following.

- In what order to implement Options 1–4?
- Do the child's presenting behaviors/symptoms (Option 2) need to be addressed through regressive work? Or . . .
- Is there another method?

Even when you see children (aged 3–10 and including teens) where you are hypothesizing or quite sure of the likelihood of Regressive Re-enactment work, you will still work to complete Option 1 first.

Guidelines for Option 1

You strive to complete Option 1 for several reasons:

- It may be all you need to do in treatment with the child—regardless of the seriousness of the trauma onto the child and regardless of whether you were sure after Phase B that regressive work was likely going to be required.
- It is a comprehensive method for completing an assessment on the child—psychological, emotional, and behavioral—that reduces the amount of question-asking dialogue that can set up a dynamic in the room of resistance and that of like pulling teeth on the part of the clinician.
- It is a powerful tool for assessing the child/teen's ability or lack thereof to regulate (with or without your prompting) their affect.
- It allows the child/teen to understand your role as container and director of the child/teen and of the treatment.
- It allows the clinician to fine tune the treatment issues and the treatment plan for the child, per the child. Directed Sand Trays 1–6 allow the clinician and the caregiver to add to or delete from the original hypothetical plan formulated as a guideline in Phase B. For example, what appears to be the most impactful aspect of the traumatic event(s) per the child, and what appears to be the primary presenting issue and theme in the child's/teen's sand trays? You will not get this information through any other option at this stage of treatment.
- It allows you to build an intense relationship with the child within a very short period.

If in the midst of Option 1 with children aged 3–10 (who have experienced caregiver-related trauma) you observe that the child really has very, very little sense of self, no sustenance, and/or a lack of ability for creating any kind of content for sand stories—then it is likely that you will need to likely move into the creation of regressive sand stories for the purpose of Regressive Re-enactment first, and assist the child in growing a sense of self (through the reflective and interactive eyes of the caregiver to the child) prior to being able to complete Option 1—the standardized 1–6 Standard Directed Sand Tray Stories with the child.

- In what order should Options 1–4 be implemented?
- Do the child's presenting behaviors/symptoms (option 2) need to be addressed through regressive work? Or . . .
- Is there another method?

If you do need to move into Regressive Re-enactment first before any depth or content or themes will be risked by the child in creating sand stories, then it will most likely be that the traumatic impact of the event (related to primary caregiver) will have been resolved; however, you will still need to go back and create the sand stories from Option 1 right through to the child's/teen's telling all the details of the Traumatic Event. The building of the child's foundation in the regressive work will sometimes need to be formulated and created prior to the child having anything to offer or willing to risk in the telling or the revealing or the creating of the Directed Sand Stories 1–6.

After Option 1 you can then decide to proceed with Option 2 (Regressive Re-enactment); proceed with Option 3 (Education), always resulting in diagrams and charting for the child; or proceed with one or more aspects of Option 4.

The clinician's job after completing Option 1 is to select the order (and the specific details) from the options list for treatment. Once the options are ordered, the clinician writes down the specific interventions to be included for the child from the options list, and this order of the options becomes the child's/teen's treatment plan. Of course, adjustments can be made to the order as treatment and treatment issues present themselves. Treatment must never end without the child's detailed account of the traumatic event and a review and restructuring of the way in which the child's belief system was affected.

All options for treatment end up back at the board with a diagram depicting the corrected/improved belief system—schemata created for the child that the child can draw back and describe to you in the context of their own past, present, and future. As well, is there any remaining action that the child needs to take (with the guidance and support of the clinician and caregiver) that will assist the child in honoring the self and the self's integrity and feeling of self-empowerment and resolve?

Option 2

When comparing the caregiver's PAST/PRESENT/FUTURE Diagrams to the child's PAST/PRESENT/FUTURE Diagrams, discuss differences/similarities and how the child's trauma has impacted the caregiver's own past experiences and belief systems. It is important to discuss with the caregiver the typical reactions and expectations that occur during Phase C and prepare the caregiver for the emotional reactions of the child (e.g. anger toward caregiver, blame toward caregiver, etc.).

In cases of sexual abuse, there are two consistent reactions in children that impact their belief systems:

- Anger toward caregivers for failing to protect them
- Difficulties trusting the caregiver to protect them in the future, which often leads to child in the lead/responsibility piece

Steps to proceed to Phase C:

1. Always develop two belief systems (minimum).
2. Read them over with the caregivers and have them rank them 1–10 of degree to which they are being acted out by the child.
3. Check with the caregiver which belief system fits more accurately for their child, and challenge any misthinking regarding their belief system or their impact in the belief system.
4. Take the primary belief system and have caregivers develop PPF diagrams for their child.
5. Make a treatment list of other interventions and issues to be addressed to resolve this belief system (e.g. overemphasizing how caregivers are competent in protecting child).
6. Compare the caregiver and child PPF diagrams for similarities and differences.

Sand Trays

While completing the Sand Tray Stories, have caregivers and clinician look for themes and FBS in each story and rate the degree to which the FBS is present in the story. Have caregivers chart the demonstration of these belief systems being acted out at home by the child to determine the most prominent belief system.

While conducting Sand Tray Stories:

1. Don't forget to integrate questions pertaining to the belief system/known experience into the story to help them unveil their FBS.
    - Who was taking care of the kids?
    - Let me guess: Mom provided you with lots of experiences that tore at your heart over the years?
    - How did you cope with that then?
2. Ask about how they are coping now with those experiences.
    - What can repair that pain?
    - How do you cope with that when you think about it now?
    - How do you cope with the little monkey when it comes up?
3. Look for the dilemma in each story and bring it to the board.
    - Not wanting foster care/not wanting home.
    - Angry with parent's choices/wanting to help them change.
    - Happy vs. sad house—what is happy about that house, and what is sad?
    - Small TFA vs. big TFA.
    - Have child chart these diagrams for homework of how he is feeling these over the week.
4. At the end of each session and beginning of next session, review and summarize what occurred in the session.

Constructing the FBS:

1. Always use specifics and then move to generalities as is more meaningful and potent for the child/person.
2. Discuss what makes them feel the FBS (e.g. powerless) and what makes them feel the corrected BS (e.g. powerful).
3. Chart FBS vs. CBS.
4. Caregiver's homework is always to do things to support the CBS (e.g. positive feedback of being powerful, situations to show this).

Other ideas:

- If the child does not identify themes in his story (e.g. Mom is perfect in the story) or rationalizes the event to the extent that they cannot acknowledge anger and other strong emotions toward the caregiver, the clinician can redo the story the following week, emphasizing common responses in similar situations. The child can then do a response story.
- Infant picture—to help the child understand that just having a baby doesn't necessarily make a good mom, make a diagram that shows how the infant's behavior is intended to encourage "good Mom" responses (crying to indicate the baby needs to be fed or changed or moved, etc.).
- Worry pie.
- Whole heart vs. half heart.
- Correct timeline of events for clarity and discuss what is expected of parent/child at each stage (e.g. babies, toddlers, young children).
- Write a regressive story for a baby doll (e.g. if child's dilemma is that they will be a bad parent).
- Therapeutic letter writing—can send or keep copy to add things through the years.

****Prior to entering Phase C work, each clinician should have a template of what the clinician can expect from child because of Phase B work completed.**

You need:

- Primary impactful traumatic event.
- Specific trauma theme.
- Faulty Belief System showing how child has most likely attached themselves to the outcomes or occurrence of the event.

The template should and needs to be crystal clear on what the primary traumatic event and likely resulting theme is for the child (according to the best guess of the caregiver and clinician). You must take 15 minutes after the last session in Phase B and write down your best guess of what the issues for this child are and what your hypothetical plan will be for the child. You describe what you expect to be the issues and in what presenting order for the child. This becomes your treatment formulation.

When you see the child in Phase C, the child then is either confirming or disproving your thinking, your treatment template, and your clinical formulation. If you ignore this step, you will not know where you are going (hence, you will not be able to direct the child towards that goal or direction), and the child will not look to you for that purpose or with confidence to do so. Nor will you be able to assess how to get to a place you're not sure of where it is in the first place, let alone get there in the shortest and most effective manner possible.

If you know where you are going in advance (with a very informed best guess), you do not have to then try to get the child over to your side through various forms of power struggles in your language with the child or in the sand tray or on the board—because you know where you are going and you know that you are going to bring the child through the other side of their experience just like you did with the caregiver. The child will tell you and show you through their revealing if you have it correct or not. This does not mean that you ignore what the child is revealing because you think your insight has to be correct. It is simply your starting guide—the child reveals to you from that point on to confirm or disconfirm your idea.

Main goals of Phase C:

1. Reduction of behaviors and symptoms of children.
2. Accurate assessment of the most impactful traumatic event according to the child and identification of the most significant traumatic theme for this child as associated with the event. When you have identified the most accurate and relevant theme for this child, all their behaviors and symptoms will fit and fall within that theme.
3. Determine the sense-making child has made of the event, using method(s) from template(s).
4. Identify the Faulty Belief System of the child (how the child has included themselves in the progression or outcomes of events), and deconstruct and reconstruct belief system using undisputable logic (using methods from templates).
5. Gather all the intricate details (bit by bit) detail by detail, step by step—leaving nothing out of the event itself. Caregiver assists clinician in the gathering of the details, but this session is child-led (not clinician- or caregiver-led).
6. Ensure the details and the ordering make sense, address FBS along the way—correct and normalize along the way as you see fit.

Upon the completion of Steps 2–6, behaviors and symptoms should be reduced by a significant degree.

Directed Sand Trays should contain 15% emotions/support/normalizing by clinician and 85% directedness by clinician. As you move towards the Traumatic Event Directed Sand Tray, clinician should be exercising 95% directedness in the telling of the story with the child.

Children's Trauma Themes

These are some common traumas for children and common themes (but not inclusive) that can emerge from caregivers' reports, sand trays, and diagrams when these traumatic events have occurred. When you are listening to the caregiver or child and/or watching the child, keep your eyes and ears open for words or feelings that are hinting or leading towards these yet to be identified themes: the themes (not the events) will likely lead you to the dilemma of the child that needs to be resolved if treatment is to be considered complete/resolved.

TABLE 6.6 List of Traumatic Events, Possible Themes, and Potential Dilemmas

Traumatic Event	*Theme*	*Dilemma*
Physical Abandonment	Loss	I want to be loyal to my mother/father regardless of what he/she did, but how can I? **Treatment:** How can the child take some form of action to demonstrate loyalty? List positive aspects of caregiver prior to getting into retelling details of the traumatic event . . . letter writing and discuss options for letter. Unknown whereabouts of caregiver . . . message in a bottle . . . higher spirit world takes over and delivers?
Physical Abandonment	Loss	I know what my mother/father did, but are they OK? He/she must be missing me. Why haven't they contacted me? **Treatment:** clarify access issues legally and in writing and share with child the outcome/choices of the caregiver after listing loving, positive aspects of the caregiver. Then affirm needs and thoughts of child. I feel mad/sad at/with my caregiver . . . but I really need to love them and see them as good and not bad. **Treatment:** Make a list of caregiver's positive and loving qualities. Diagram a woman . . . fact: almost all women can have children . . . one woman who has a child is a loving, giving mother; the other is not. Just because most women have children does not mean they are able to be good, loving mothers. Sperm and egg analogy . . . same process . . . for father figures who do not follow through. Most important that a child has one loving and nurturing caregiver . . . does not need to be one's Mom or Dad if not there.
Real or Perceived Threat to Caregiver's Life	Fear of Loss	I know that adults keep saying it will not happen again, but what I feel I know is that it will happen again, it is just a matter of when, and I must be ready for it when it does happen again, so I won't be surprised, and I will be ready. **Treatment:** demonstrate logically and visually what is different now with the caregiver, then at the time of the trauma, and prove to the child through examples that the caregiver is the one who is always going to be looking out for and protecting the child. This may not be 100% true; in fact, the child cannot imagine that which has not yet occurred (nor can we protect the child from future trauma; therefore, we must help rebuild a formula in their mind that they can have some faith in and move on). As such, the caregiver's ability to protect is the best chance to move the child through the trauma, and the dilemma.

Identified Traumatic Event: Witness to Domestic Violence
Traumatic Theme: Not Important (Insignificant)

Case History

Hannah—10 Years Old

Hannah had seen her Dad hit her Mom numerous times. Hannah would ask her Dad, beg her Dad, not to hit her Mom. Her Dad would tell her that he would stop but would never keep his word to her for longer than a day. Hannah's Dad has moved out of the house. Hannah has seen her Dad once a week over the past month, and he has called almost every night to talk to her.

Hannah's presenting behaviors are: fighting with other students, defiance, and not eating.

Supportive grandparents and Mom.

Hannah's Negative Self-Belief System

If I ask and beg my Dad to stop yelling and hitting my Mom and he always ends up hitting her anyway, then that must mean I am not important enough to my Dad to make him stop hurting my Mom.

Theme: Not Important

Corrected NSBS: Even though my Dad could not stop hurting my Mom and the police told him he had to move out of our house, he still makes sure that he sees me every week and calls me every night, and this must mean I really am important to him after all.

Corrected Theme: **Important**

The Whiteboard Option With Older Children

Returning to the example of Jaime, whose case history provided the last Phase C training example, the group suggested ideas as to what this child's dilemma might be.

At this point, we can hypothesize about the theme, the belief system at work, the dilemma and its impact.

Jaime was then asked to make a list of positives and negatives about Mom. He was left alone to do this because his initial response was "I don't know." He knows where we are heading and is resistant. I name the resistence and address his anger at missing sessions and interrupting the momentum due to family cancellations.

The child makes a list. We view it and ask him to read it.

Question to the child: How did they cope with these dualities? It must have been hard work . . . He says: "I don't know." He is getting even more angry. I address the difficulty of the child knowing where we are heading and how hard this is for him to go through the middle of it. But he agrees to trust me, and I give him all sorts of encouragement and praise at this point, because I can intuit his fear.

Sentence completion exercise: Review sentences . . . incomplete. Review sentences, complete.
People pleasing theme confirmed: Scaling question: 9/10.

Jaime says that he sometimes hides in the basement when guests are there to avoid going upstairs and feeling like he must please them.

The treatment issue is clear: the commitment to treatment is clear from the child. I assure him we can help make this feel better and much less exhausting for him. I give lots of encouragement.

Treatment options:

- Sand Tray Stories (ideas for resolving/reworking traumatic events related to caregiver abandonment, neglect, abuse history, alcohol addiction).
- PAST, PRESENT, FUTURE Diagram—Charting.
- What does a people-pleaser look like—very specifically, day to day?
- This is how I feel letter, hello/goodbye letter.
- Anger release program, otherwise known as the Emotional Regulation Program (ERP) (admits getting angry too quickly).
- Tell the sand story of what kind of life the child wished for with her family (unmet dreams). Or have the child tell this story.
- Tell the "what may happen in the future" sand story. Or have the child tell this story. How do we decide if we or the child should tell the story?
- Which sand stories might we want to choose to complete for this child? Why?
- You then tell the next story, or the child tells it.
- If you have been the one to tell the story (make sure the child can tell the story back to you), then what do we need to do next? . . . Why?
- How do we use the whiteboard after the sand trays have been completed? As a way for the child to say back to you what they/you have been creating or re-creating in the sand tray.
- Will we decide upon a goodbye letter written to her mother and father via the computer? Directed by clinician. (Aunt completed this . . . we could read that letter to the child).
- List of possible sand trays to complete . . . some if not all.

Clinicians prepare to do the following:

- Rework details of story to include what should have happened for the safety and love of the children by the parents. Or have child tell this story. Normalize child's ideas and/or correct them.
- Tell the story that depicts child's emotions that she must have been having through all of this fear/anxiety/survival show every day. Look for child to add to this story.
- Tell the story of how the child coped behaviorally with this life. How they managed to get through it—behavior-wise—day . . . how they acted to keep the stress and chance of violence/abuse down. Or have the child tell the story, and you correct or adjust it along the way.
- Tell the good story of the days that were not bad. This child feels the need to say it was *all* bad (especially for Aunt and Uncle's sake). Welcome the good with the bad. Or see if the child can tell this story.
- Tell the "There are days when I miss my Mom and Dad" story. Or have the child tell this story.

Which Story Should I Start With? How Do We Decide?

Factors to Consider: Clinician's Brainstorm List

What stories do I absolutely need? Do I have all trauma details I need? Has the belief system of the child identified in Phase B been confirmed or denied? At what age would regressive work likely begin with this child? Are the caregivers in a position of readiness? Does the child have a strong enough foundation to enter the traumatic details now with, or do we need to create that foundation first (i.e. Regressive Re-enactment)? Does the order not matter with this child? If so, which one do I prefer?

FIGURE 6.1 Thoughts, Feelings, and Actions of Child Witness/Victim of Family Child/ Adolescent Completion

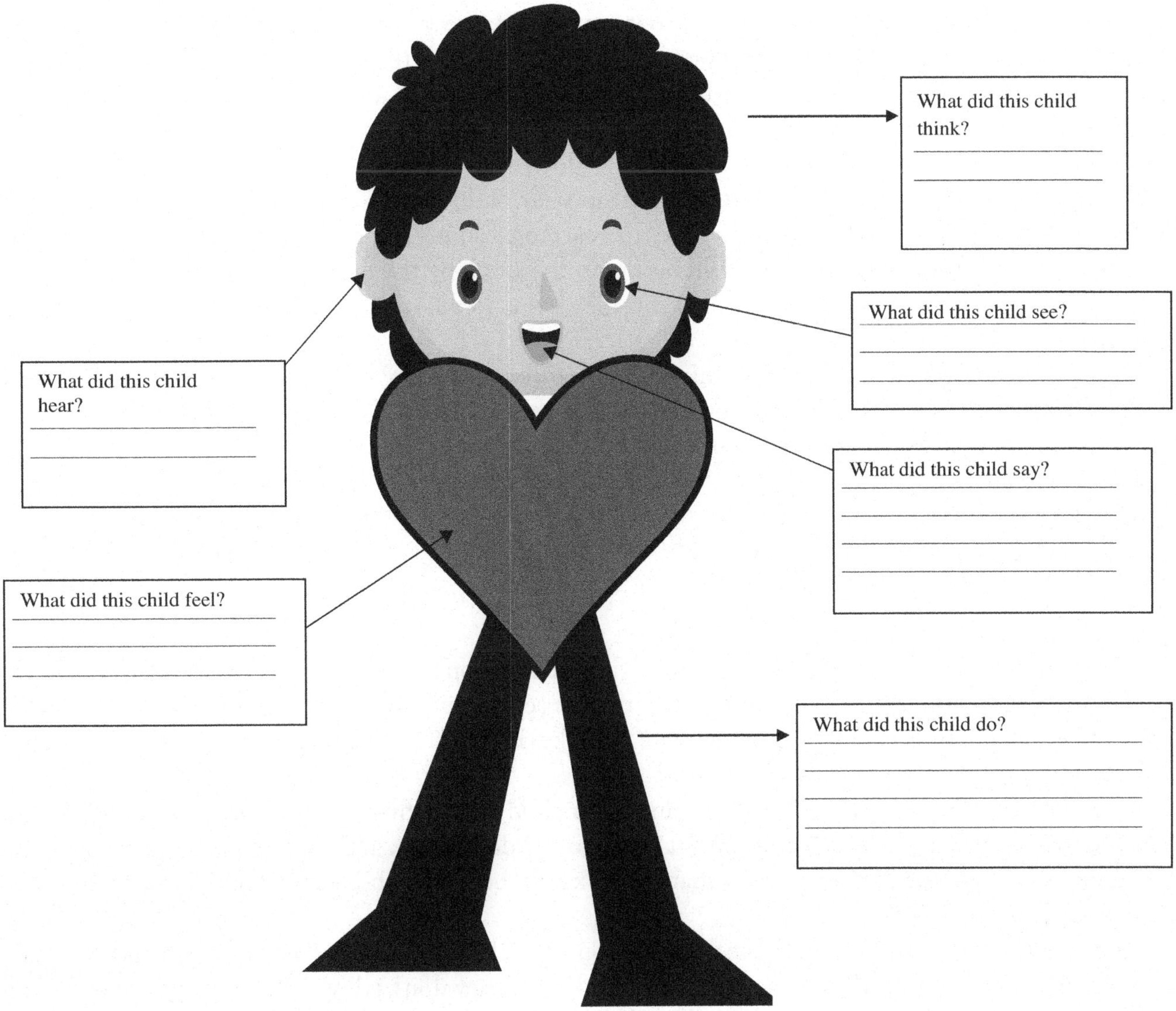

The Behavioral Choice Program—the language of choice

- The *language* of choice really matters. You are trying to convince your children that *they* have a choice, and that it's of no consequence to *you* which they pick.
- Choice is neither *good* nor *bad*. The language of choice says, "Either choice you make is OK."
- "Tomorrow is a brand-new day." The choices a child makes are for *today*; they can make other ones tomorrow.
- It is important for the caregiver *not* to react to the child's choice with suggestions or comments. The child needs to believe that their choice is really *their* choice.
- Just before the time you have decided upon, you say, "The choice program is about to begin!" At the right time, you say, "The choice program has begun."
- If your child says, "I'm not doing it!" Your response will be, "That is your choice. *You* get to make that choice."
- The caregiver must not indulge in hints, prompting, or giving clues about the time or the choice.

How the Behavioral Choice Program Works

You will have already listed the behaviors that you would like your child to increase and/or decrease and have ranked them in order of importance. The next step is to pick a behavior to change that is manageable. This would be a behavior that is not an issue of high importance, and has an extra high chance for success. This is important because you want the child to see that it is possible for them to make their own choices, and that their choice determines what happens next. You don't want to pick something too hard and inadvertently set up your child to fail. You must be extremely specific about what you want done. You may need to rearrange some things to make this doable for the child. Example: "Your coat needs to be hung up on the hook by the door when you come home from school." If you have more than one child, you may want to color-code the hooks so that each child has their own hanger.

After you have picked out what you think are the three most important things to your child in their daily life, you will need two envelopes to put in an easily accessible place such as on the fridge door. One envelope will have a checkmark on the front and the other will have an X.

For example:

1. Nintendo: least important
2. T.V. time: second least important
3. Telephone: most important

You rank them in order of importance, and write each one on a separate index card that will fit in the envelopes. The program is divided into three, 5-minute segments (total of 15 minutes). For younger children who can't tell time, it is important to have a clock with the 5-minute segments marked in different colors.

After you say "the choice program has begun," your child has the first 5 minutes to *choose* to do the task and *keep* all three things on the cards, or to choose to *not* do the task and *lose* the least important of the three items or activities. If they tell you that the task is done before the end of the first 5 minutes, they have chosen to keep all three.

At this point you can say, "That's great—I see you have chosen to keep all three things and you know how to choose to keep the things you enjoy in your day." If they don't tell you the task is done before the completion of the 5 minutes, you can say, "That's OK. I know that you made the choice that was best for you at the time. You have two other times that you can choose to lose or keep. Either choice is OK." If they have not told you that the task is done in the next 5 minutes, they have chosen to lose the second most important thing or activity.

If they choose to lose all three, then you can say, "Tomorrow is another day. You have new choices tomorrow. Whatever choice is best for you is the one you should pick."

> *Remember that it is extremely important for you, the caregiver, not to show in any way that you have an opinion about the rightness or wrongness of the child's choice. The child needs to experience the results of their choice for themselves. It need to* truly *be their choice, without influence from you.*

The behaviors and choices should only be used at the agreed-upon times in the context of the Behavioral Choice Program. Other behaviors should be dealt with as you would normally. You will need to chart the progress of your child in the program. When he/she has been able to go for 14 days without choosing to lose anything, it will be time to add on the next behavior.

The Behavioral Choice Program checklist:

- Anger/release (punching bag or something similar).
- Mark-able clock.
- Two envelopes per child: one marked with a checkmark and one with an X.
- Three cards per child: the caregiver and clinician decide together what is marked on these.
- The caregiver's trust in and hope for the program's positive results for themselves and their child.

Specific behaviors list:

- I would like my child to increase: list 15 as you think of them.
- I would like my child to reduce: list 15 as you think of them.

Behavioral goals list:

- Make bed.
- Up for school on time.
- Stop swearing.
- Stop hitting.

TABLE 6.7 Behavior Choice Program Chart (Agreed on With the Child/Teenager)

Behavior	*Time*	*Choice*	*Activity (least to most important)*	*Outcome*	*Length*	*Next Step*
1. Make bed	8 a.m.	Yes	3. Phone 2. TV 1. Computer	Keep Keep Keep	2 weeks	Add on behavior goal 2.
2. Up for school on own	7:30 a.m. 7:40 a.m. 7:50 a.m.	No No Yes	3. Phone 2. TV 1. Computer	Lose Lose Keep	1 week	Stay on behavioral goal #2 until child has chosen not to lose any activities for 2 weeks.

Examples: An Adolescent's PAST, PRESENT, and FUTURE Diagram; First Week of Charting

FIGURE 6.2 Adolescent Example of PAST Trauma #1 Diagram

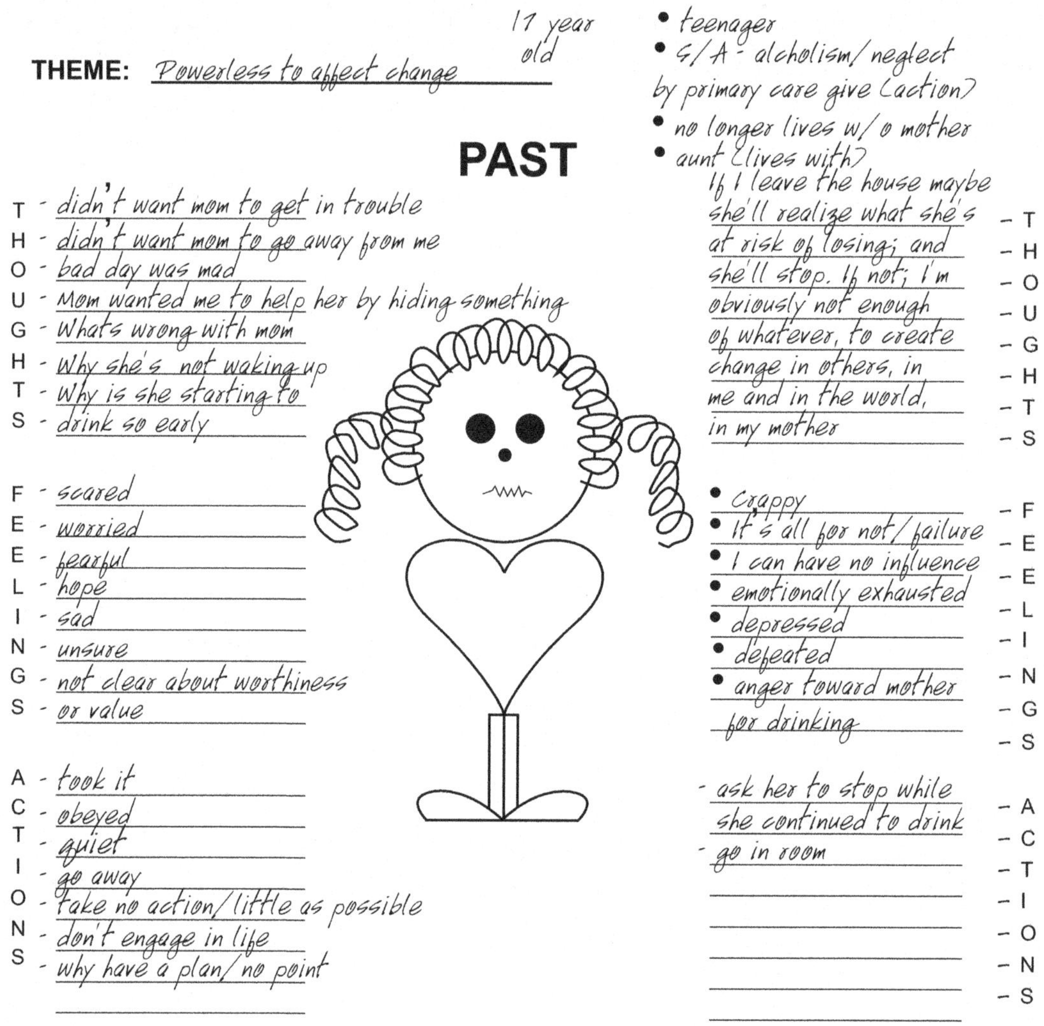

	MON	TUES	WED	THURS	FRI	SAT	SUN	
PAST	I	I			II	II	I	
PRESENT		I				II	II	
FUTURE					III		I	

FIGURE 6.3 Adolescent Example of PAST Trauma #2 Diagram

THEME: *Powerless*

PAST

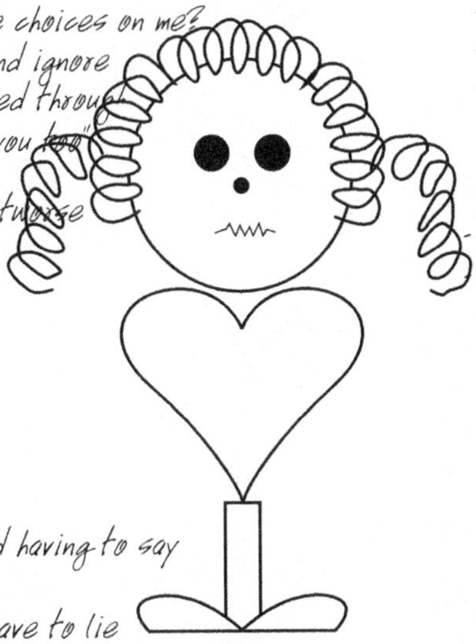

THOUGHTS (left):

- (why is she doing this?)
- what is she going to do next? when will it happen?
- If she's working - how come she's always on the computer?
- Why does she want to talk to me all the time?
- What is she up to if she's spending all her time waiting for me to get on the comp?
- Saying "I love you" changes what choices she's made in her life and the effect of those choices on me?
- Am I supposed to violate and ignore how I feel and what I've lived through
- Saying back to her "I love you too"
- How can you embarrass me like this? You are making it worse

FEELINGS (left):

- Frustrated
- Angry
- Confused
- Anxious
- Worried

ACTIONS (left):

- Avoid her in order to avoid having to say something
- Don't want to feel like I have to lie to myself or to her.
- Refuse to minimize it to myself
- Create an excuse to leave

THOUGHTS (right):

#2

- How dare she?
- Trying to figure out why she's doing it.

FEELINGS (right):

- Infuriated
- Overwhelmed

ACTIONS (right):

- Blocked

	MON	TUES	WED	THURS	FRI	SAT	SUN	
PAST	II	III		III	III			
PRESENT	~~IIII~~	I		II	I			
FUTURE	IIII	II	III		II			

FIGURE 6.4 Adolescent Example of PRESENT Trauma Diagram

THEME: ____________________

PRESENT

T – When my mom afront on line or in person
H – I tell her to stop I will approach her when I'm
O – ready.
U – I won't say "I love you"
G – if I dont mean it
H – I'm not emborrassed
T – for who I am because
S – I'm not you

F – Relieved
E – Unburdened – not worried
E – about her life but my own
L – happy
I – I feel a sense of closure
N – and resolution about my former feelings
G – at peace
S –

A – I say no to her face
C – I don't allow her to walk
T – all over me.
I – letting her know it doesn't
O – draw boundaries for mothers behaviour
N – ask her to leave
S – refuse to minimize

–She did that – T
to herself, its not – H
my responsibility to – O
fix her problems – U
– it turns out my mom – G
was unfit to mother. – H
–too bad for her – T
that she lost me. – S

– Powerful – F
– Content – E
– In control – E
– L
– I
– N
– G
– S

– Communicate to – A
bosses and power – C
people effectively – T
– not intimidated – I
– O
– N
– S

	MON	TUES	WED	THURS	FRI	SAT	SUN	
PAST	I	II	I	I		I		
PRESENT	𝍸	II		I	II			
FUTURE		IIII	𝍸	III	𝍸	III		

FIGURE 6.5 Adolescent Example of FUTURE Trauma Diagram

THEME: *NOT GETTING INTO POWERLESS SITUATION FROM THE BEGINNING*

FUTURE

– *Ultimately*

T – *I'll allow a new beginning*
H – *with mother on my terms only.*
O –
U – *My mom's only escape*
G – *was alcohol – thats not*
H – *for me*
T – *Proud that I have*
S – *a career.*

I know bull when I see it

– I know the boss – T
cant push me around – H
because he needs me – O
– U
I'm not afraid to – G
say how I feel to – H
boyfriend etc. – T
– my boyfriend respects – S
my boundaries whatever
they are

F – *JOB*
E – *appreciated*
E – *proud of career*
L – *confidence*
I – *content*
N – *needed*
G – *relieved*
S –

– F
– E
– wise – E
– L
– enlightened – I
– N
– G
– S

A – *RELATIONSHIPS*
C –
T – *talk about concerns*
I – *and feeling at beginning*
O –
N – *I don't stifle my feelings;*
S – *express them effectively*

I leave before or – A
whenever the bullshit – C
starts – T
– I
– O
– N
– S

	MON	TUES	WED	THURS	FRI	SAT	SUN	
PAST								
PRESENT								
FUTURE								

Conclusion

This chapter emphasizes my view that therapeutic commitment to beginning treatment with the child alone needs to be reconsidered, especially when the child or teen is living with their parent(s) or another adult caregiver. The person with whom the child most needs to have a trusting and openly communicative relationship is the parent or caregiver. In most situations, we would be hard-pressed to find parents who did not want their children to communicate whatever is going on their lives with them. Children and youth—and even adult offspring—generally find comfort, and even take pride in, acknowledging a respectful dialogue with their parents/caregivers: open communication is one of the hallmark signs of positive relations between parents and their children (of all ages). If such communication—and consequently such a quality of relationship—is not happening between parent and child, isn't this exactly what one of the primary goals of any treatment should be?

The leading assumption of the Intergenerational Trauma Treatment Model is that parental response patterns can be intercepted when the parent receives treatment for unresolved childhood trauma prior to commencing treatment with the child. It is entirely possible that the "child alone" practice began because clinical training for intense parent-child work (outside of attachment therapy) isn't generally a component of post-graduate psychology and social work programs (in large part because there are so few models available with which to train students). Most psychology or social work students never learn the rationale or process—the neuroscientific basis—and what treatment would look like *in practice* with both parent and child/youth in the room.

Again, for the most part, with some modifications to account for age and developmental stage, the therapeutic practices designed for individual adults (and couples) are applied to children and teenagers *as a group*. Or, perhaps to acknowledge that teens are in the sensitive period of individuating from their parents, seeing them alone to communicate with someone other than their parents (or if the teen is living outside the family home) was held to reinforce the value of providing them with at least one adult ready to listen. In my view, even teenagers do not benefit from having their primary relationship be with their therapist. If a child does not have any adult in their life, then the treatment goal could reasonably be to set about establishing a primary relationship with someone in the child's life—not the therapist. Over twenty-some years of practice, I've never encountered a teenager who refused or contested the inclusion of parents in their treatment, whether the identified treatment issue is related to the parent(s), especially when the difference in their own short- and long-term outcomes are clearly and confidently explained. I believe this is because all teenagers long for and would prefer a positive, healthy, and healed relationship with their caregiver. I may negotiate with the teenager to see them alone once or twice to solidify the strength and connection of our therapeutic relationship, but only once the teenager understands and agrees that the parent *will* be brought in for most treatment sessions. The parent is involved from the start in each session with the child when the child is between the ages of 3–14 years. In the ITTM process, the parent will have already received treatment—that the child has observed and experienced—prior to the child even being seen, so they have already developed some measure of hopefulness about the parent's capacity to continue with positive change. The importance of paying close attention to the mediating effects of caregiver mental health issues has been thoroughly considered in earlier chapters, and is supported by recent research, as noted (McCormack & Thomson, 2017; McCarty & McMahon, 2003; Baker-Ericzen et al., 2010, p. 401).

At base, the ITTM contends that the child/teen does not need to form a relationship with the therapist nearly as much as they need to experience their parent or caregiver undergo healing from their own issues (guided by the therapist in the room) and consequently be positioned as the most important "healer" for the child. The model was specifically created to offer clinicians in complex Trauma II treatment a method that addresses how negative impact can be resolved at its core in adults, caregivers, and children. It is also intended to assess, indicate effective treatment, and help to resolve the Primary Negative Belief System that is the core of parent/caregiver and child relationships. Given that the individual's core belief systems—usually formulated in childhood—inform and shape the thoughts, behaviors, and symptoms of all individuals at all ages and stages, this is a fundamental therapeutic objective.

References

Baker-Ericzen, H. M.-F., et al. (2010). Comparing child, parent, and family characteristics in usual care and empirically supported treatment research samples for children with disruptive behaviors. *Journal of Emotional and Behavioral Disorders* 18:2, pp. 82–99.

McCarty, C. & McMahon, R. J. (2003). Mediators of the relation between maternal depressive symptoms and child internalizing and disruptive behaviors disorders. *Journal of Family Psychology* 17:4, pp. 545–556.

McCormack, L. & Thomson, S. (2017). Complex trauma in childhood, a psychiatric diagnosis in adulthood: Making meaning of a double-edged phenomenon. *Psychological Trauma: Theory, Research, Practice, and Policy* 9:2, pp. 156–165.

Appendix 6.1

Adult Therapeutic Letter

Dear Mom,

There are some things I need to say.

It's hard for me to start because all of the things I want to say just swirl around and around in my mind.

What keeps poking out, though, is what happens next?

What are you going to do?

What are you going to do to make this better?

You're the Mom. You're supposed to protect all of your children. You're supposed to be hardwired to protect all of us.

As mother hen, all of us should be welcomed under your wing. Yet, the majority of us are left out in a storm, a storm we did not create.

And then I think, you just aren't capable—you're not capable of anything different.

You are your mother's daughter—fueled by anger, resentment and a burden too huge to shake, a burden whose power trumps all.

I am living in a tornado, and the bigger and more destructive that tornado becomes, the bigger and more destructive that tornado becomes!

This is your tornado. Yet you've taken shelter behind a curtain of ignorance, and behind it you're protecting Julie.

If this tornado kills her, I don't care, not right now, I don't. But I want it to hurt you. I don't want it to kill you because that would be too easy.

I enjoy hearing feedback that you're not doing well.

"Good," I think. You deserve this.

You've always turned your back.

You turn your back on so many responsibilities. You want to be the Mom when it's easy, when it means you get to spend happy time with my family and me. But you don't want to be the Mom when it's hard.

Because you can't?

As part of Mya's Beyond Borders program last semester, she had to write a letter to someone who inspires her, who empowers her. She wrote that letter to me. And in that letter she highlighted all the ways I make her a better, stronger person.

And in that letter, I did not recognize you or your relationship with me.

Your "empowering"—it you want to call it that—was to not make me strong for the sake of feeling strong, but to feel strong because you were weak. I had to be strong. I had no choice.

In a situation of survival, if there are two people and one is not strong, the other one, by default, has to be.

I carried you. I have carried you and carried this mother/daughter relationship. I have made this happen, this relationship of ours.

Your emotional selfishness made me do it.

If I wanted a relationship with you, I had to make it happen.

I supported you when you were sick. I believed you. I always believed you. I had to. You were weak . . . the weakest. If I didn't believe you, then what? Would you, could you have gotten weaker? Would you have died? You sure tried.

You put all of your weakness on us. We were made to be the strong ones. Your kids, the strong ones. And now, as adult kids, you're weak still . . . or again. And we just have to let you be weak because poor old Heather can't. She just can't. This is your shit.

Not mine. Yet I am in it.

Where do we go from here?

Right now, I don't want to go anywhere from here.

I want to see you suffer. I want to know you miss me, you miss Mya and Emm. I want you to know you're fucking all of this up.

Your weakness is fucking all of this up.

Your weakness makes Julie stronger (but in the wrong way), and makes Dad build stronger walls.

Your weakness now, however, can either make me weak or make me not care. I don't see it making me stronger. I got nothing to give you. No more free passes, no more forgiveness. No more compassion because to have compassion for you means I have to honor you. I don't.

When friends talk about their mothers now I cannot relate. I can't even contribute. You embarrass me. I am ashamed of you.

Mark tried to reach out to you, to make amends—I haven't a clue where he gets his patience and compassion—and you told him to never call you again. And that there is no "I" only "we"—you three.

Holy. Shit.

If I was thinking of having a relationship with you again, that thought was immediately snuffed out.

I know this all makes me sad, but I'm so angry right now that I don't have time for sadness.

Maybe it's easier to be angry. You're angry. Am I weak if I remain angry? Or does it just make me indifferent?

What happens if I allow myself to be sad? What happens if I allow myself to go there?

There is sadness, but I keep pushing it out of the way and the big monster truck of anger drives me through my days.

Why am I sad? I know why I am sad, but *why* am I sad??

I'm sad because I'm not important enough. Mya isn't special enough. Emmitt isn't special enough.

None of us deserve your time.

I'm sad because I know I can't even talk to you—you'll throw up anger and your anger always wins. Always. Slicing through me in one blow.

I'm trying to remember when times were good. What were my milestones in life?

My first marriage? You were angry.

My marriage to Owen? You were frail, and too proud. Boastful.

The birth of Mya? I don't remember.

The birth of Emmitt? You were afraid and needy.

I do remember coming home from school, sitting at the island, watching you make dinner, eating a sleeve of Premium Plus and butter.

That's how I remember us.

I remember getting dressed for my high school graduation and you told me I was beautiful. But it made me feel uncomfortable. I felt bad for being beautiful because you thought you weren't.

I remember giving you a Mother's Day card years ago as a young adult. It was filled with all the reason you were a good Mom, but it was hard to write because it wasn't written with true intentions. It was written to make you feel better about yourself. Like I was *your* mother.

That's it!

You were/are only my mother because you gave birth to me. Not because you empowered me or inspired me. Not because you instilled confidence in me, but because I had no choice.

What do you think in your quiet moments?

Do you miss me?

Do you allow yourself to miss me?

Do you know why I said my relationship with you is over? Because for me to maintain that, I have to remain angry at you.

If I don't maintain my anger then all I have left is sadness and disappointment and a void—a void that now has a name, that's now recognized for what it is—I don't have a mother. I don't know if I ever did.

But we pretended. You were all I had.

And now I don't even have that. I don't have anywhere to play my fix-it mothering skills because they don't work anymore.

You don't need me. You don't want me.

Never mind that I need you.

You don't need me.

All of your failures, insecurities, and inadequacies are being replaced by and compensated for now. You feel like a mother now. You're now responsible for Julie and her happiness, not her recovery, and it's 43 years too late. You're not responsible for her recovery because that's too hard and you're not prepared to remove that curtain of ignorance and face the demons. And by default, you're now responsible for Izaiah. So all of the love and caring and compassion a grandmother is supposed to give all of her grandchildren, you are giving it all to Izaiah.

Conclusion: Re-Circuiting Trauma Pathways

> I hate it. I have a hard time thinking about things. They make me feel all mixed up and sad. After I'm done though I feel so much better. It really does help. Talking about the accident was the best part for me. It made me feel so awful but I needed to talk about it. . . . I'm more in control. That's a good thing. I'm maturing and need to make good choices.[1]

These are 10-year-old Ned's reflections on the ITTM treatment as he experienced it. By the time he entered the program with his mother, they had already seen a number of mental health professionals and had unsuccessfully tried various therapies and medications to address his behavioral symptoms, which included attention deficit, lashing out in anger, and most notably, regression. During his regressive episodes, he declared that he was 3 years old, spoke "baby talk" in a "baby voice," crawled on the floor, and wanted to drink from a baby bottle. Ned's most significant trauma impact occurred at the age of 15 months: his actual memories of the event are nebulous due to his age and the trauma circumstances. After a Christmas visit to his grandparents, the family was involved in a serious car accident that killed his twin brother, sparing him, his older siblings, and their mother, who was at the wheel. Ned's father, intermittently hospitalized for bipolar disorder, left the family shortly afterwards; he was abusive on his visits with his three young children. Thus, in the first five years of his life, Ned had experienced a traumatic event (the accident) that brought about a traumatic loss (his twin brother); he was further affected by his father's sudden unexplained absences (his hospitalization), the breakdown of his family (divorce), maltreatment, and witnessing maltreatment (by his father). He was desperately attached to his mother and her every brief absence terrified him.

Not at all surprisingly, on entering ITTM treatment, his Ned's mother described herself as "exhausted, overwhelmed, out of my league and terrified." We will return to her story later; at this moment, the words of a traumatized "in treatment" 10-year-old boy capture the essential ambivalence about therapy common to all participants, of all ages. Yet what matters here is that, while "hating it," Ned was still keenly aware that he "felt so much better" after a session, and that his participation in treatment "really does help." It would be challenging to find a more honest, direct, and incisive assessment of the therapeutic process and self-progress within it than through the eyes of a child in the midst of treatment.

This book is an introduction to the ITTM's principal objectives, operations, and desired outcomes. It is a concise explanation of the method that I developed, over years of personal research and clinical practice, to contend with complex trauma and its intergenerational manifestations for readers drawn largely from the ranks of mental health and child welfare professionals (in various disciplines) or students working toward those ends. I argue, and reiterate here, that the long-standing therapeutic commitment to commence treatment with the child—alone and on their own—needs serious re-evaluation. The primary caregiver (most often but not necessarily the mother) is obviously the person with whom the child most needs to have a secure, trusting, open, and supportive relationship. In most situations, caregivers want their children to disclose to them whatever is going on in their lives, especially concerning traumatic events. In many such cases, however, the child/adolescent finds themself unable to articulate "the problem." They will disclose the traumatic impact to their self-belief system by "acting out" symptoms and behaviors that cannot be ignored due to their disruptive and harmful, or at least risky, nature. Preempting or interrupting this negative mode of disclosure by recircuiting the brain—reconstructing negative self-beliefs to a healthier form—is an enormous challenge for the child, caregivers, clinicians, and all others affected. But there can be no disagreement that it is one worth taking up. Unresolved trauma impact is not simply an individual issue, even though individual costs are high, and potentially fatal. It affects all relations and interactions at all times, damaging their positive potential, with further damage to the traumatized individual. Its unrelenting grip is transmitted generationally, to affect even those yet unborn well into the future. The individual, familial, and social costs—in every sense—are incalculable (Van der Kolk, 2014; Vachon et al., 2015; Maté, 2003).

As I have noted, the present situation of Indigenous communities in Canada, due to the traumatic intergenerational legacy of over 100 years of abusive residential school experiences, constitutes the most persistent and encompassing state of complex trauma impact in North America. It is critical that any treatment implemented with Indigenous children and their caregivers is, above all else, responsive to their exclusive needs. Because of the origins of the physical and mental trauma that characterized their childhood, they suffered an identity loss that has fractured, if not outright destroyed, their cultural security and compromised their cultural safety. Thomson (2005) provides a useful definition of cultural security as "a commitment to the principle that the construct and provision of services offered by the health system (or child welfare system) will not compromise the legitimate cultural rights, values or expectations of Aboriginal people" (Thomson, 2005; cited in Carriere, 2008, p. 72). Cultural safety is accomplished by designing child welfare policies and procedures "that will not stray from the critical importance of culture as a determinant of resilience for Indigenous children" (Thomson, 2005; cited in Carriere, 2008, p. 72).

The ITTM's flexibility and adaptability make it an especially useful therapeutic method in situations such as this. Group discussion (in the Trauma Information Sessions) lends itself to the circle structure that, along with story-telling and picture-making, are significant cultural practices in many Indigenous communities. Elders are respected and valued community members: they are, in effect, caregivers to all and not simply to those with biological or legal ties. They are vital sources of cultural knowledge as well as guidance and comfort, and must be included in treatment. Mothers are considered particularly important in the shaping of children's resilience, a core belief that the ITTM also underscores by centering caregiver involvement (Carriere, 2008, p. 76; Blackstock, 2005; Anderson & Lavell-Harvard, 2014).

Indigenous clinicians trained in the ITTM are ideally positioned to provide culturally appropriate and culturally secure treatment. Adrian Jacob, currently Keeper of the Circle for Sandy-Saulteaux Spiritual Centre (Manitoba, Canada), undertook the ITTM 30-hour training course to assist in his community liaison work with the Mobile Diabetes Screening Initiative in Alberta. Type 2 Diabetes is endemic among Indigenous peoples in Canada. Chronic unrelieved stress is an important determinant of diabetes, alongside other chronic stressors such as poverty and childhood trauma. Consequently, as he explains it, "The idea of treating the caregiver before treating children in crisis made sense to our work," especially in view of the continual uncovering of intergenerational trauma among residential school survivors, a high proportion of whom are located in the western provinces. As his own words indicate:

> I have sought to find ways to incorporate both the clinical training I've received in my own work and to bring this training to other Indigenous leaders. Adaptations of the ITTM to the Indigenous community will be key to addressing in a deep way the underlying causes of many chronic problems.[2]

The Intergenerational Trauma Treatment Model's leading assumption is that caregiver response patterns can be intercepted when the caregiver receives treatment for unresolved childhood trauma *prior* to commencing treatment with the child. It is entirely possible that the "child alone" practice began because clinical training for intense parent-child work (outside of attachment therapy) isn't generally a component of post-graduate psychology and social work programs: there are few models available with which to actually train students. Most psychology or social work students never learn the rationale or process, the neuroscientific basis, and how treatment would unfold in practice with both caregiver (and/or elder) and child/youth in the room. Treating caregivers first gives them the (likely rare) opportunity to resolve the lifelong repercussions of their own childhood trauma. Furthermore, and perhaps for the first time, their own treatment—and their continued and consistent involvement in their child's treatment—encourage their hope and motivation for their child's recovery and their important role in it. This rising hope and motivation in turn improve the likelihood that they will see the program through to its successful end, and that they will apply what they have learned in the home. Obviously, this can only improve the child's outlook and healing prospects.

In my view, neither children nor teenagers benefit from having their primary relationship with their therapist. If a child does not have any supportive adult in their life, the treatment goal could reasonably be to set about establishing a primary relationship with someone already in the child's life, such as an elder or other concerned adult—not the therapist. Over twenty-some years of practice, I've never encountered a teenager who refused or contested the inclusion of caregivers in their treatment, whether or not the identified treatment issue is related to the caregiver(s). I may negotiate with the teenager to see them alone once or twice, but only if the teenager understands and agrees that the caregiver will be brought in for most treatment sessions. The caregiver is involved from the start in each session with the child when the child is between the ages of 3–14 years. As such the caregiver is positioned to be the child's focal "healer." The importance of paying close attention to the mediating effects of caregiver mental health issues has been thoroughly considered in earlier chapters, and, also as noted, is validated by current research.

The ITTM was specifically created to offer clinicians in Complex Trauma II treatment a method that addresses negative impact at its core. Its various components assess, indicate the form and structure of effective treatment, and work to resolve the Primary Negative Belief System that grounds unhealthy caregiver-child relationships. Having located the source and nature of the most impactful trauma effect(s), the clinician applies ITTM methods, derived from logic and mathematics, to systematically deconstruct and reconstruct the primary negative self-belief system in both caregiver and child. Charting and diagrams are central to this process. Under clinician direction, clients (adults and children) create and update these as "homework." The results constitute tangible evidence of progress in a manner that even young children can appreciate. Given that the individual's core belief systems are formulated in childhood and thereafter inform and shape the thoughts, feelings, and actions of all individuals at all ages and stages throughout the life course, this is the fundamental therapeutic objective.

The practices that I have detailed, with illustrations, in Part 2 of this book take the reader methodically through each of Phase A, B, and C. These outlines of practices *in no way substitute* for the detailed instructions provided in the ITTM training manual, which are delivered by trained ITTM clinicians. Nonetheless, singly and together, the three chapters focus on a number of points that clinicians should emphasize with clients as they embark on this program. I will conclude by reiterating these.

To begin, the brain is physiologically and neurologically structured *from birth* to engage in a process of selection and assimilation that ensures an individual's capacity for generating belief systems. Infants and children are 100% dependent on their primary caregiver(s) for survival, and the caregiver's behavior constitutes the child's only known world. In the first four years of life, children define the primary caregiver and themselves to be "as one and the same" to meet the child's innate survival needs. When these basic human needs are coupled with a child's ongoing brain development as they incrementally build the capacity to reason, their automatic inclusion of the "I" within all caregiver-related conclusions is the only possible result. Put simply, the child's inclusion of the "I" increases their chances for survival.

The caregiver's behavioral responses, then, are the concrete proof required by the brain to generate the premises of logic-based self-conclusions. The brain accepts only evidence-based truths as premises. The rules of the most elementary form of logic presuppose that the premises will combine and result in a logical conclusion. For young children, this evidence is actually the under-developed child-brain's *grasp* of what is happening. Children have no inclination to question negative self-schemata conclusions because they lack the capacity to do so. Their unquestioning internalization of untenable, false, negative self-beliefs has lasting, often lifelong, detrimental effects for self-formation. These negative impacts are reinforced—"proved"—when they, as children and into adulthood, invariably process subsequent trauma as their own "fault" and thus their "deserved consequences."

The most important question comes at the very end: what are the real-life experiences and outcomes for the adults and children who undertake ITTM therapy? Ned's testimony that opens this chapter, as I have observed, is an eloquent example of the child's-eye view. There is clearly no "one experience fits all" category. Although much depends on the caregiver's commitment and cooperation, since most children/teenagers do not initiate treatment on their own, overall findings based on client reports indicate that the ITTM functions as a viable brain-based therapy.

One mother entered ITTM treatment to help her 10-year-old son, Paul. Her son had seen seven different mental health practitioners from the time he was 3, when he had begun expressing the impact of his parents' divorce at that time by acting out. His enraged outbursts increased in magnitude and frequency as he got older. Each of the clinicians had diagnosed ADHD. Then his entire known world—family, home, community, school—was upended. He suddenly had to adjust to a new stepfather and blended family, a new home in a new town, a new school, teacher, and peers. By the time of referral, Paul had already presented symptoms severe enough to be heavily medicated. His medication had triggered a substantial weight gain, further worsening his negative self-beliefs. Attempts to wean him from the drugs precipitated intense outbursts. He was hospitalized. A new psychiatrist prescribed several different medications in a few months, the last of which sent Paul to hospital once again, with life-threatening anaphylactic shock. The psychiatrist then recommended placement in a boys' home. This is a fairly typical case history.

It was at this point that I met with this besieged mother and suggested that she and Paul try the ITTM treatment. Here is how she describes her experience of the opening Trauma Information Sessions' "re-programing" (her term) of her thoughts and feelings about her son's behavior:

> As we began the trauma treatment program, I was learning to replace my "knowledge" of ADHD with knowledge of trauma. I had no realization at first of what was happening to my thinking, but I

> slowly began to "get it." I had to let go of all my thoughts related to my son's behavior, and re-program my thinking. I replaced thoughts like "he's hyper" with thoughts of "he's stressed," [of] "he needs a consequence" with "he needs me," [of] "he needs time-out" with "he needs time-in," [of] "he's driving me crazy" with "I am too stressed right now. I need to calm myself."[3]

Her metacognitive learning process continued through the charting and diagramming exercises. She not only acquired the knowledge, but became increasingly aware of how her own thinking/feeling/acting responses were changing accordingly:

> The information on thoughts, feelings and actions, and examining loops of thinking and interacting, really helped me to understand how to change my reactions to my child's behaviors. To fully appreciate that my thoughts led to my feelings and then actions, and that of course the same was true for my child, was truly enlightening. . . . I was so focused on his behavior . . . in my belief that he had ADHD [and was acting impulsively as a result] . . . that I neglected his thoughts and feelings. . . . When I started replacing my own thoughts, my reactions changed, and the loops between him and myself ended.[4]

By the time that we arrived at the co-creation of a PAST/PRESENT/FUTURE Diagram of her son's thoughts and feelings, she had finally broken through the stasis of her own anxiety and hopelessness:

> It was encouraging to see, in his present, that his thoughts, feelings and actions were getting better. When we were nearing the end of our program, I looked back at this diagram. It was with tremendous joy that I realized that the hopes and goals for my son's future thoughts, feelings and actions had become his new present—what a beautiful gift![5]

Even as their treatment was in process, this mother/client was already feeling a long dormant upsurge of "great hope for his future." Most gratifying from the clinical perspective is how she expressed the outcome of their participation in the ITTM treatment: "Our child is healed. Our step family is healed."

This, too, is a not untypical participant reflection in respect to the ITTM's outcomes when caregiver and child treatment is implemented and carefully directed by trained clinicians. Any step taken toward healing intergenerational trauma and lightening the prospects for hopeful and healthy lives within and across generations is inarguably the only point and purpose of designing and delivering therapeutic models. In re-circuiting trauma pathways, the Intergenerational Trauma Treatment Model is supported by neuroscience, logic, and mathematics as a workable and sustainable means toward that end.

Notes

1. "Ned's" testimony while undergoing ITTM treatment with his mother. Copping, "Our Trauma Treatment," personal file, 2014. Used with permission; names and potentially revealing details have been changed to protect privacy and confidentiality.
2. Adrian Jacob, personal letter to the author, 2016. Jacob (clan name: Ganosono) is a member of the Turtle Clan of the Cayuga Nation of the Six Nations Haudenosaunee Confederacy.
3. Copping, "Our Trauma Treatment," personal file, 2014. Used with permission; names and potentially revealing details have been changed to protect privacy and confidentiality.
4. Ibid.
5. Ibid.

References

Anderson, K. & Lavell-Harvard, D. M. (Eds.). (2014). *Mothers of the Nations: Indigenous Mothering as Global Resistance, Reclaiming and Recovery*. Bradford, ON: Demeter Press.

Blackstock, C. (2005). The occasional evil of angels: Learning from the experiences of Aboriginal peoples and social work. Special edition "World Indigenous Peoples Congress on Education," *Journal of Entrepreneurship, Advancement, Strategy and Education* 1, pp. 1–50.

Carriere, J. (2008). The soul work of adoption and Aboriginal children. *Pimatisiwin: A Journal of Aboriginal and Indigenous Community Health* 6:1, pp. 61–78.

Maté, G. (2003). *When the Body Says No: Understanding the Stress-Disease Connection*. Hoboken, NJ: J. Wiley.

Thomson, N. (2005). Cultural respect and related concepts: A brief summary of the literature. *Australian Indigenous Health Bulletin* 5:4, pp. 1–11.

Vachon, D. D., Krueger, R. F., Rogosch, F. A., & Cicchetti, D. (2015). Assessment of the harmful psychiatric and behavioral effects of different forms of child maltreatment. *JAMA Psychiatry* 72, pp. 1135–1142.

Van der Kolk, B. (2014). *The Body Keeps the Score: Brain, Mind and Body in Healing Trauma*. Oxford, UK: Wiley Publishing.

Index

Note: Page numbers in *italics* indicate figures and page numbers in **bold** indicate tables on the corresponding pages.

access visits **120**
ADHD *see* Attention Deficit Hyperactivity Disorder (ADHD)
adolescents: female delinquents 34; PAST, PRESENT, and FUTURE Diagram *184–187*; psychotherapy for 3; *see also* childhood
adopted children 30
adults: behavior loops 113; therapeutic letter 190–192
alcohol effects 157
American Academy of Child and Adolescent Psychiatry 5
amygdala 27, 30
anger: assessment 134–135; concerns in home **119**; cycle 93; loop 93; release program 134, 158
anticonvulsant phenytoin 35
anxiety 29, 61, **120**
assessment sessions 151
assimilation 51
Attention Deficit Hyperactivity Disorder (ADHD) 33
attunement 123, 158, 159
autonomy 17

basal ganglia 27
behavioral loop 87–89; chart *91*; diagram 87–89, *90–91*; examples *90*, 92
Behavior Choice Program (BCP) 153, 158, 169, 181–183, **183**
Betty's case history 160–163
"big-T trauma" 37
bio-psycho-social factors 115
bipolar disorder (BPD) 34
boundary diagram 159
brain: automatic pattern-seeking process 44; childhood maltreatment 35; development 27; inherent capacity to reason 46–49; plasticity 29; requisites of reason 49–50; sensitivities 28

cardiovascular diseases 28
caregiver-child-clinician relationship 18
caregiver-child/family therapy 61
caregivers 118; abandonment 159; assessment 113; behavior loop 113; "best guess" 149; childhood trauma impact *77*; and child joint sessions 151; child trauma treatment, involvement in 17–18; core treatment 134; as co-therapist 6; depression 61; discord 27; involvement 61; motivation 15; neuroplasticity and 30; orientation to Phase C 149–151; positive and negative aspects list of 159; recollection 150; selection 121; Self-Determination Theory 22; stress levels 17; treatment, drop out of 15
caregivers and children 62–63; advanced CBT diagrammatic structures 68–71; caregiver's unresolved childhood trauma impact 80–89; diagrams *76–77*; implementation 109–110; metacognition, role of 63–65; testimonial from a parent 96–105; therapeutic activities **63**; Trauma Information Sessions (TIS) 65–68; Trauma Information Sessions checklist 73–75; trauma treatment 106–108
caregiver sessions 118; anger assessment 134–135; barriers to treatment and recommendations **119–120**; caregiver-directed "one-on-one" quality time with the child 130–134; case history 135–148; diagram examples *125–129*; reviewing caregiver's Trauma Information Session responses 122–124; Session 1 assessment goals 119–122; task online 124
caregiver's loops, reviewing with caregiver 93
cell membranes *125*
cerebral cortex 27
C-ET *see* Cognitive-Experiential Theory
charting follow-up homework 156, 159
charting homework 141–142

chart of treatment options **171–172**
child-focused trauma treatments 18
childhood: abuse 28; amnesia period 46; trauma: in adults 1; mentalizing processes 36; *see also* adolescents
child-identified traumatic event 164
children: abandoned by their caregiver 169; brain and complex trauma 26–29; chronological age 151; day-to-day thoughts 151; joint sessions, and caregivers 151; mental health 166; of sexually abused caregivers 27; welfare authorities 2
children's trauma themes: adolescent's PAST, PRESENT, and FUTURE Diagram *184–187*; Behavioral Choice Program (BCP) 181–183, **183**; clinician's brainstorm list 180; family cancellation 179; language of choice 181; negative self-belief system 179; sentence completion exercise 179; thoughts, feelings, and actions of child witness/victim *181*; traumatic events, possible themes, and potential dilemmas **178**; treatment options 180; whiteboard option with older children 179
Child Witnesses of Domestic Violence Diagram 157
chronic pain syndrome 28
cognitive behavioral diagrams 5, 158, 159
Cognitive Behavioral Theory (CBT) 23, 56, 62; advanced diagrammatic structures 68–70
cognitive consciousness **44**
cognitive distortions 2, 162
Cognitive-Experiential Theory (C-ET) 45
cognitive tools 69
cognitive unconsciousness **44**
competence 18
complex post-traumatic disturbance 26
complex trauma in childhood: children's regulated stress response system and 30–32; child's brain and 26–29; defined 1; evidence-based treatments 4; forms of 2; phase-based treatment method 5, 22, 62–63; treatment, best-practice guidelines 5; treatment, to caregivers 6
Concrete IMBP 20, 21; criteria 21
conscious thinking 45
containment and self-regulation 67–68
contaminates 27
coping strategies 151
cortisol 31, 32
custody access battle **120**

"dandelion" diagram 70, *70*; charting *71*
decentering 43
Delicate IMBP 20, 21; criteria 20
depression 29, 61
"Developmental Trauma Disorder" 115
developmental traumatology and neuroscience 32–37
diagrams 158
dialectical method theory 55
Directed Sand Tray, story-making 155
"disembedded" thinking 43
dissociation 2, 30, 55, 68
distressing symptoms 135
drug and alcohol addiction 29, **119**
DSM-V disorder 21
dual-processing theories of higher cognition 44
dysfunctional sexual behavior 2
dysregulation 37

Early Childhood Deductive Reasoning Theory (EC-DRT) 6–7, 45, 52, 53–56
eating disorders 2
EC-DRT *see* Early Childhood Deductive Reasoning Theory (EC-DRT)
education 157
egocentrism 43
"embedded" thinking 43
emotional attachment 156
emotional attunement 113
emotional intensity 14
emotional self-expressiveness 118
emotions, dimensions of 14
epigenome 29
event-specific abuses 5
evidence-based interventions 31, 37
experience-dependent brain plasticity 29
experience-expectant brain plasticity 29
externalizing behaviors 2, 30
extrinsic motivation 16

family cohesion 118
family stress 27
family violence: parent completion *129*; power **119**
faulty belief: statement 156; system diagram 155
Ferguson, C. R. 14
fibromyalgia 28
first-level order behavioral loops 93–94
FUTURE Diagram 56, 145–148, *147*, *187*

gastrointestinal disorders 28
gene-environment interactions 27
genetics and mental health 29
group discussion 80; containment 81; emotional attunement 81–83; impact scale 80

higher order cognitive (HOC) processes 36, **44**
high road/low road diagram 157
hippocampal abnormalities in adulthood 32
hippocampal neurogenesis 35
hippocampal sensitivity 32
hippocampus 27, 32
homeostasis 50
human behavior 85
hyperarousal symptoms 61
hyper/hypo-responsiveness 32
hypothalamic-pituitary-adrenal (HPA) system 31–33

identified regulation 16
identity 2, 37; conclusions of 37, 113; detrimental, loss of 3; development of 26; loss of 194
implicit beliefs 45
individual self 50
individual trauma impact resolution 173
individual traumatic events 54
"Inside the Teenage Brain" documentary 157
integrated theory of personality 45
integration 51
intergenerational therapeutic method 26
intergenerational transmission of abuse 34
intergenerational trauma 13
Intergenerational Trauma Treatment Model (ITTM): brain-based method 6–7; complex trauma 3; current child trauma treatments 6; defined 1; Early Childhood Deductive Reasoning Theory (EC-DRT) 6–7, 45; endorsement 117; implementation 109–110; Indigenous communities 3, 4; phases 62–63; phases treatment *77*; reflections 111–116
Intergenerational Trauma Treatment Model (ITTM) Phase A 62–63; advanced CBT diagrammatic structures 68–71; caregiver's unresolved childhood trauma impact 80–89; diagrams *76–77*; implementation 109–110; metacognition, role of 63–65; testimonial from a parent 96–105; therapeutic activities **63**; Trauma Information Sessions (TIS) 65–68; Trauma Information Sessions checklist 73–75; trauma treatment 106–108
Intergenerational Trauma Treatment Model (ITTM) Phase B 63, 118; anger assessment 134–135; barriers to treatment and recommendations **119–120**; caregiver-directed "one-on-one" quality time with the child 130–134; case history 135–148; diagram examples *125–129*; reviewing caregiver's Trauma Information Session responses 122–124; Session 1 assessment goals 119–122; task online 124; therapeutic activities **63**
Intergenerational Trauma Treatment Model (ITTM) Phase C 63; adolescent's PAST, PRESENT, and FUTURE Diagram *184–187*; Behavioral Choice Program (BCP) 181–183, **183**; clinician's brainstorm list 180; diagrams *77*; family cancellation 179; language of choice 181; negative self-belief system 179; sentence completion exercise 179; therapeutic activities **63**; thoughts, feelings, and actions of child witness/victim *181*; traumatic events, possible themes, and potential dilemmas **178**; treatment options 180; whiteboard option with older children 179
inter-relatedness 17
interventions types 153
intrinsic motivation-based platforms (IMBPs) 18, 19, 23
ITTM *see* Intergenerational Trauma Treatment Model (ITTM)
ITTM trauma treatment 166, 170; checklist **153–154**; training and training manual 156

knowledge of person variables 64

language of choice 181
letter writing 159
life experiences and neuroplasticity 29–30
limbic-hypothalamic-pituitary-adrenal axis 27

maternal depression 27, 118
Membrane Diagram **120**, *125–126*, 126, 157
memory, recalling child's impactful: Behavior Choice Program (BCP) 153; Betty's case history 160–163; caregiver and child joint sessions 151; caregiver orientation to Phase C 149–151; children's trauma themes 178–187; ITTM trauma treatment checklist **153–154**; Phase C 159; Phase C treatment options 173–177; regressive work template **169**, 169–173; Sand Tray Stories 152–159; traumatic events not directly involving caregiver abandonment, abuse, or neglect 164–169
memory work 140
mental health: clinicians 15; system 18; treatments 2
mentalizing 35–36
mental models 54
metacognition 63–65, 67
Monoamine Oxidase-A (MAOA) 34–35
motivation: building 14; defined 14; in trauma treatment theories 14–17
motivational interviewing (MI) 15
myelin 27

negative-experience recall 46
negative self-belief system (NSBS) 38, 50–53, 135, 139–140, 158, 179; formulation 137; of parents 135
negative self-deductions 2, 44, 137
negative self-generalizations 46
negative self-schemata 69
neglect variables 118
neurodevelopmental disorders 29
neurons 31
neuroplasticity, life experiences and 29–30
neuroscience: children's regulated stress response system 30–32; child's brain and complex trauma 26–29; developmental traumatology and 32–37; life experiences and neuroplasticity 29–30; neuroplasticity, life experiences and 29–30
non-stressful day diagram 140–141
norepinephrine (NE) 33

"one-on-one" quality time with the child 130
Organismic Integration Theory (OIT) 16
organism's genetic code 29

parent-child loops 113
parenting pathways 113
PAST/PRESENT/FUTURE Diagrams 159, 161, *184–187*

PAST TFA Diagram 135–139, *138*, 166; adolescent's *184–185*
Pathways Diagram 157
personal boundary issues **120**
pharmacotherapy 35
physiological dysregulation 31
Piaget's theory 43
playing dress-up 130
poly-victimization 33
poly-victimized adolescents 33
positive and valid self-beliefs 46
positive self-deductions 38, 49–50
post-traumatic stress disorder (PTSD) 3, 33, 35
Power and Control Hypothesis: Men's Diagram version *128*; Women's Diagram version *127*
practice-based evidence 4
prefrontal cortex 27, 30
PRESENT Diagram 56, 139, 140, 142–145, *143–144*, *186*
primary caregiver-related trauma 169–170
primary emotion 165
Primary Negative Belief System (PNBS) 5, 6
progesterone 34
propositional calculus 56
psychiatric consultation 151
psycho-educational material 66
psycho-educational sessions 61
psychosis 29
psychotherapy 35; for adolescents 3

quality time program 130–132; chart and explanation *132–133*, 134

Regressive Re-enactment (R-E) 156, 160, 174
regressive work template **169**, 169–173
regulation disturbance 2
"re-impactments" 135
relational sensitivity 2, 17, 63, 111
Rogers's self-concept theory 45

Sand Tray methods 63
Sand Tray Stories 152–159, 162–163
Schema Therapy 56
Seasonal Affective Disorder (SAD) 33
second-level order 94–95
"Secrets of the Silver Horse" cluster dolls 157
selection 49
selective serotonin reuptake inhibitors (SSRIs) 35
self-belief formulation 44
self-belief systems 3, 26
self-capacity 18
self-deductions 26, 56
self-defeating behavioral loops 86–87
self-determination 65
Self-Determination Theory 16–17, 18, 23; caregiver motivation 22; evidence-based application 19
self-esteem 158
self-incurred competence platform 19
self-isolation 18
self-mutilation 2
self-questioning 64
self-representations 69
sense of powerlessness 137
sense of self 16
sentence completion exercise 179
sexual abuse effects 157
Shattered IMBP 19, 20
"Sixties Scoop" 3
"small-t trauma" 37
social isolation 27
somatization 2
"stand-alone" depiction 139
strategy variables 64
substance abuse 2, 35, 166
suicidal ideation 121
susceptibility to revictimization 2
sympathetic nervous system (SNS) 33

task variables 64
testosterone 34
therapeutic letters 158, 159
thoughts, feelings, and actions of child witness/victim *181*
trait 30
trauma, 26, 78; resolution of 158, 159
Trauma Information Sessions (TIS) 6, 62, 65–68; checklist 73–75; responses 122
traumatic bereavement 2
traumatic events: not directly involving caregiver abandonment, abuse, or neglect 164–169; possible themes and potential dilemmas **178**
traumatology and neuroscience 32–37
trauma treatment 106–108; caregiver involvement in child trauma treatment 17–18; goals 151; intrinsic motivation-based platforms 18–22; medical model version *76*; motivation in 14–17
treatment diagram 151
Truth and Reconciliation Commission in Canada 3

un-mentalized children 37
unresolved trauma impact 27

victimization 164
violence 2; community 33; counseling 146; domestic 3, 25, 33; family 22, 119, 129, 135, 136; preschoolers' physical and emotional ailments 33
visual learning techniques 64

"Western" science 4
wet cement analogy 78–79
whiteboard option with older children 179
witnessing other traumatic events 157

Made in the USA
Las Vegas, NV
26 February 2022

44634362R00116